IMAGES
of America

CHINESE MILWAUKEE

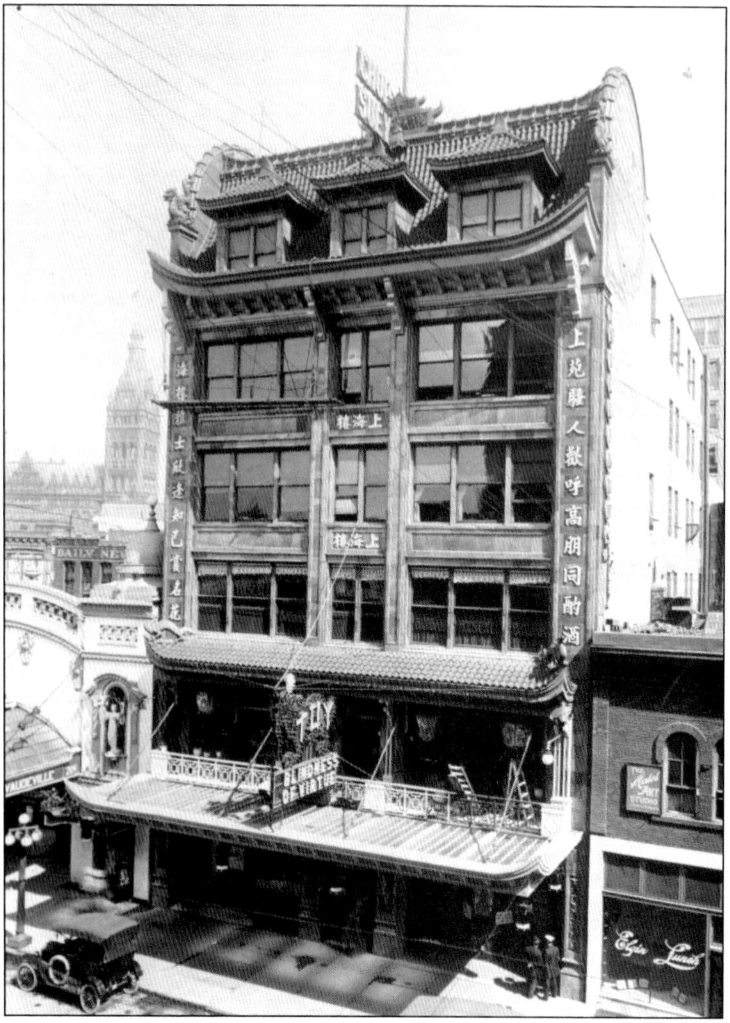

At the time of its opening in 1913, the Toy Building at 172–174 Second Street (later renumbered 716–718 North Second Street) in downtown Milwaukee was described as the largest and most luxurious Chinese restaurant building in the world. The building was a popular entertainment destination for Milwaukeeans in the 1920s and 1930s and included a 460-seat theater (first floor); Toy's Restaurant, band stage, and ballroom (second floor); and the Hascall Billiards Hall (third floor). Offices and living quarters filled out the fourth through sixth floors. It was demolished in 1937 and replaced by a parking structure. (Courtesy of the Milwaukee Public Library.)

On the cover: This photograph was taken at a farewell dinner given to Charles (Charlie) Toy on March 17, 1946, at Toy's Chinatown Restaurant on the corner of North Third Street and West Wisconsin Avenue. Toy, born Moy Toy Ni, immigrated to the United States in 1880 and became a multimillionaire and one of the most successful Chinese American businessmen of the early 20th century. At the time of the photograph, Toy, age 86, was preparing to fulfill a longtime dream of returning to his native China to live out his retirement years. An earlier attempt in the mid-1930s was cut short by the Japanese invasion of China. Toy returned to China shortly after this photograph was taken, where he remained until his death in 1955 at age 95. The takeover of China by the Communist government in 1949 presented additional challenges for Toy, given his position as an enormously successful Chinese American capitalist. (Courtesy of the Toy family.)

IMAGES
of America

CHINESE MILWAUKEE

David B. Holmes and Wenbin Yuan

ARCADIA
PUBLISHING

ISBN 978-0-7385-5224-8

Published by Arcadia Publishing
Charleston, South Carolina

Printed in the United States of America

Library of Congress Catalog Card Number: 2008921569

For all general information contact Arcadia Publishing at:
Telephone 843-853-2070
Fax 843-853-0044
E-mail sales@arcadiapublishing.com
For customer service and orders:
Toll-Free 1-888-313-2665

Visit us on the Internet at www.arcadiapublishing.com

This book is dedicated to the Chinese residents of Milwaukee, who for 130 years have turned adversity into opportunity and in the process succeeded in building better lives for their families and future generations.

Contents

Acknowledgments 6

Introduction 7

1. First Arrivals: 1874–1889 11
2. Chinese Medicine and Other Curiosities: 1890–1899 21
3. A Growing Community: 1900–1929 31
4. Depression and World War: 1930–1949 57
5. Family Reunification: 1950–1959 77
6. Changing Patterns: 1960–1975 89
7. New Arrivals: 1976–1989 107
8. The Rise of China: 1990–2007 115

Acknowledgments

The authors are grateful to the following individuals who contributed to the research or writing of this book: Xiaoqing Wang, Margie Li, Judy King, Ann Yuan, Philip Wang, Dr. Guanyuan Jin, Gene Moy, Yi Hong, Yang Chen, Dr. Roger Zhong (coauthor of chapters 7 and 8), Dr. Dian Wang (coauthor of chapter 2), and Dr. Chia Vang. Special thanks are given to Maurine Huang, Ph.D., whose 1988 doctoral dissertation on the Milwaukee Chinese community was one important source of information and inspiration for this project and who was the author of chapters 4 and 6. Special thanks are also given to Katherine Toy, who shared information from her research on the Toy family, as well as contributed a personal perspective on the significance of Milwaukee's Chinese community as part of the introduction for the book.

We are grateful to the following individuals and organizations that provided photographs, drawings, or other materials that were used as illustrations in the book: Jennie Chan, Yang Cheng, Joyce Knoch, Sally Moy Klatt, Elinor Lee Cheung, Dr. David Toy, Dr. Dennis Toy, Katherine Toy, Lulin Chang Walter, Larry Widen, Paul Wong, Dr. Jiang Hsieh, Rev. Joshua Yu, Dr. Guanyuan Jin, Dr. Thomas T. Tang, Yi Hong, Zhengjiang Sun, Dr. Mingtao Jiang, the Chinese American Museum of Chicago, the Frank Lloyd Wright Foundation, the International Institute of Wisconsin, the Chinese Christian Church of Milwaukee, the Milwaukee Journal Sentinel, the Milwaukee Public Library, and the Wisconsin Historical Society. We wish to express special thanks to the staff at the Milwaukee Public Library who assisted in the production of the numerous digital images of photographs and provided access to other materials in their collections for use in the book. Special thanks are also given to Laura Toy, who shared not only many treasured family photographs, but who also provided many delicious glasses of iced tea.

We thank Arcadia Publishing for their commitment to local history and providing a means to bring to light many small, but never-the-less significant stories from our nation's history.

Finally we thank our wives (Irene Alarcon and Qi Zhang) and daughters (Ann and Reena Yuan) for their patience, support, and encouragement throughout this project.

INTRODUCTION

The history of the Chinese residents of Milwaukee is a remarkable story that has been neglected both in previous histories of the City of Milwaukee and of Chinese Americans throughout the United States as a whole. It is uncertain when the first Chinese arrived in Milwaukee, but by the end of 1874, at least four Chinese laundries were open for business in Milwaukee. These residents were part of a major influx of Chinese immigrants to the United States that began in 1848 with the discovery of gold in California. In addition to the lure of riches, hardship in China pushed many to leave their native country. The preceding decade, as well as the decades to follow, were a time of great turmoil in China, beginning with the First Opium War between the British and Qing Empires, from 1839 to 1842, and continuing between 1842 and 1852 with a series of floods and crop failures that ravaged southern China and resulted in periods of famine among peasant farmers. This in turn was followed between 1851 and 1864 by the Taiping Rebellion, which resulted in an estimated 20 million deaths in China.

It is estimated that more than 300,000 Chinese immigrated to the United States during the period 1850 to 1882. These immigrants left a significant mark on the American landscape, with the most well-known examples being the transcontinental railroad, constructed between 1865 and 1869 primarily through the labor of Chinese immigrants, and Chinatown districts that were created in San Francisco, New York, Chicago, and other major United States cities and which remain in existence to this day. Remarkably, virtually all the Chinese immigrants during this period came from eight districts in two provinces in southern China, Guangdong and Fujian, with a collective area smaller than the state of Rhode Island. The importance of this area to the United States dates back even earlier to before the Revolutionary War, at which time Canton (now known as Guangzhou) in Guangdong Province was a major destination for New England trading ships. The importance of this area continues to the present day, with the more than 60,000 factories in Guangdong Province representing a major source for low-cost imports to the United States.

Life for the first Chinese residents of Milwaukee was challenging in ways that are difficult to fully appreciate today. The first residents were almost universally involved in the laundry business, which was one of the few occupations where Chinese could find employment during the 19th century. Aside from the hard work associated with washing and ironing clothes by hand for 10 to 16 hours a day and six days per week, the residents had to deal with the loneliness associated with, in a majority of instances, leaving a wife and children behind in China (a separation that in some cases lasted a lifetime) and the racist attitudes of the time, during which Chinese were frequently portrayed in the press as heathens, rat eaters, opium addicts, and other negative stereotypes.

Within two years of the period of major Chinese immigration that began in 1848, the first anti-Chinese law was passed in America—a tax in California that applied only to miners of Chinese ancestry. This was followed by a series of increasingly restrictive immigration and other anti-Chinese laws, culminating in the Chinese Exclusion Act of 1882, which virtually ended

Chinese immigration to the United States for more than 60 years. Although Milwaukee appears to have provided a relatively friendly environment for the early Chinese residents, anti-Chinese incidents did occur. The worst incident occurred in 1889, following the arrest of two Chinese laundrymen who were charged with having "enticed" several "white" girls aged 14 or younger for "immoral purposes." With public anger spurred on by sensationalized newspaper accounts, four days of protests on March 11, 1889, exploded into a 12-hour riot by an estimated 3,000 Milwaukee men of Euro-American ancestry that targeted Chinese laundries and their owners. Although significant damage was done to at least a dozen Chinese laundries, it should be noted that no Chinese were apparently injured, and the laundry owners were eventually compensated for their losses by the United States government.

Although the Chinese community in Milwaukee has always been relatively small in number compared to the major Chinese population centers on the West and East Coasts of America, the Chinese residents in Milwaukee still managed to make a distinct contribution to the cultural and social heritage of Milwaukee, and in some ways, distinct contributions to both American and Chinese history. One example of this influence occurred during the period 1937 to 1940, when the Milwaukee Chinese community of some 300 residents, led by the longtime community leader Jack Wong, raised more money to support the Chinese war effort against Japan than any Chinese community in the United States, except San Francisco (which at the time had a Chinese population that was at least 50 times greater than that of Milwaukee). A 1932 article had noted that at least 10 Chinese from Milwaukee were training to be pilots to join the fight against Japan following the Japanese invasion of Manchuria. At a time when nearly all categories of Chinese were generally banned from coming to the United States, the Chinese residents of Milwaukee were in some ways leading the effort in America's eventual war against Japan.

The story of the Milwaukee Chinese community has also been characterized by many examples of extraordinary individual achievement. Perhaps the best example of this achievement is the story of Moy Toy Ni, better known by his adopted American name of Charlie Toy. Arriving in San Francisco in 1880, Toy reportedly owned nothing more than a sack of cotton clothes and a piece of wood inscribed in Chinese with the words that became his motto: Honesty Endures. Toy lived in several cities throughout the United States before finally making his way to Milwaukee in 1904, where he opened a restaurant at 199 West Water Street (now North Plankinton Avenue). By 1912, Toy's restaurant, import, and other businesses were successful enough that he was able to construct a six-story building in downtown Milwaukee that included a restaurant and ballroom and a 460-seat theater, as well as offices and living quarters. The building, which was designed in a Chinese architectural style, was reported at the time to be the largest and most luxurious Chinese restaurant building in the world. By 1923, Toy had become known internationally as the Chinese Rockefeller and had constructed a 50-room mansion on the outskirts of Canton, China, where he entertained visitors from Milwaukee. Remarkably, Toy's home was one of several in the same area owned by Milwaukee area Chinese families, creating what was in effect a Milwaukee neighborhood in Canton, China, more than 80 years ago.

China's influence on Wisconsin's economy dates back to at least 1864, at which time an article in the *Milwaukee Sentinel* noted a rush by residents of Dunn and surrounding counties to collect ginseng for sale and export to China. Ginseng was reportedly the first major product exported from the United States to China. Ginseng-related trade between China and Wisconsin continues to this day, with Wisconsin-grown ginseng currently accounting for 95 percent of the ginseng produced in the United States, and Wisconsin ginseng considered to be the highest quality in the world.

The role of the Chinese community continues to evolve as the Milwaukee area strives to build institutional and business ties with China in recognition of the significant challenges and opportunities associated with China's increasing importance to the Milwaukee economy, especially for a city that has been one of the most important manufacturing centers in the United States. While some businesses such as leather tanning have almost vanished in response to Chinese competition, other businesses such as mining equipment manufacturing have experienced record growth and profitability attributable in large measure to direct or indirect demand from China. The importance of China to Milwaukee and Wisconsin's economic future has been recognized by leaders such as Wisconsin governor Jim Doyle, who in 2004 and 2007 led what were reportedly two of the largest state-sponsored business delegations ever to visit China. It is estimated that as of 2008, several hundred Milwaukee area businesses have established manufacturing or other business operations in China.

Another milestone for Milwaukee's Chinese community occurred in October 2007 with the arrival of Chinese basketball star Yi Jianlian, who was drafted by the Milwaukee Bucks professional basketball team. Yi Jianlian shares a link with many of the first Chinese residents of Milwaukee in being a native of Guangdong Province. However, Yi's arrival contrasted dramatically with that of earlier Chinese immigrants, with his arrival at Chicago's O'Hare Airport qualifying as an international news event and covered by reporters from more than 40 news organizations. With only two Chinese players currently playing for teams in the National Basketball Association (NBA), and an estimated 1.2 billion Chinese who watched at least one NBA game within the last year, Yi Jianlian may already be the most widely known Milwaukee resident in the world.

Following is a personal perspective on Milwaukee Chinese history from March 24, 2008, provided by Katherine Toy, a fifth-generation Chinese American, as well as a great-great-granddaughter of Charlie Toy:

> Upon meeting someone new, I have often been asked, "Where are you from?" "San Francisco," I reply, but like most Chinese Americans, I am already suspicious that what the questioner really wants to know is my ethnicity. "Oh, I mean where were you born?" I continue to play along and say, "Redwood City, California." "Really? Well then your parents, where were they born?" When I answer that my father and grandfather were born in Milwaukee, I can pretty much guarantee a look of surprise every time. Chinese American history is largely unknown by most people in the United States, but even among those who have some familiarity with the field, the fact that Milwaukee's Chinese community is more than 130 years old comes as a surprise. For my family, however, this history is our history. By the mid-1880s, my great-great-grandfather Charlie Toy called Wisconsin his American home.
>
> As a child, one of my favorite things to do on a rainy day was to take down the old box that lived on the back shelf of my father's closet. For me, that box was a treasure chest and its contents kept me occupied for hours at a time. The treasures inside were dozens of yellowed newspaper clippings and sepia-toned photographs that told the story of my family's history in the United States.
>
> When my grandfather would visit from Milwaukee, he would bring the photographs to life for me by telling stories about the people and places they represented—some of them were entertaining vignettes of childhood: the photograph of the family's mansion on Fourteenth Street elicited a story about how Grandpa and some of his siblings and cousins were playing in the ballroom one day when the door suddenly slammed shut and locked them inside. They were convinced that it was a ghost who did it.
>
> Other photographs and documents brought forward stories that revealed how the family's wealth and privilege could not completely erase the discrimination then faced by all Chinese in America, even those who were American born. Members of the Toy family traveled extensively between the United States and China during the time in which the Chinese Exclusion Act (1882–1943) was in effect. Before every trip, each traveler undertook a lengthy investigation with the immigration service to secure the necessary papers to reenter the United States. Today the records of these investigations, along with those of other Milwaukee Chinese, are being preserved by the National Archives and Records Administration.
>
> In many ways, the story of my great-great-grandfather is the quintessential American dream story—that of a poor immigrant who arrives with nothing, but through hard work and determination becomes a wealthy man. I have no doubt that my great-great-grandfather

was an extraordinary and accomplished individual. Yet I also believe that Milwaukee itself played a leading role in the story of his life. I wonder if Charlie Toy's success would have been possible had he stayed in the city where he first landed—San Francisco. California was home to the largest number of Chinese immigrants during this time, and anti-Chinese sentiment was at its strongest in that state, making it less likely that Charlie Toy would have secured business relationships with white Americans on the same level that he was able to secure in Milwaukee.

For more than 130 years, a Chinese community has contributed to the diversity of the Milwaukee experience. In this book, David Holmes and Wenbin Yuan bring this story to a greater audience, allowing the story of Milwaukee's Chinese community to finally be told.

Katherine Toy made her own contribution to Chinese American history through several years of service as executive director of the Angel Island Immigration Station Foundation, during which time she led an eight-year, $32 million effort to help preserve the historical landmark that is considered by many to be the Ellis Island of the West Coast and a place of great historical significance to Chinese Americans.

One

FIRST ARRIVALS
1874–1889

It is unknown when the first Chinese set foot in Milwaukee. One early visitor was John Assam, who in 1870 was noted in newspapers as being a Chinese cook visiting Milwaukee as a product demonstrator for a stove company at the Wisconsin State Fair. The earliest documented Chinese resident of Milwaukee was Wing Wau, whose arrival in Milwaukee was noted on July 3, 1874, in the *Milwaukee Daily Sentinel*, announcing the opening of his Chinese laundry at 86 Mason Street. Other Chinese laundries soon followed.

The *Milwaukee Republican Sentinel*, on August 15, 1882, described a Fourth of July celebration by 12 of the estimated 23 Chinese who were living in Milwaukee at that time. The group gathered early at the laundry of Ring Shane, where a feast of apple pie with roast chicken, beef, and pork was prepared. Dressed in blue blouses, white shirts, and straw hats, they hired carriages and traveled to their chosen picnic ground—Union Cemetery—where they enjoyed their meal and a rare day of leisure.

By 1887, there were 30 Chinese laundries listed in the Milwaukee City Directory. At least half of the laundries and other Chinese businesses of this era were located within a six-square-block area bounded by West Water, Fourth, Wells, and Sycamore Streets (now named North Plankinton Avenue, North Fourth Street, West Wells Street, and West Michigan Avenue). There was at least one Chinese and Japanese import store (owned by Sam Ring Kee), located on the ground floor of the luxurious Plankinton House hotel. Most Chinese business owners and workers were male and lived within the same buildings as their business.

Although the 1880 United States Census recorded only two Chinese residents in Milwaukee, various newspapers estimated the city's Chinese population to be 12 in 1881, and increasing to 90 by 1887. Possibly the number of Chinese residents was significantly underrepresented by the official census data due to persecution and discrimination experienced by both legal and illegal Chinese immigrants. Milwaukee was not immune from anti-Chinese violence. In March 1889, two Chinese laundrymen named Sam Yip Ya and Hah Ding were arrested and charged with "enticing" several "white" girls aged 14 or younger for "immoral purposes." With public anger spurred on by sensationalized newspaper accounts, four days of protests exploded into a 12-hour riot targeting Chinese laundries on March 11, 1889.

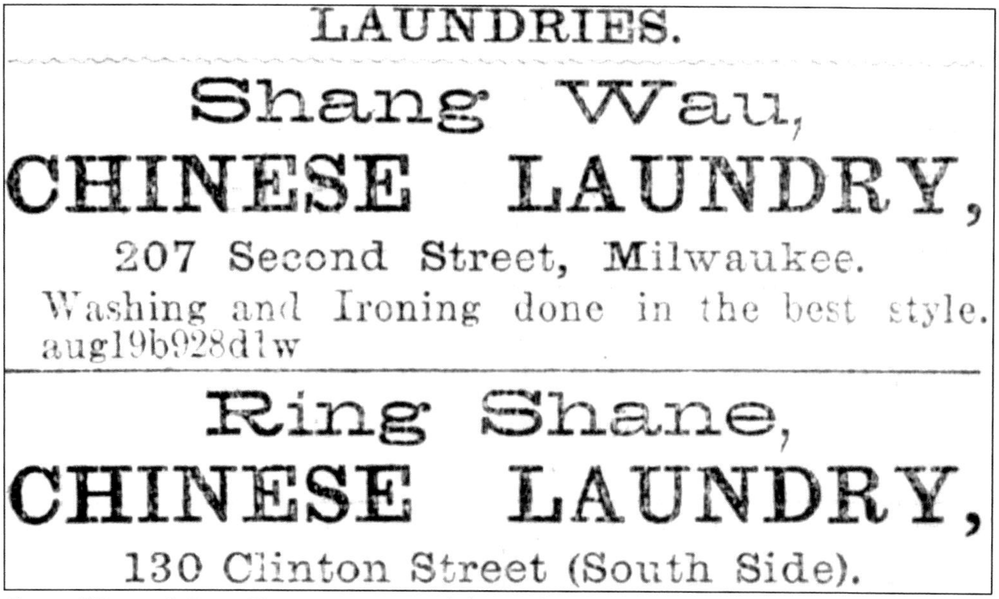

Shang Wau and Ring Shane were two of the earliest Chinese residents of Milwaukee. Like nearly all the first Chinese residents of Milwaukee, they made their living as laundrymen. This advertisement appeared in the *Milwaukee Daily Journal* on August 22, 1874. By late 1874, there were at least four Chinese laundries operating in Milwaukee. Ring Shane was exceptional for this era in having his Chinese wife living and working with him in Milwaukee. (Courtesy of the Milwaukee Public Library.)

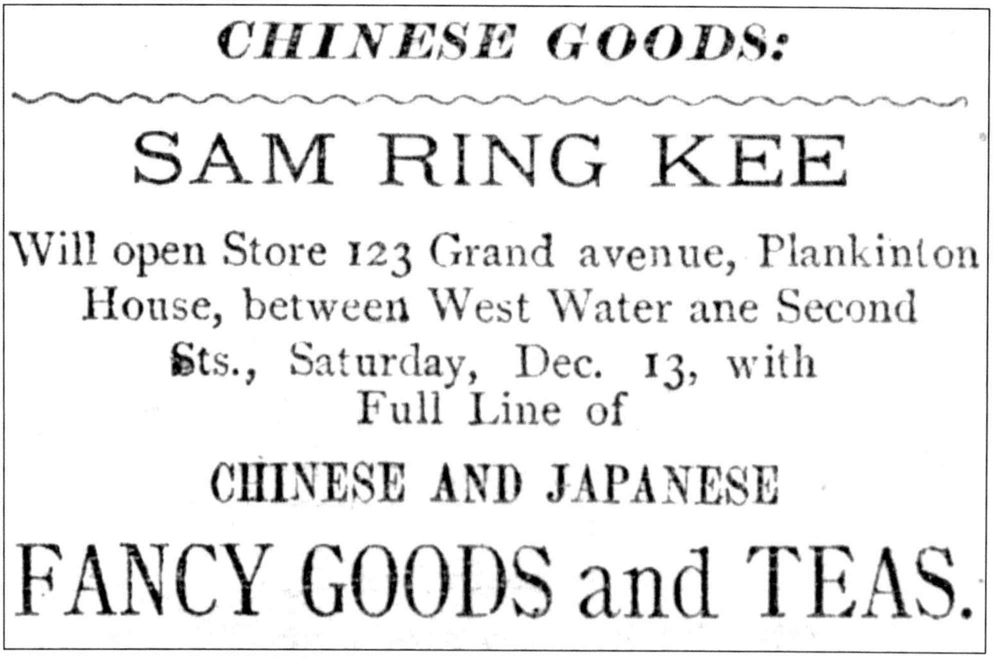

Sam Ring Kee was an early leader of the Milwaukee Chinese community who owned several businesses, including a Chinese and Japanese import store that opened in December 1884, as announced by this advertisement that appeared in the *Milwaukee Sentinel* in December 1884. (Courtesy of the Milwaukee Public Library.)

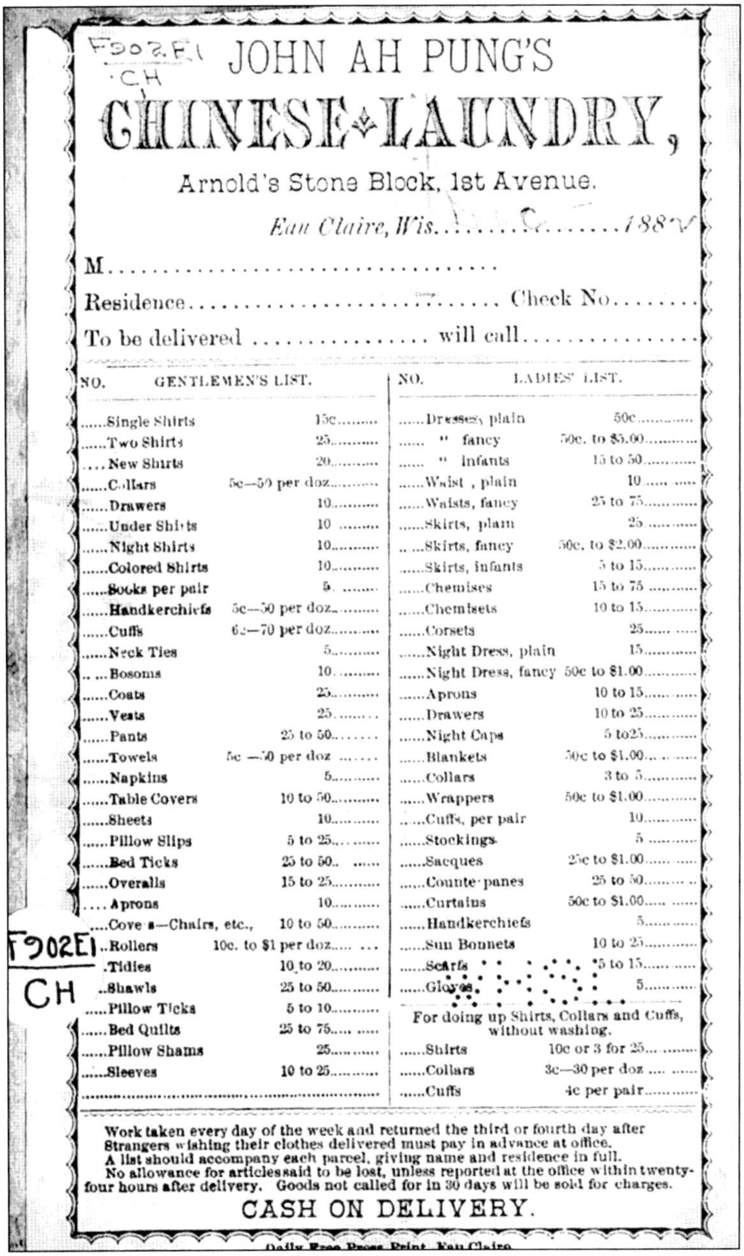

F902.E1 CH

JOHN AH PUNG'S

CHINESE LAUNDRY,

Arnold's Stone Block, 1st Avenue.

Eau Claire, Wis. 188

M....................................

Residence.............................. Check No.........

To be delivered .... will call................

NO.	GENTLEMEN'S LIST.	
......	Single Shirts	15c
......	Two Shirts	25
....	New Shirts	20
......	Collars	5c—50 per doz
......	Drawers	10
......	Under Shirts	10
......	Night Shirts	10
......	Colored Shirts	10
......	Socks per pair	5
......	Handkerchiefs	5c—50 per doz
......	Cuffs	6c—70 per doz
......	Neck Ties	5
......	Bosoms	10
......	Coats	25
......	Vests	25
......	Pants	25 to 50
......	Towels	5c—50 per doz
......	Napkins	5
......	Table Covers	10 to 50
......	Sheets	10
......	Pillow Slips	5 to 25
......	Bed Ticks	25 to 50
......	Overalls	15 to 25
....	Aprons	10
....	Covers—Chairs, etc.,	10 to 50
..	Rollers	10c. to $1 per doz
	Tidies	10 to 20
..	Shawls	25 to 50
.....	Pillow Ticks	5 to 10
......	Bed Quilts	25 to 75
......	Pillow Shams	25
......	Sleeves	10 to 25

NO.	LADIES' LIST.	
......	Dresses, plain	50c
......	" fancy	50c. to $5.00
......	" infants	15 to 50
......	Waist , plain	10
......	Waists, fancy	25 to 75
......	Skirts, plain	25
......	Skirts, fancy	50c. to $2.00
......	Skirts, infants	5 to 15
......	Chemises	15 to 75
......	Chemisets	10 to 15
......	Corsets	25
......	Night Dress, plain	15
......	Night Dress, fancy	50c to $1.00
......	Aprons	10 to 15
......	Drawers	10 to 25
......	Night Caps	5 to25
......	Blankets	50c to $1.00
......	Collars	3 to 5
......	Wrappers	50c to $1.00
......	Cuffs, per pair	10
......	Stockings	5
......	Sacques	25c to $1.00
......	Counte-panes	25 to 50
......	Curtains	50c to $1.00
......	Handkerchiefs	5
......	Sun Bonnets	10 to 25
......	Scarfs	5 to 15
......	Gloves	5

For doing up Shirts, Collars and Cuffs, without washing.

......	Shirts	10c or 3 for 25
......	Collars	3c—30 per doz
......	Cuffs	4c per pair

Work taken every day of the week and returned the third or fourth day after
Strangers wishing their clothes delivered must pay in advance at office.
A list should accompany each parcel, giving name and residence in full.
No allowance for articles said to be lost, unless reported at the office within twenty-four hours after delivery. Goods not called for in 30 days will be sold for charges.

CASH ON DELIVERY.

F902E1 CH

Fourteen of the 16 China-born residents recorded by the 1880 United States Federal Census as living in Wisconsin were located in cities other than Milwaukee, including Fond du Lac, Green Bay, Janesville, La Crosse, Oshkosh, Portage, and Racine. By the time of the 1900 United States Federal Census, the 214 Chinese residents were located in 59 separate Wisconsin cities and towns, with fewer than 10 percent of those residing in Milwaukee. Although Milwaukee still recorded the highest number of Chinese residents (21), Madison and Oshkosh both recorded 18 Chinese residents. The city of Eau Claire, with 10 Chinese residents, was the fourth-largest Chinese population center. Little is known of John Ah Pung, who operated a laundry in Eau Claire in 1882 and produced this order form and price list for laundry services provided by his business. (Courtesy of the Wisconsin Historical Society.)

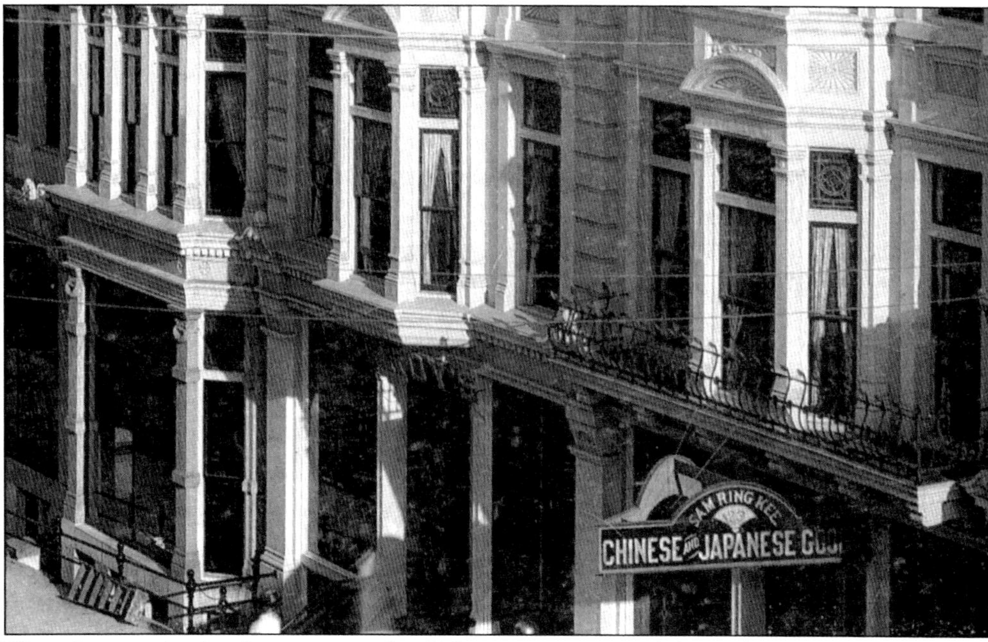

This photograph, dated approximately 1885, represents one of the earliest known images of a Chinese business in Milwaukee. Shown in the lower right-hand corner of the original photograph (below) and the detailed view (above) is the Chinese and Japanese goods store opened by Sam Ring Kee, one of the earliest leaders of the Milwaukee Chinese community. The store was located in the Plankinton House, which at this time was considered to be the most luxurious hotel in the city of Milwaukee. The Plankinton House, which opened in 1883, was torn down in 1915 and replaced by the Plankinton Arcade, which still exists as part of the Grand Avenue Mall. (Courtesy of the Milwaukee Public Library.)

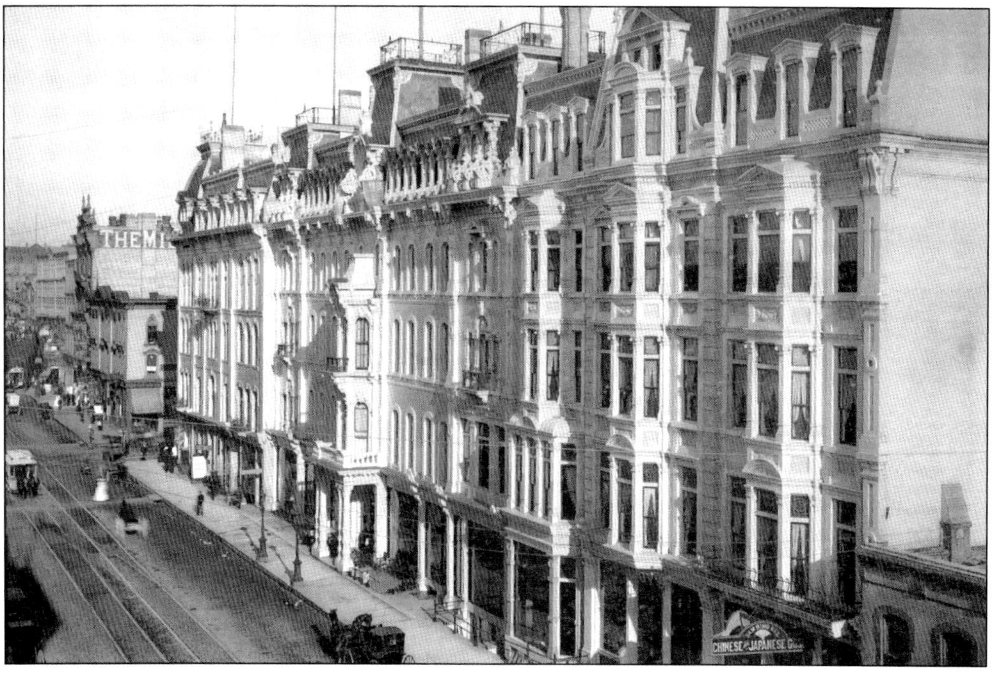

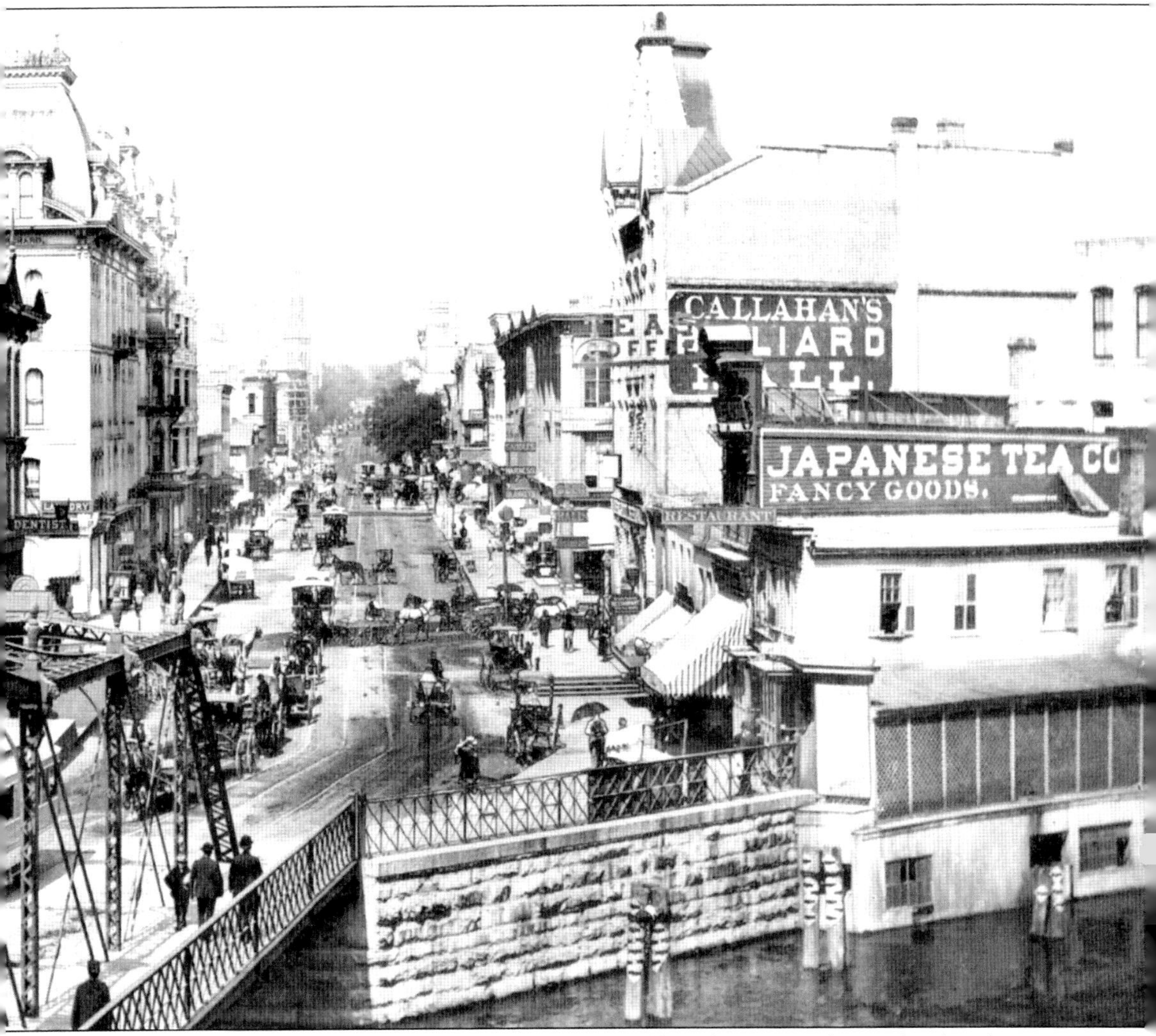

A majority of the laundries and other businesses owned by Chinese residents of Milwaukee in the 1870s and 1880s were located in an area extending several blocks west from the Milwaukee River and north from Grand Avenue (later renamed West Wisconsin Avenue). This photograph provides a view facing west along Grand Avenue from the bridge over the Milwaukee River. At least three Chinese-owned businesses were located in a several-block section along the south side of Grand Avenue at the time of this photograph, about 1885. (Courtesy of the Milwaukee Public Library.)

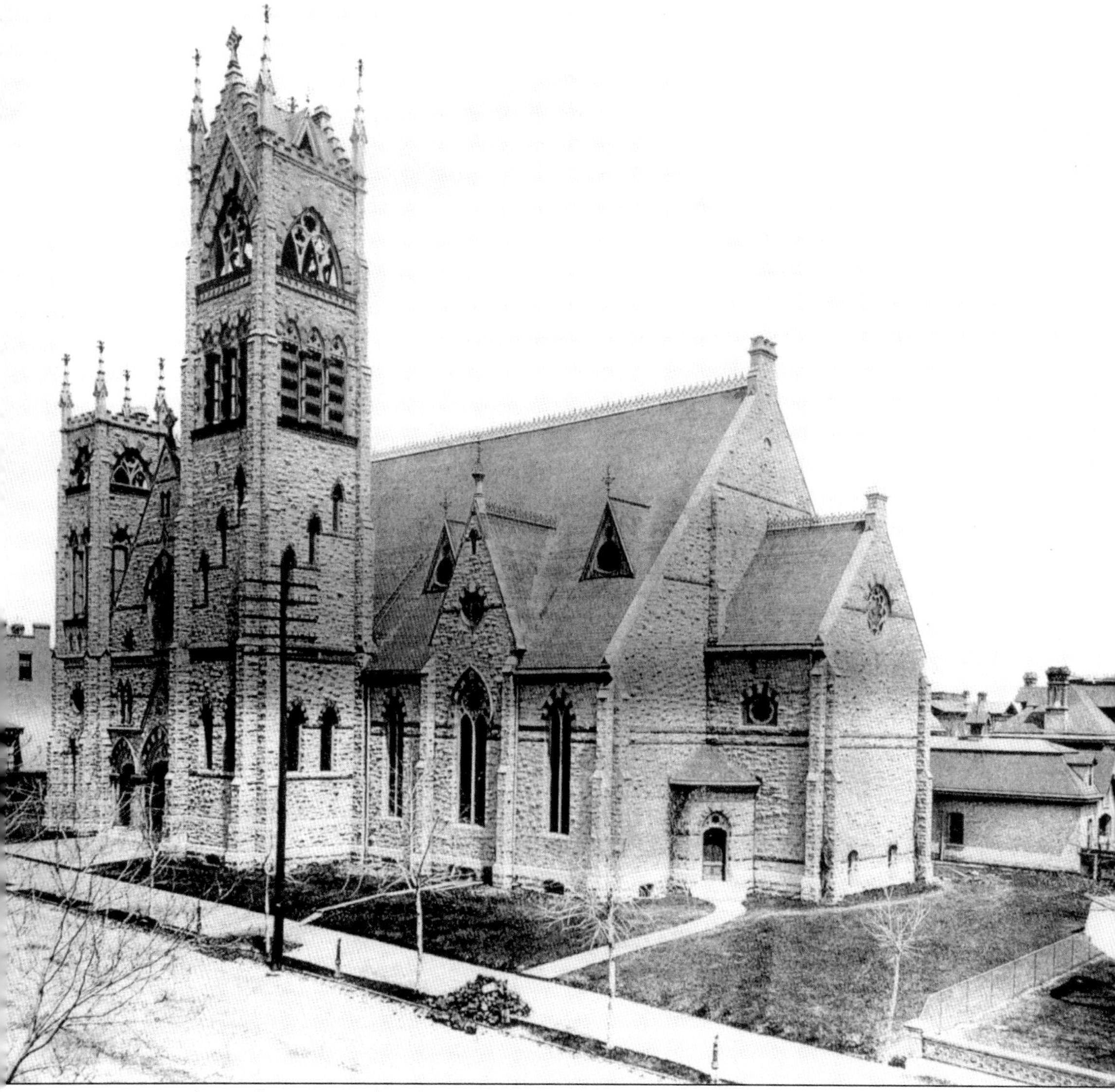

Immanuel Presbyterian Church organized one of the earliest missions for the Chinese residents of Milwaukee. An article in the *Milwaukee Journal* dated April 24, 1884, reported that missionaries from Immanuel Presbyterian Church had converted 17 of the 24 Chinese residents in Milwaukee to Christianity and that the work of conversion was still being carried on, with many of the Chinese attending Sunday school and an "intellectual course" that was being taught. The results were described as "as satisfactory as could be expected." A later article in the *Milwaukee Sentinel* dated April 18, 1887, described the Chinese as having a room of their own decorated in a Chinese style on the fourth floor of the YMCA. By this later date, the number of Chinese in the city of Milwaukee was estimated at 90, and 18 were reported in the article to be attending Sunday classes at which individualized English classes were provided by ladies from the church who were described as being of the highest social standing. (Courtesy of the Milwaukee Public Library.)

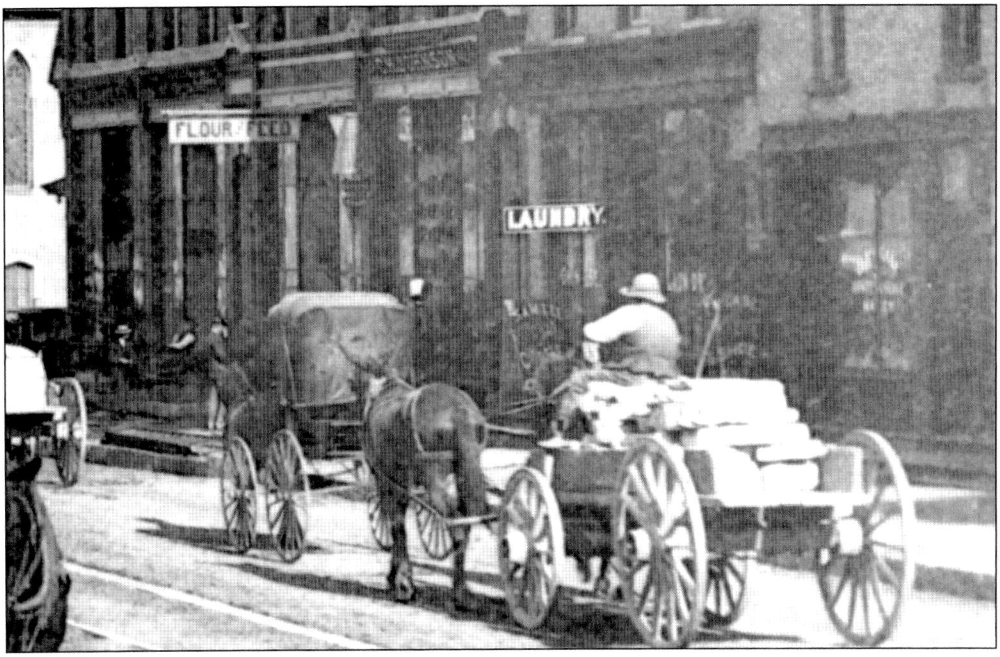

This *c.* 1885 photograph includes the earliest known image of a Chinese laundry in Milwaukee, the Sam Lee Chinese Laundry located on the right side of the photograph in the 500 block of Grand Avenue (now West Wisconsin Avenue). Although a laundryman using the name Sam Lee was quoted in an article in the *Milwaukee Sentinel* dated October 5, 1885 (in which he estimated that there were approximately 50 to 55 Chinese laundrymen living in the city), it should be noted that Sam Lee was a common name used for Chinese laundries in America, reportedly because the pronunciation of *Sam Lee* is very similar to the Cantonese word for "family laundry." (Courtesy of the Milwaukee Public Library.)

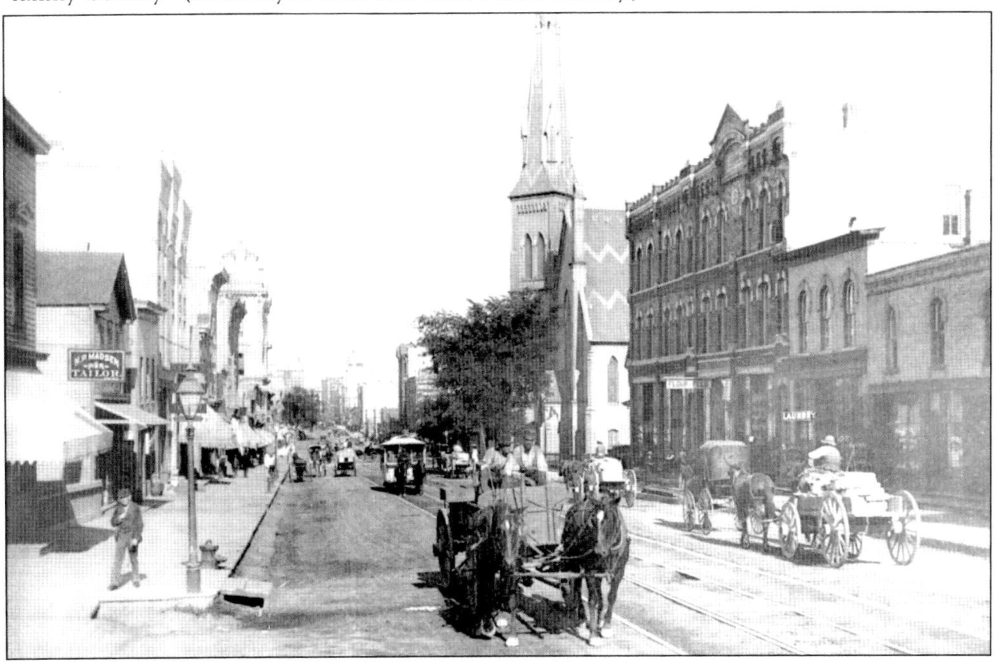

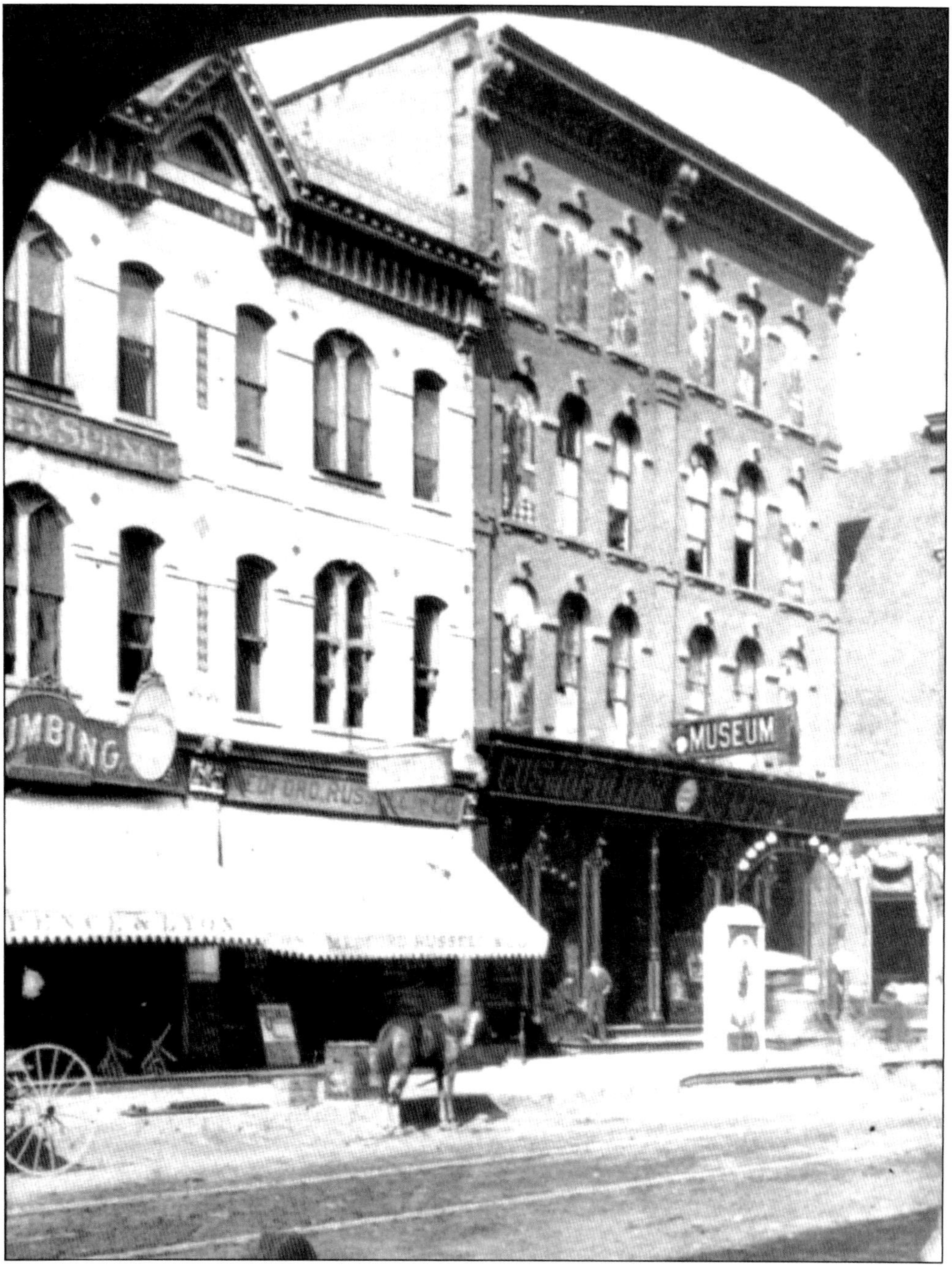

The Milwaukee Dime Museum at 128 Grand Avenue (now West Wisconsin Avenue) was located in the general area where a majority of Chinese businesses in Milwaukee were located in the 1870s and 1880s. This photograph is half of a stereographic image pair created by an unknown photographer in 1885. The Milwaukee Dime Museum opened in 1883 and went out of business in 1890. The performers who appeared at the Milwaukee Dime Museum during this period included a number of Chinese performers, such as Chang Woo Gow, as noted on the advertisement presented on page 19. (Courtesy of the Milwaukee Public Library.)

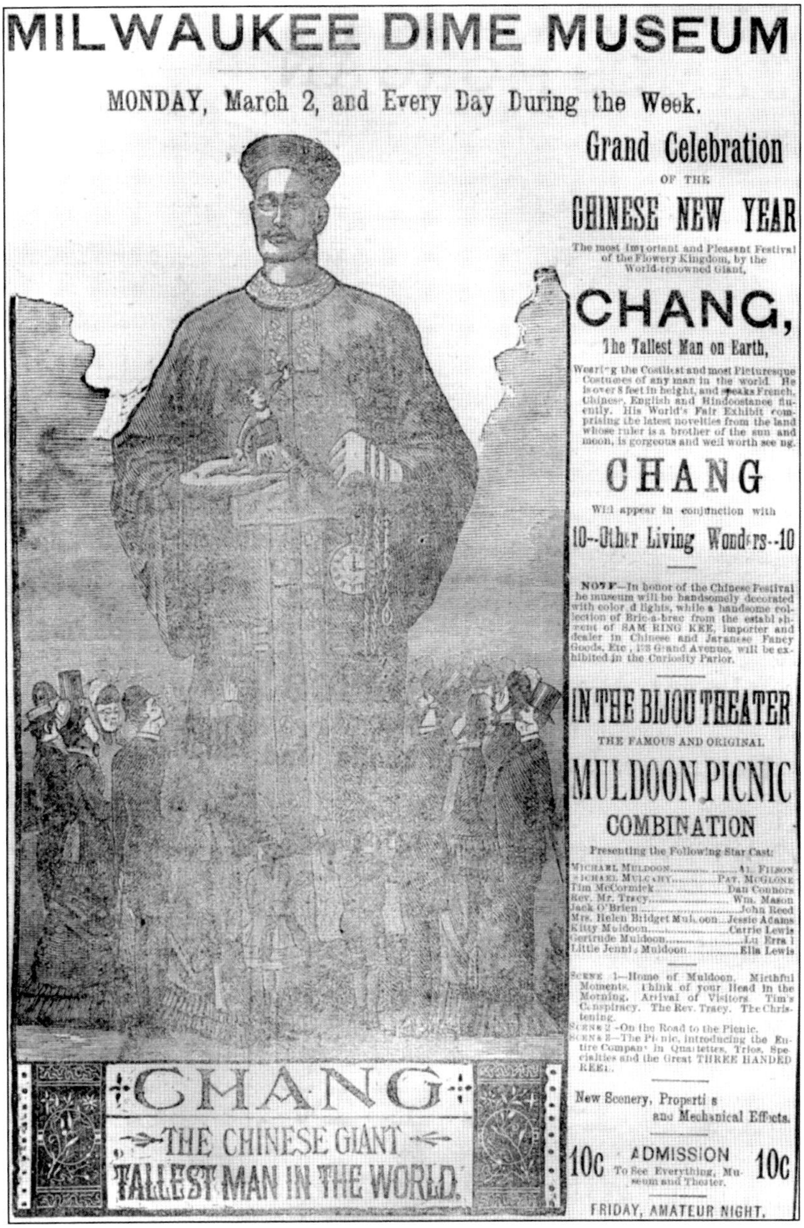

It is likely that few Chinese visitors to Milwaukee during the 1870s and 1880s made as big of an impression on the general population as Chang Woo Gow, better known at that time as "Chang the Chinese Giant" or simply "Chang." In 1885, Chang Woo Gow visited Milwaukee for two weeks as part of an appearance at the Milwaukee Dime Museum coinciding with the Chinese New Year. Although advertisements at the time claimed that his height was eight feet four inches, his documented height of seven feet eight inches likely still makes him the tallest person of Chinese heritage ever to visit Milwaukee, even in the modern era of seven-foot-tall Chinese basketball stars. This advertisement appeared in the *Milwaukee Daily Journal* on March 2, 1885, and also notes a display of Chinese bric-a-brac available for viewing, from the store of Sam Ring Kee, which was located directly opposite from the Milwaukee Dime Museum at 123 Grand Avenue. (Courtesy of the Milwaukee Public Library.)

DEED OF A HEATHEN

Testimony Against Hah Deng in the Municipal Court.

CROSS-EXAMINATION DOES NOT SHAKE IT.

On March 7, 1889, two Chinese laundrymen, Hah Ding and Sam Yip Ya, were arrested and charged with having "enticed" several young "white" girls for "immoral purposes." On March 11, 1889, the *Milwaukee Daily Sentinel* reported the purported incident (above), the same day on which an estimated 3,000 residents of the city rioted across the city, damaging at least a dozen laundries owned by Chinese residents. On March 16, 1889, the *Milwaukee Daily Sentinel* noted the arrival of Chinese officials from Washington, D.C., to assess the damages (below). The laundry owners were later compensated by the United States government. Similar compensation was provided during this era by the Chinese government to American residents living in China, who were the target of several anti-American riots by Chinese residents during the 1880s. Chinese laundries in the city decreased from 28 in 1888 to 13 in 1889, and remained fewer than 20 in number until the 1920s. (Courtesy of the Milwaukee Public Library.)

APPEALING TO LAW

A Representative of the Chinese Government Coming.

MILWAUKEE HAS AN INTERNATIONAL CASE

Two

CHINESE MEDICINE AND OTHER CURIOSITIES 1890–1899

The two laundrymen who were a catalyst for the anti-Chinese riot of 1889 were released from custody in 1890, after the Wisconsin Supreme Court determined that the age of consent law, under which they had been charged, was flawed. However, the riot had a lasting effect on the Chinese community, as measured by the number of Chinese laundries listed in Milwaukee City Directory. Whereas a total of 30 laundries were listed in 1887, the number during the 1890s ranged from 10 to 12. As 90 percent or more of the Chinese residents in the city were employed in the laundry trade during this period, the decrease in the number of laundries likely reflects a proportionate decrease in the population of the Milwaukee Chinese community.

The complex attitudes other residents held toward the Chinese is illustrated by an incident that occurred in 1890, within one year of the riot. In March 1890, a Chinese herbal medicine clinic opened in downtown Milwaukee, accompanied by a daily barrage of advertisements in the Milwaukee newspapers. The advertisements claimed that the proprietor, a Chinese doctor by the name of Gun Wa, could cure a wide range of "American diseases" using Chinese herbal remedies. By 1891, an investigation by the Milwaukee police had determined that the herbal medicines were little more than colored water and that "Gun Wa" had been impersonated by at least four different Chinese laundrymen with no Chinese herbal medicine or any other type of medical training. Even with advertising expenses that averaged $3,000 to $4,000 per month, the clinic had a net profit of approximately $4,000 per month, attesting to a high level of interest by Milwaukeeans in Chinese traditional medicine even at this early date.

Milwaukee has been the home of several of the most successful and influential Chinese Americans in the United States. One of these was Dr. Gee Wo Chan, who moved to Milwaukee in 1894, one year after having headed the Wah Mee Exposition Company, which financed, constructed, and operated the Chinese concession at the 1893 World's Columbian Exposition in Chicago. The exposition, which was attended by an estimated 27 million visitors, was significant in Chinese American history in providing the first broad exposure of Americans to Chinese theater, religious architecture, and other components of Chinese culture. During his three years in Milwaukee, Dr. Chan practiced Chinese herbal medicine in a clinic located in downtown Milwaukee.

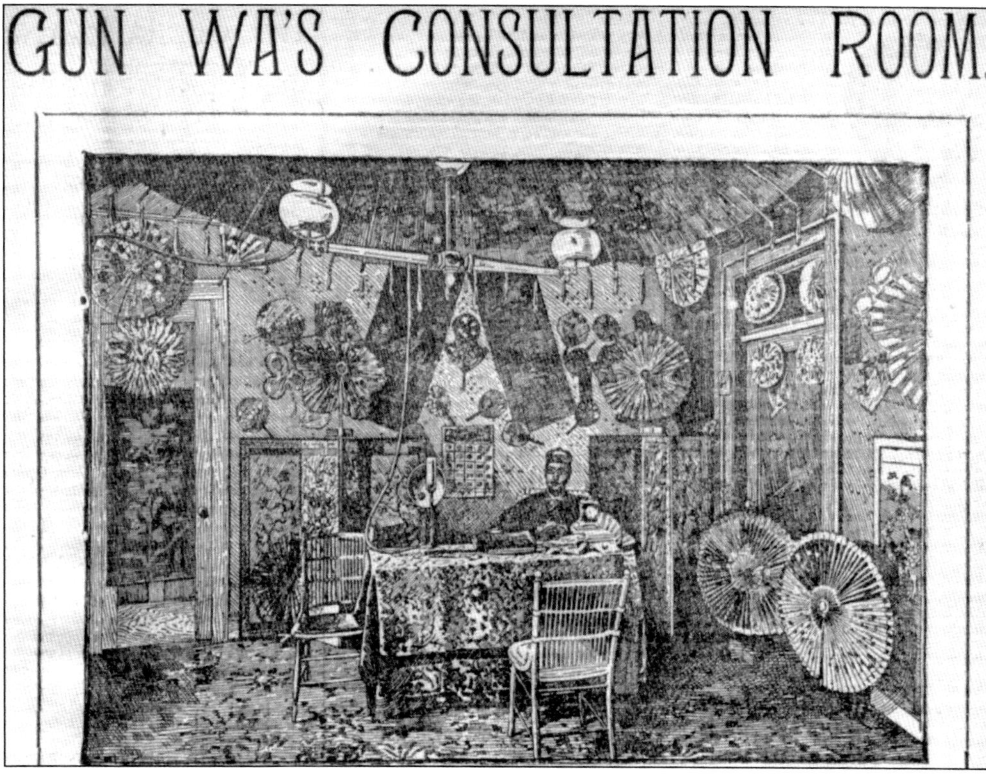

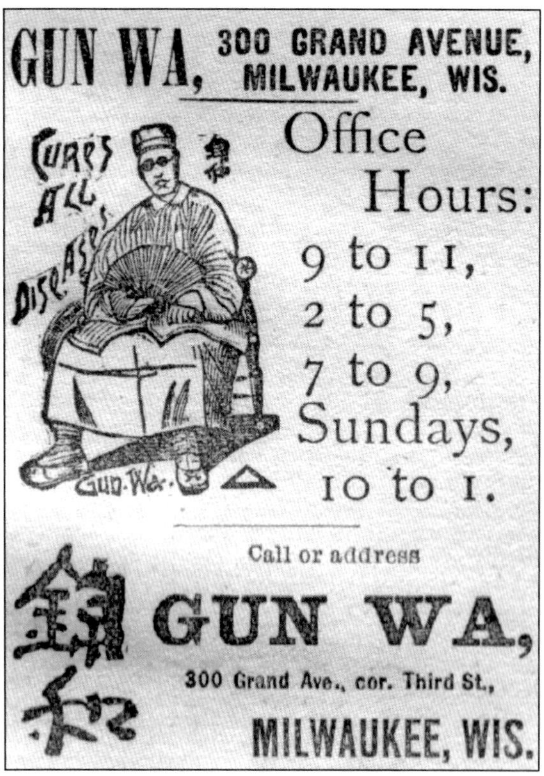

In August 1889, advertisements in Milwaukee newspapers announced the arrival in Milwaukee of a Chinese doctor named Gun Wa. These advertisements appeared in the *Milwaukee Sentinel* in March 1890. In June 1890, the office was shut down and the proprietors arrested and charged with fraud. Subsequent investigations by authorities determined that the business had made a net profit of approximately $4,000 per month while open, even after deducting advertising expenses that averaged $3,000 to $4,000 per month. An article in the *Milwaukee Journal* dated March 23, 1891, noted that up to four different Chinese laundrymen from Milwaukee had pretended to be Gun Wa at various times. The initial success of this business, less than five months after the anti-Chinese riots in March 1889, is an expansion of the mixed and sometimes conflicting attitudes toward the Chinese during this era. (Courtesy of the Milwaukee Public Library.)

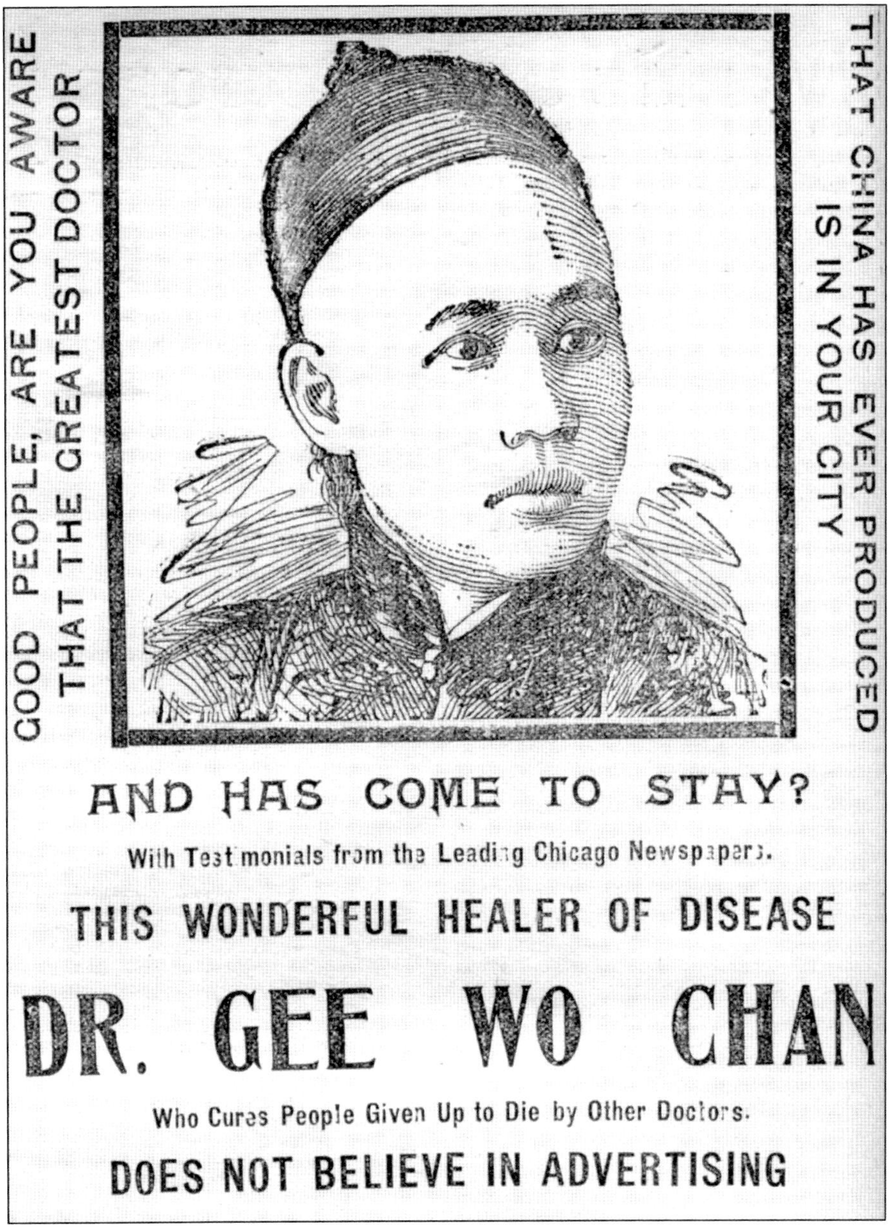

Dr. Gee Wo Chan was possibly the first authentic practitioner of traditional Chinese medicine in Milwaukee, as well as one of the most influential Chinese Americans of his era. Dr. Chan was born into a wealthy family in Foo Chow, China, in 1858, and came to the United States in 1884 to visit the New Orleans Exposition, as an emissary of the Chinese emperor. This drawing is part of an advertisement for Dr. Chan with testimonials that appeared in the *Milwaukee Journal* on September 14, 1894. Note that although the advertisement states Dr. Chan "does not believe in advertising," this advertisement was one of several hundred placed in Milwaukee newspapers between 1894 and 1897, when Dr. Chan left Milwaukee. Dr. Chan was recently "reincarnated" by author Steve Hockensmith as a character (Dr. Gee Woo Chan) in a series of detective novels set in the western United States and San Francisco's Chinatown in the 1890s. (Courtesy of the Milwaukee Public Library.)

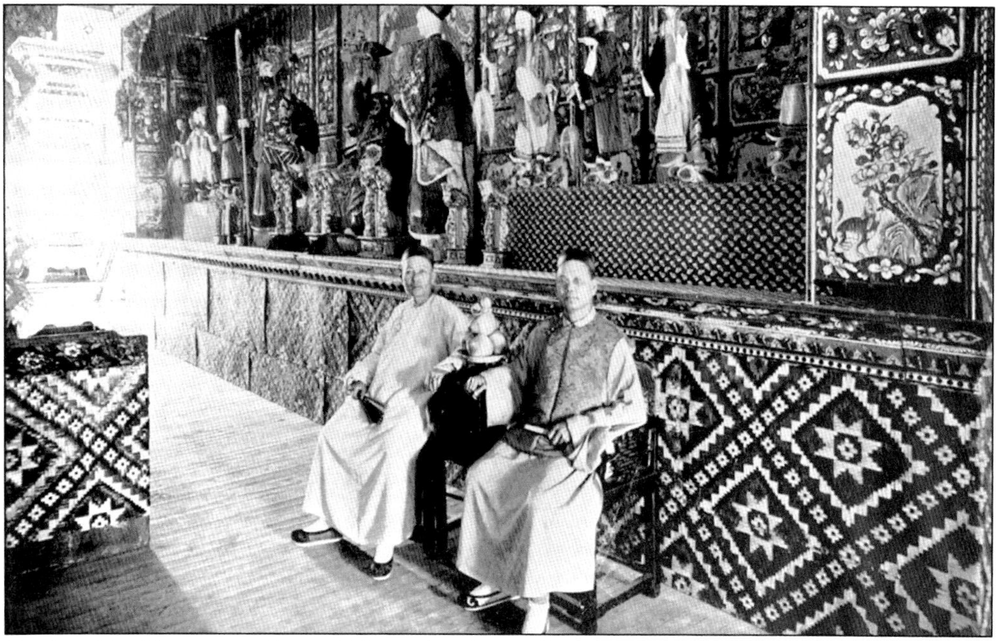

Dr. Gee Wo Chan, a resident of Milwaukee from 1894 to 1897, is shown on the right together with his business partner, Hong Sling, in this 1893 photograph taken in a joss house constructed as part of a Chinese village complex on the midway area of the 1893 World's Columbian Exposition in Chicago. A joss house is a traditional Chinese place of worship or temple. The lower photograph shows an exhibit of a Chinese farmhouse interior, which was a part of the Chinese village complex. The 1893 exposition was attended by an estimated 27 million visitors (equal to approximately one half of the United States population at that time). The Chinese village was significant in providing the first major public display in the Midwest (and possibly the United States as a whole) of Chinese theater, religious architecture, and other components of Chinese culture. (Courtesy of the Chinese American Museum of Chicago.)

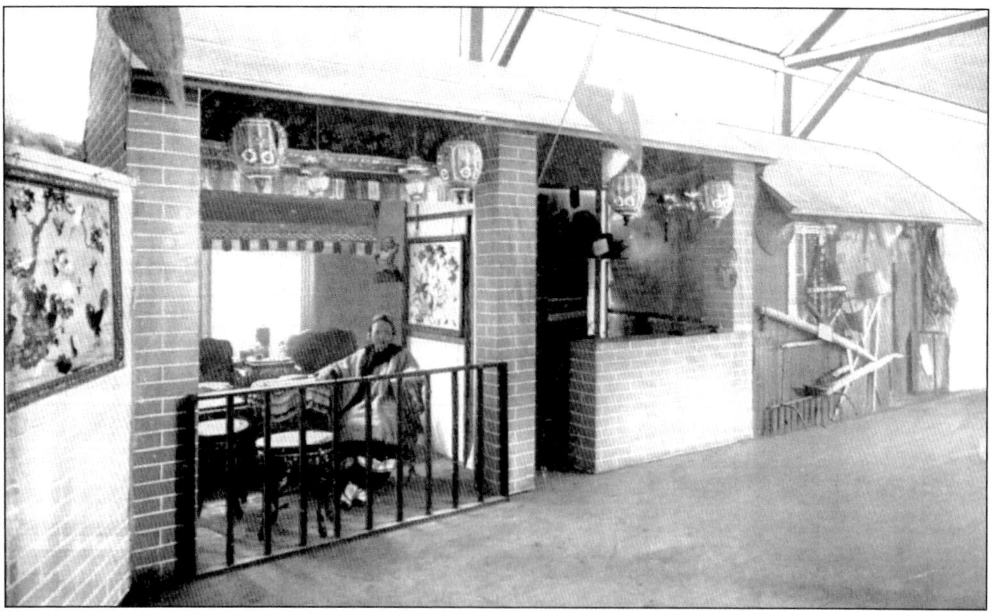

This Chinese village complex (right), constructed by the Wah Mee Exposition Company, includes a combination Chinese theater, joss house (temple), bazaar, and café. More than 200 actors from China were brought to Chicago to perform in the theater during the exposition. The Chinese theater is on the left (below), the Austrian pavilion is on the right, and the 264-foot-high Ferris wheel (the world's first) is in the background. The president of the Wah Mee Exposition Company, and arguably the most influential Chinese American associated with the exposition, was Dr. Gee Wo Chan, who moved to Milwaukee in 1894, the year after the exposition ended. Dr Chan's business partners included Wong Kee, a grocer who was reportedly the wealthiest Chinese in Chicago, and Hong Sling, owner of the Sam Lung Company, who among other accomplishments was reportedly the first Chinese to introduce chop suey to the Midwest. (Courtesy of the Chinese American Museum of Chicago.)

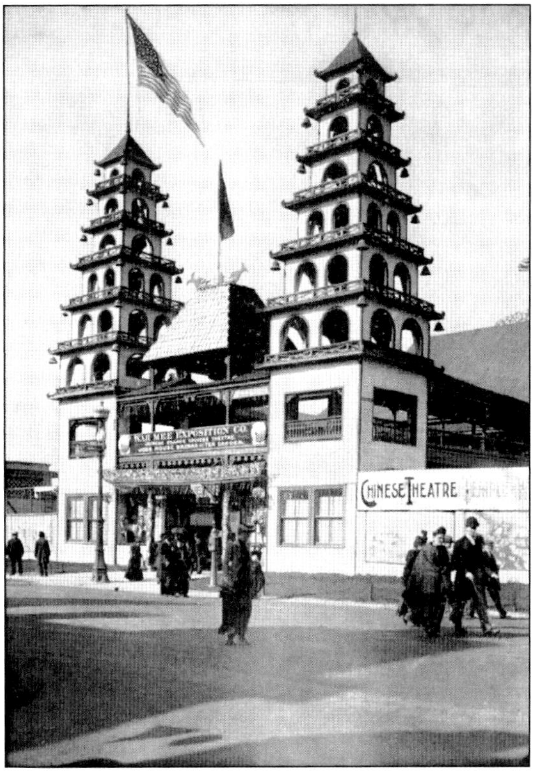

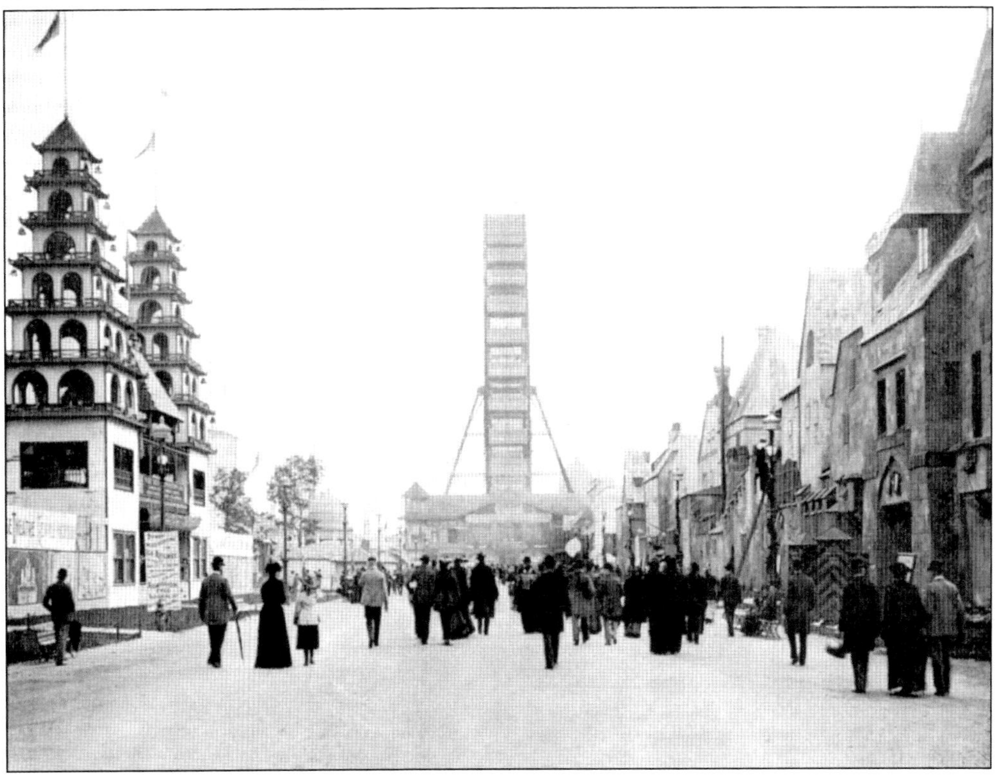

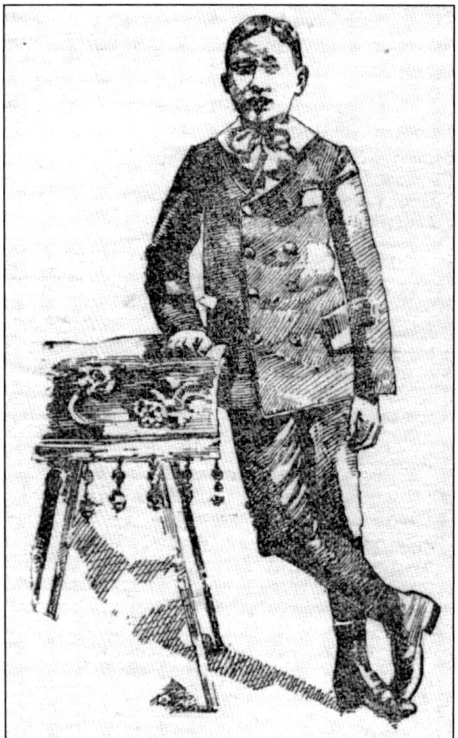

IN AMERICAN CLOTHES.

Chan Yoke was a nephew of Dr. Gee Wo Chan, who in 1895, at age 13, came to Milwaukee to spend the summer in the home of his uncle. These drawings of Chan Yoke in his "American clothes" and "native garb" appeared in the July 27, 1895, edition of the *Milwaukee Journal*. The accompanying article described Chan Yoke as having been in the United States for approximately two years and living with a family in Chicago while attending school. Dr. Chan, Chan Yoke's uncle, reportedly was one of the wealthiest and most influential Chinese in the United States during this era. (Courtesy of the Milwaukee Public Library.)

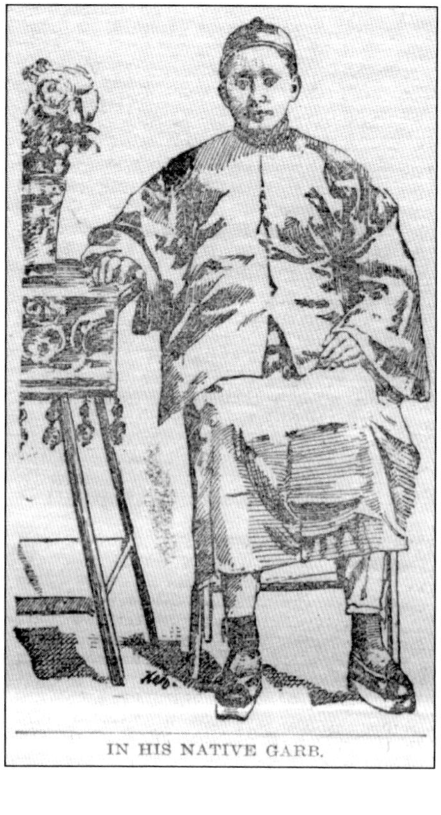

IN HIS NATIVE GARB.

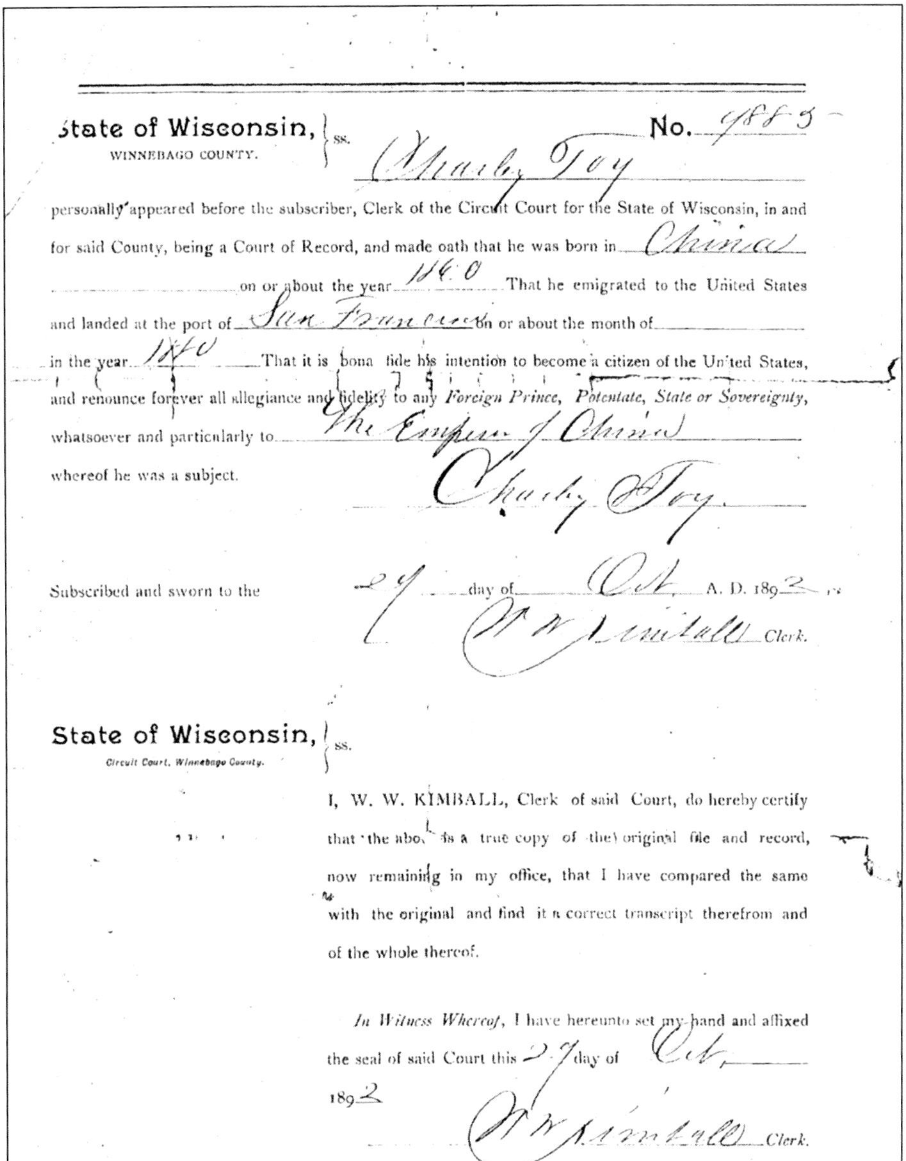

State of Wisconsin, } ss. No. 9883

WINNEBAGO COUNTY.

Charley Toy

personally appeared before the subscriber, Clerk of the Circuit Court for the State of Wisconsin, in and for said County, being a Court of Record, and made oath that he was born in China on or about the year 1860 That he emigrated to the United States and landed at the port of San Francisco on or about the month of ______ in the year 1880 That it is bona fide his intention to become a citizen of the United States, and renounce forever all allegiance and fidelity to any *Foreign Prince, Potentate, State or Sovereignty,* whatsoever and particularly to The Emperor of China whereof he was a subject.

Charley Toy

Subscribed and sworn to the 27 day of Oct A. D. 1892

W. W. Kimball Clerk.

State of Wisconsin, } ss.

Circuit Court, Winnebago County.

I, W. W. KIMBALL, Clerk of said Court, do hereby certify that the above is a true copy of the original file and record, now remaining in my office, that I have compared the same with the original and find it a correct transcript therefrom and of the whole thereof.

In Witness Whereof, I have hereunto set my hand and affixed the seal of said Court this 27 day of Oct, 1892

W. W. Kimball Clerk.

This sworn statement, signed by Charlie Toy on October 27, 1892, states his intention to become a citizen of the United States, renouncing allegiance and fidelity toward the emperor of China. The Geary Act of 1892, approved on May 5, 1892, extended the Chinese Exclusion Act of 1882 an additional 10 years. The act also stripped Chinese of protection in court, denied bail to Chinese in habeas corpus cases, and required all Chinese residents to obtain and carry a resident permit at all times with the failure to do so being punishable by deportation or a year at hard labor. It is uncertain whether filing of this statement by Charlie Toy was in response to the Geary Act, but this and other anti-Chinese laws would continue to present challenges and humiliations to the Chinese residents of Milwaukee until the Chinese Exclusion Act was at last repealed in 1943. (Courtesy of Katherine Toy.)

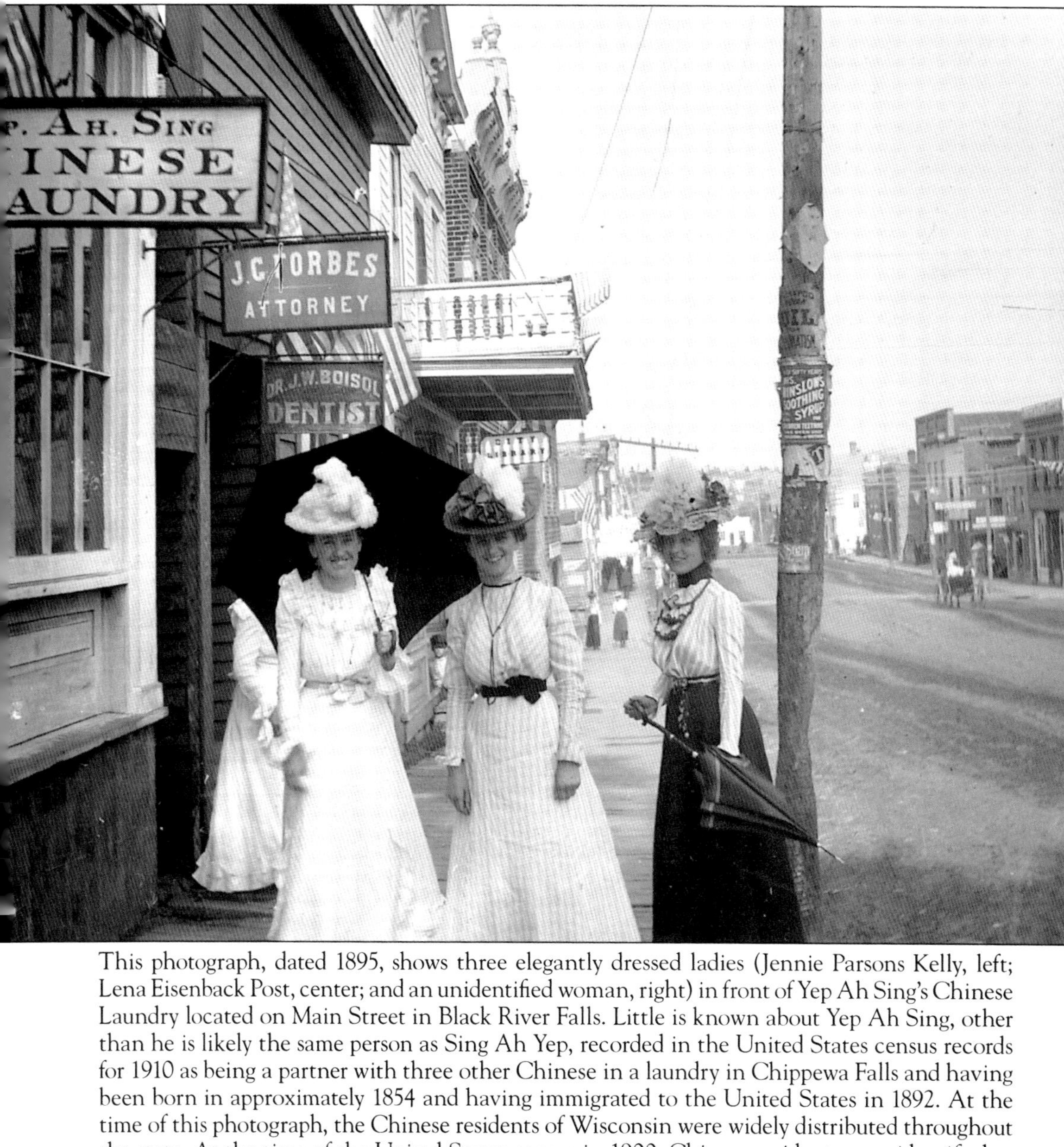

This photograph, dated 1895, shows three elegantly dressed ladies (Jennie Parsons Kelly, left; Lena Eisenback Post, center; and an unidentified woman, right) in front of Yep Ah Sing's Chinese Laundry located on Main Street in Black River Falls. Little is known about Yep Ah Sing, other than he is likely the same person as Sing Ah Yep, recorded in the United States census records for 1910 as being a partner with three other Chinese in a laundry in Chippewa Falls and having been born in approximately 1854 and having immigrated to the United States in 1892. At the time of this photograph, the Chinese residents of Wisconsin were widely distributed throughout the state. At the time of the United States census in 1900, Chinese residents were identified as living in 59 different cities throughout Wisconsin, with less than 10 percent of the population located in the city of Milwaukee. By 1940, the percentage of Wisconsin Chinese residents living within the city of Milwaukee had increased to more than 50 percent. (Courtesy of the Wisconsin Historical Society, image No. 24389.)

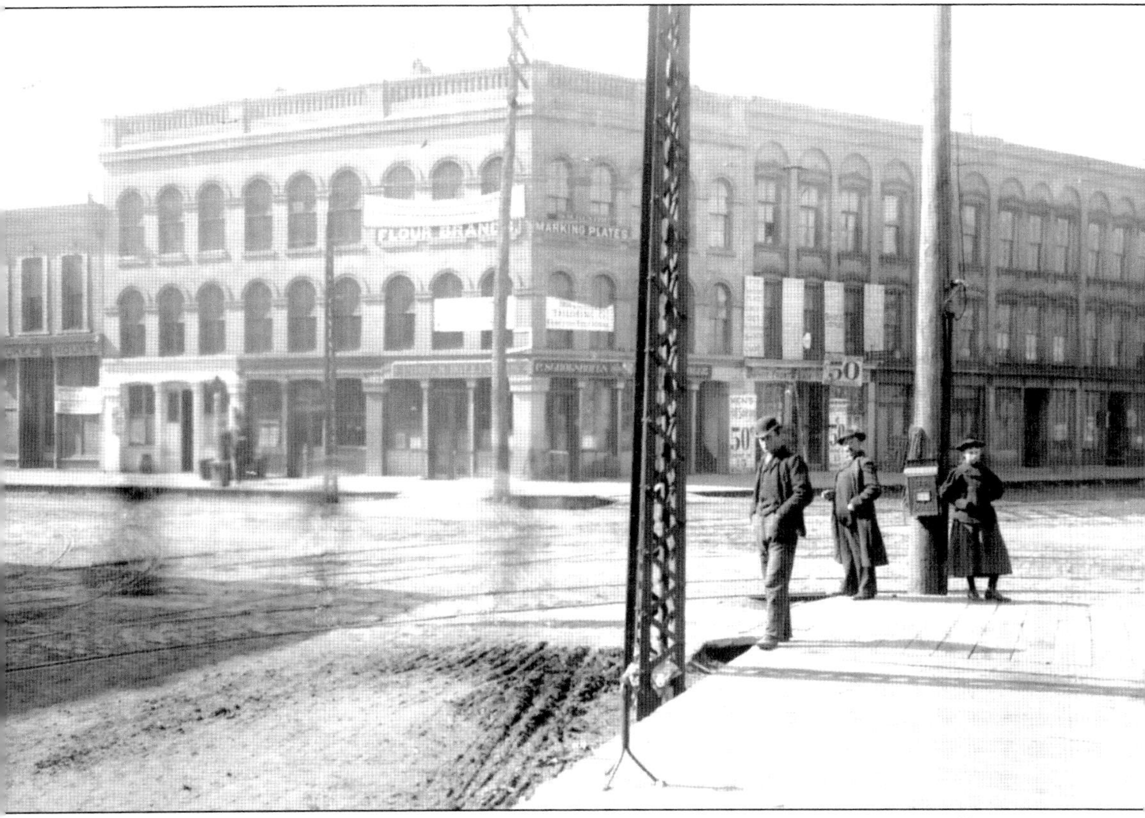

Although it is uncertain whether the Sam Kew that owned this store at 105 West Wells Street (between North Second and North Plankinton Street) was of Chinese ancestry, the store was located within a six-square-block commercial area west of the Milwaukee River within which a majority of the Chinese businesses of Milwaukee in the late 1800s were located. This photograph was taken in 1895 by an unidentified photographer. (Courtesy of the Milwaukee Public Library.)

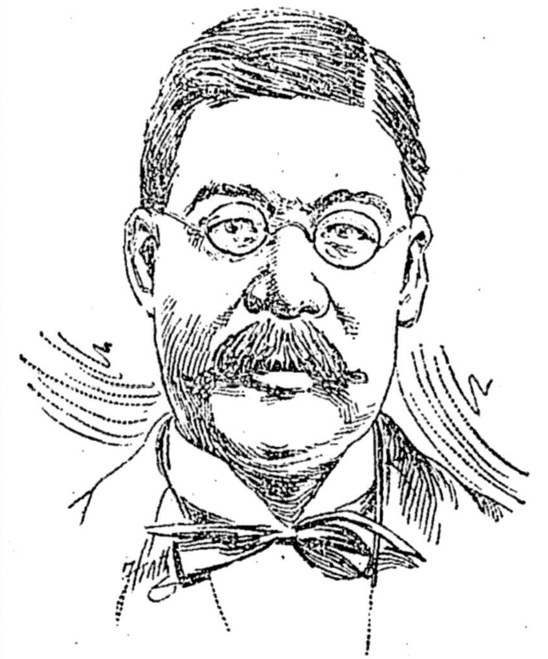

Gong Hoar of New York,
Head of the National Organization of Chinese Masons.

A meeting of Chinese Free Masons held in Appleton on October 8–9, 1898, was attended by approximately 50 members from throughout Wisconsin as well as two newspaper reporters. Gong Hoar, grand master of the Chinese Free Masons in the United States, led the meeting. Sam Wah Kee, an early leader of Appleton's Chinese community, hosted the meeting and was appointed the first master of the state lodge. Both drawings appeared as part of an article in the October 12, 1898, edition of the *Milwaukee Sentinel*. The delegation from Oshkosh was reportedly represented by a Chinese brass band. The Wisconsin group had first met in 1897 and was given a formal charter at the meeting in 1898. Fourteen members were reportedly initiated in an all-night ceremony at the meeting and a lodge of 55 members organized. (Courtesy of the Milwaukee Public Library.)

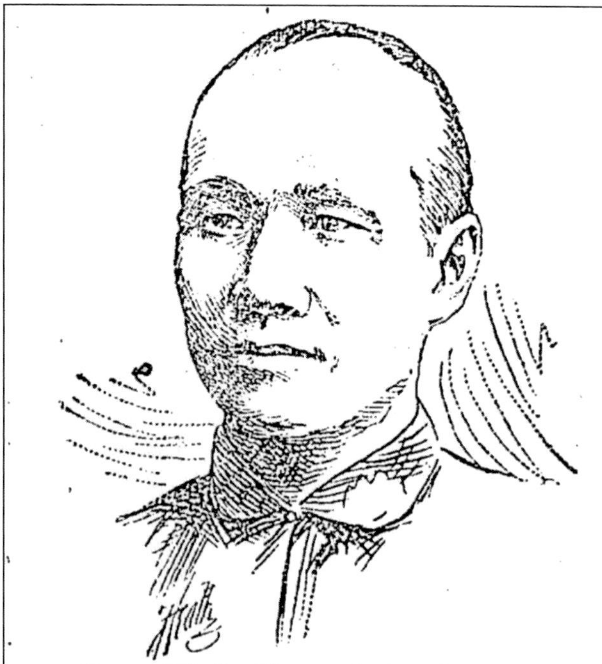

Sam Wah Kee of Appleton,
Head of the Chinese Masonic Organization in Wisconsin.

Three

A GROWING COMMUNITY 1900–1929

The period 1900 to 1929 was one of relative prosperity for Milwaukee's small Chinese community. Based on United States census records, the population increased during this period from 23 in 1900, to 51 in 1910, 65 in 1920, and 176 in 1930. The number of Chinese laundries listed in city directories also increased significantly during the latter part of this period, increasing from 12 in 1900 and 1910, to 16 in 1920, to 58 in 1930. One economic development was an increased focus on the restaurant trade. The year 1900 marked the opening of the first of several large Chinese restaurants that would eventually become institutions in Milwaukee. Based on restaurants with obvious Chinese names listed in city directory records, the number of restaurants increased from 1 in 1900, to 2 in 1904, 6 in 1910, 11 in 1920, and 14 in 1930.

In terms of the United States as a whole, anti-Chinese laws remained in effect and in some ways worsened. In 1902, the Chinese Exclusion Act was extended for another 10 years, and in 1904, the Chinese exclusion was made indefinite. By 1924, the Immigration Act was passed, which not only denied entry into the United States by virtually all Asians, but also forbade Asians from marrying Caucasians or owning land. In spite of these laws, several Chinese families flourished in Milwaukee, with the best example being Charlie Toy, who moved to the Milwaukee area from Oshkosh and in 1904 opened the Shanghai Chinese Restaurant at 199 West Water Street. In 1905, Toy obtained approval for his wife of six years to immigrate to Milwaukee. Toy's restaurant, import, and other businesses flourished to such a degree that in 1912, he constructed a six-story building in a Chinese architectural style in downtown Milwaukee that at the time was claimed to be the largest and most luxurious Chinese restaurant building in the world.

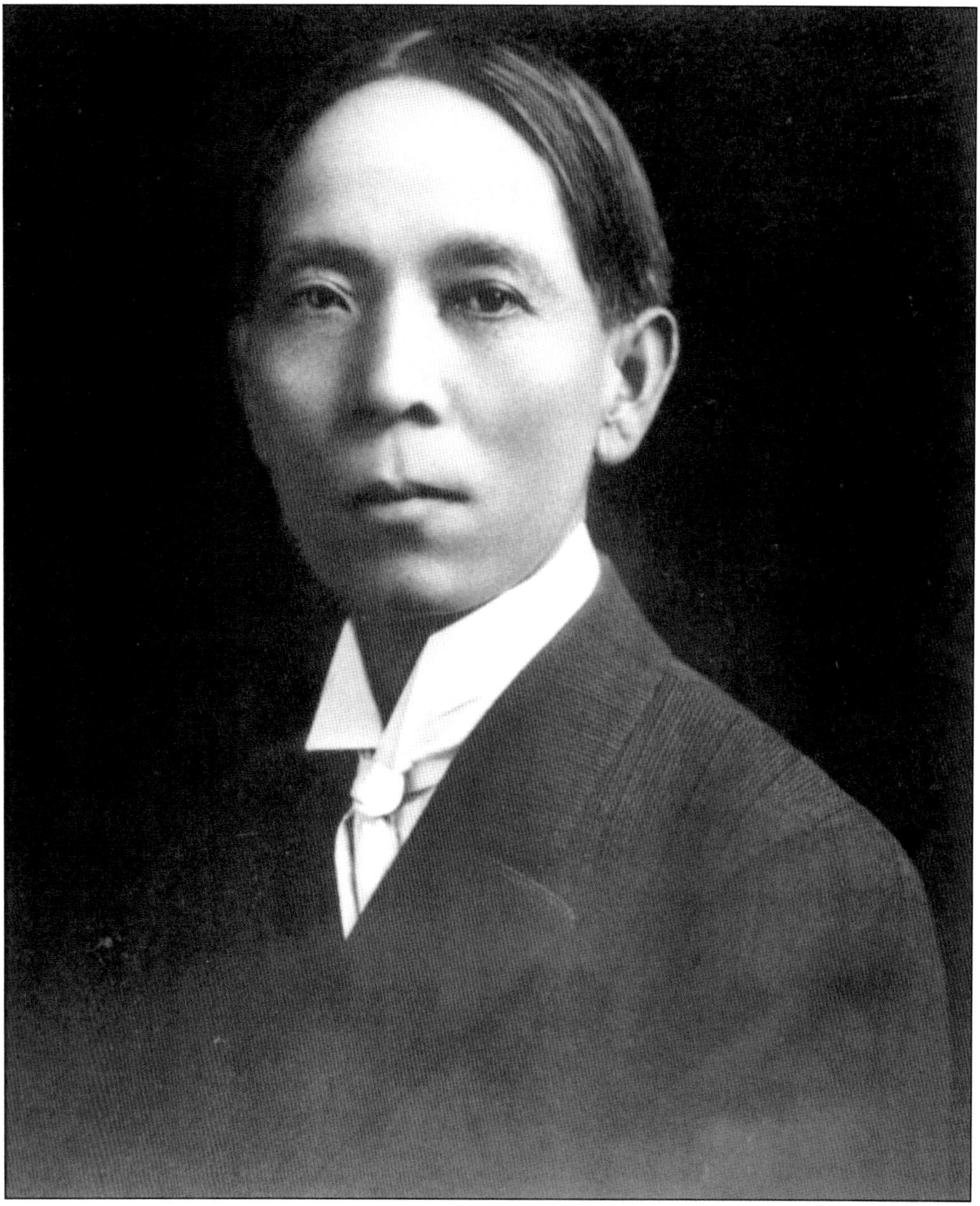

Charlie Toy was considered by many to be a patriarch of Milwaukee's Chinese community in the early 20th century. Toy (whose Chinese name was Moy Toy Ni) immigrated to the United States in 1880 at age 18, bringing no possessions other than a backpack, some blue cotton clothing, and a piece of wood engraved in Chinese with the motto Honesty Endures. Toy worked in various jobs in San Francisco, Portland, Chicago, Appleton, and Kaukauna before moving to Oshkosh in 1890 where he established several businesses. A success, Toy decided to take on the larger market of Milwaukee, and in 1904, he opened the Shanghai Chinese Restaurant at 199 West Water Street. By 1906 when this photograph was taken, Toy was well on his way to becoming one of the most successful Chinese businessmen of his era in the United States. The "Chinese Rockefeller," newspapers reported, was never too proud to lend a hand in the kitchen peeling water chestnuts or to take on other chores with his employees. (Courtesy of the Toy family.)

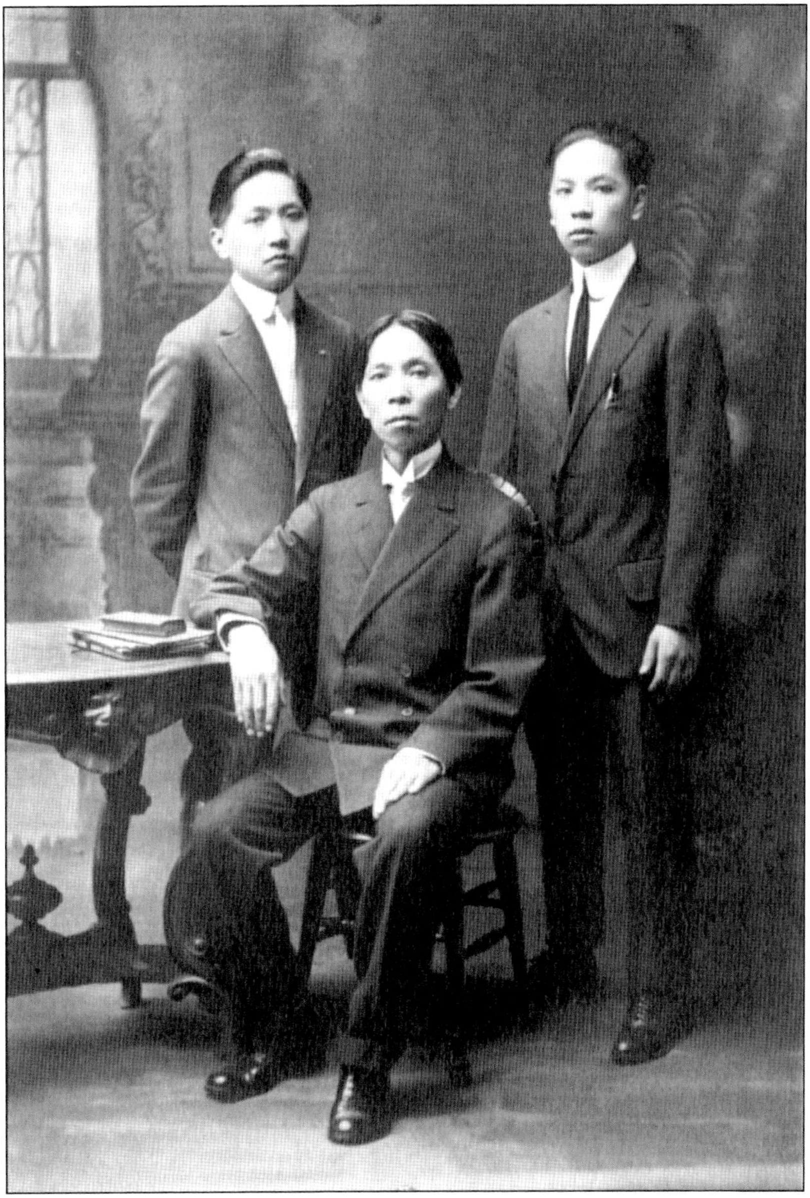

Charlie Toy (center); Moy Bock Ton, Charlie Toy's second-oldest son (left); and an unidentified relative are shown in this 1906 photograph. Moy Bock Ton, known by most Milwaukeeans as Moy B. Toy, was born in 1891 in Gum Ping village in the Sunning District of Taishan, in Guangdong Province in southern China. In 1901, at the age of 10, Moy B. Toy left his homeland to join his father in America. Being the minor son of a Chinese merchant, Moy B. Toy was a member of one of the few categories of Chinese allowed to immigrate to the United States under the Chinese Exclusion Act. Chinese children were rare, and the boy's presence attracted much attention. Newspaper reports of the "Celestial boy" and his activities were recorded in the *Oshkosh Daily Northwestern*—including accounts of Toy getting a suit of Western clothes, having his queue cut off by the local barber, and riding his bicycle around town. Toy attended the Oshkosh Normal School and later the Milwaukee Normal School. (Courtesy of Katherine Toy.)

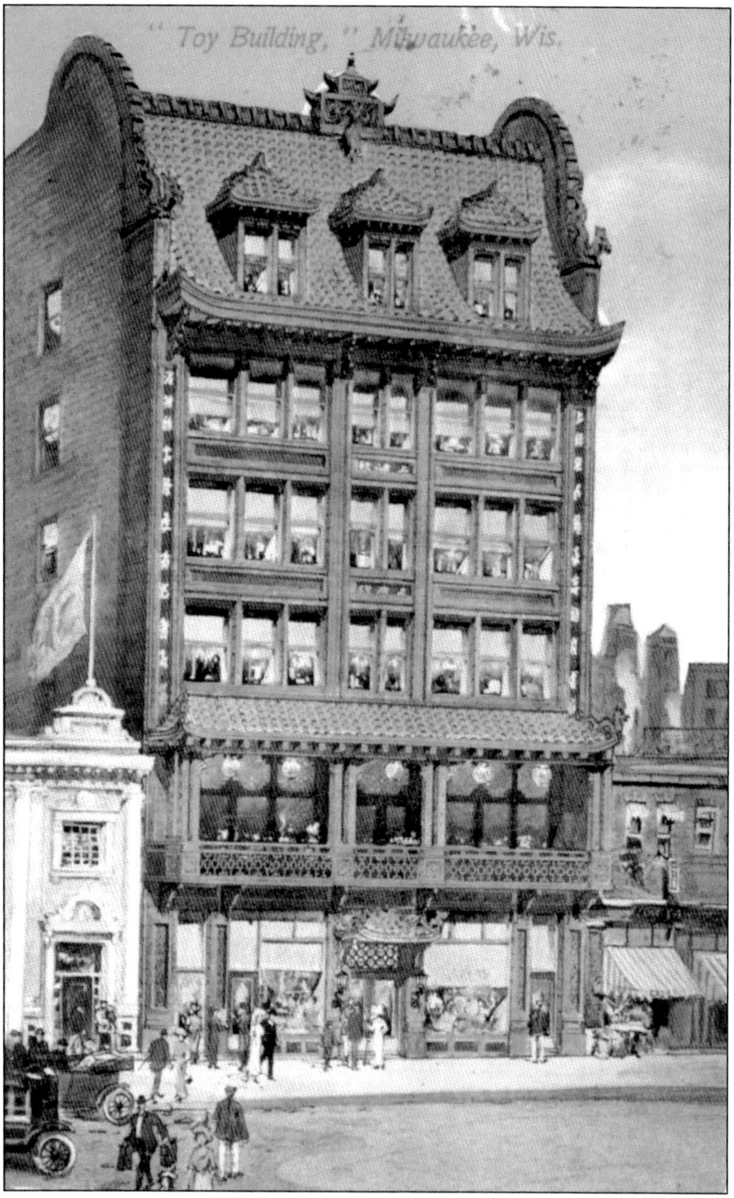

The Toy Building at 172–174 Second Street (later renumbered 716–718 North Second Street) opened in March 1913. The building was designed by Milwaukee architect Alexander Guth in a Chinese architectural style that included large green dragons along the roofline and an exterior of green terra-cotta brick. At the time of its construction, the building was described as being the largest and most luxurious Chinese restaurant building in the world. The building included the 460-seat Toy Theatre on the first floor; the popular Toy's Restaurant, band stage, and ballroom on the second floor; and the Hascall Billiards Hall on the third floor. Offices and living quarters filled out the fourth through sixth floors. Two earlier restaurants by Charlie Toy were located one block to the east at 199 and 207 West Water Street. This postcard was printed shortly after the building's construction and was mailed in 1915. The figures in the foreground include a man with a pigtail or queue in the traditional Chinese style. (Courtesy of David B. Holmes.)

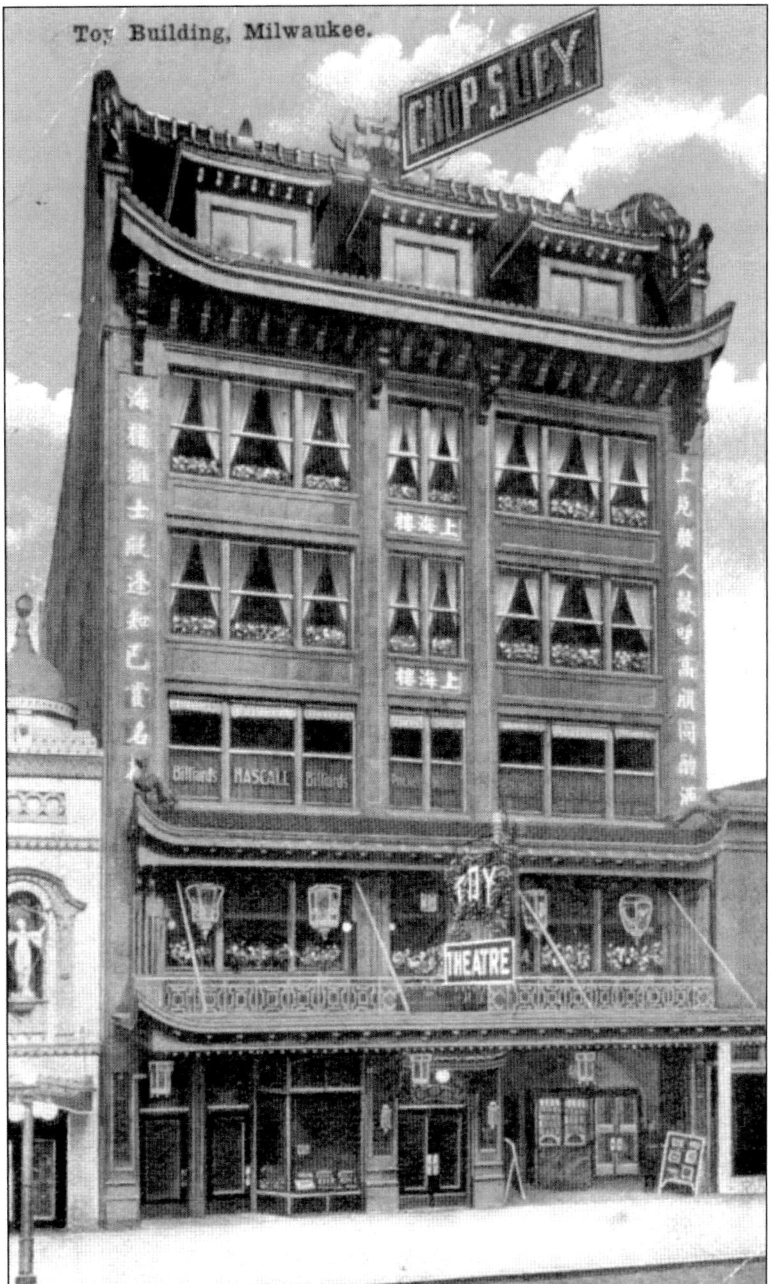

This postcard presents a view of the Toy Building dating from the early 1920s. The Toy Theatre reportedly was closed by 1924 after becoming outdated due to the presence of larger theaters designed to show talking movies. The white building to the left of the Toy Building was the Crystal Theatre, which opened in 1904 and was razed in 1927. According to a newspaper article dated 1923, the Crystal Theatre was acquired by Charlie Toy in 1921 and managed for a period by Moy B. Toy, Charlie's second-oldest son. The third floor of the Toy Building at the time this postcard was produced was occupied by the Hascall Billiards Hall, as shown by the sign on the window. (Courtesy of the Toy family.)

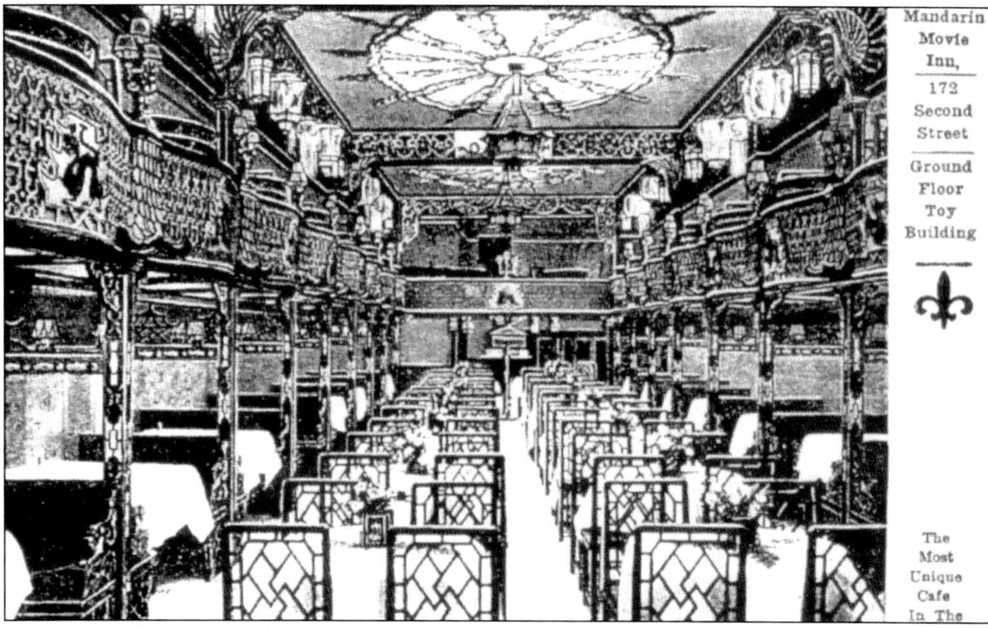

The Toy Building housed a 460-seat movie theater and café known as the Toy Theatre, or at the time this postcard was produced, as the Mandarin Movie Inn. Interestingly the concept of combining fine dining with a movie theater experience has recently made a comeback in the Milwaukee area, almost 90 years after the concept was being implemented at the Toy Theatre/Mandarin Movie Inn. (Courtesy of Larry Widen.)

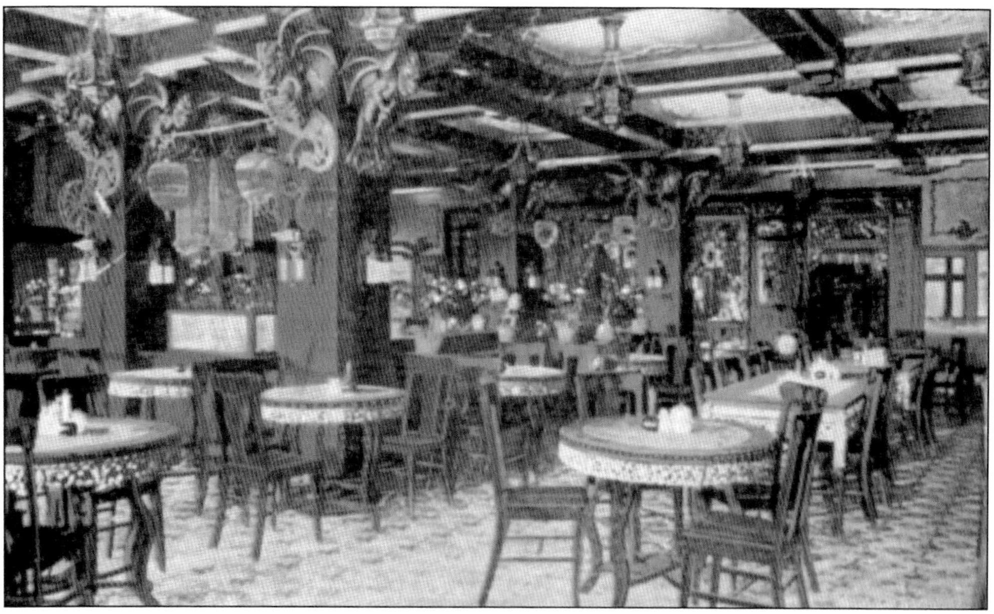

The interior of Toy's Restaurant located on the second floor of the Toy Building was elaborately decorated, as shown on this 1913 postcard. Although Charlie Toy's first restaurant at 199 West Water Street opened in 1904, as one of the earliest Chinese restaurants in Milwaukee, the first Chinese restaurant in Milwaukee appears to have opened in 1900. (Courtesy of David B. Holmes.)

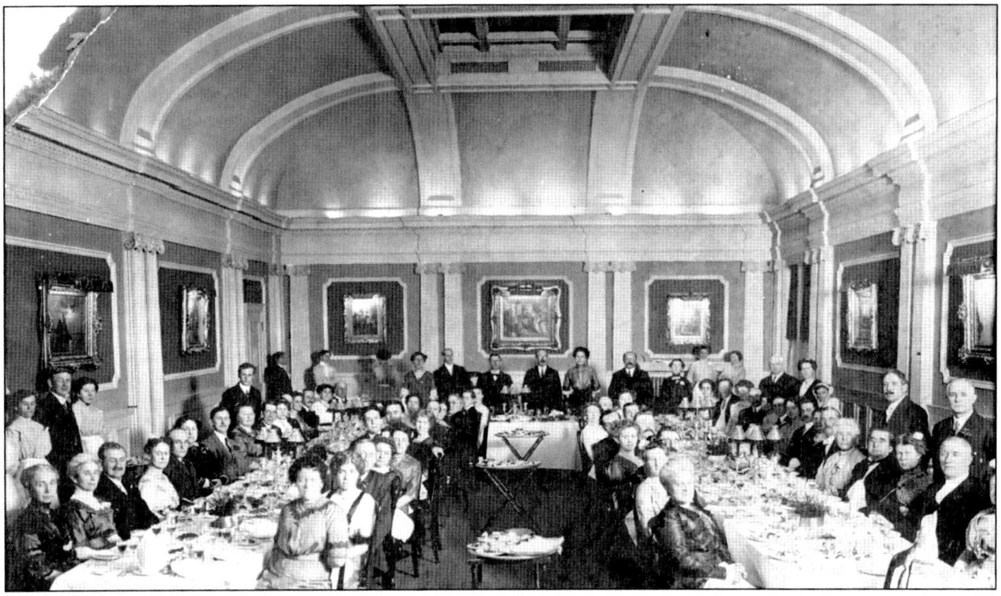

The lack of Chinese faces in this 1913 photograph despite the presence of at least 10 Chinese laundries in Milwaukee hints toward the exclusionary membership practices at the Milwaukee Laundry Men's Club during this era. At the time of the 1889 riot, Milwaukee newspapers reported that approximately 20 of the Caucasian proprietors petitioned the city to license all city laundries, with an aim of excluding many of the Chinese. To Milwaukee's credit, the licensing scheme was never implemented. (Courtesy of the Milwaukee Public Library.)

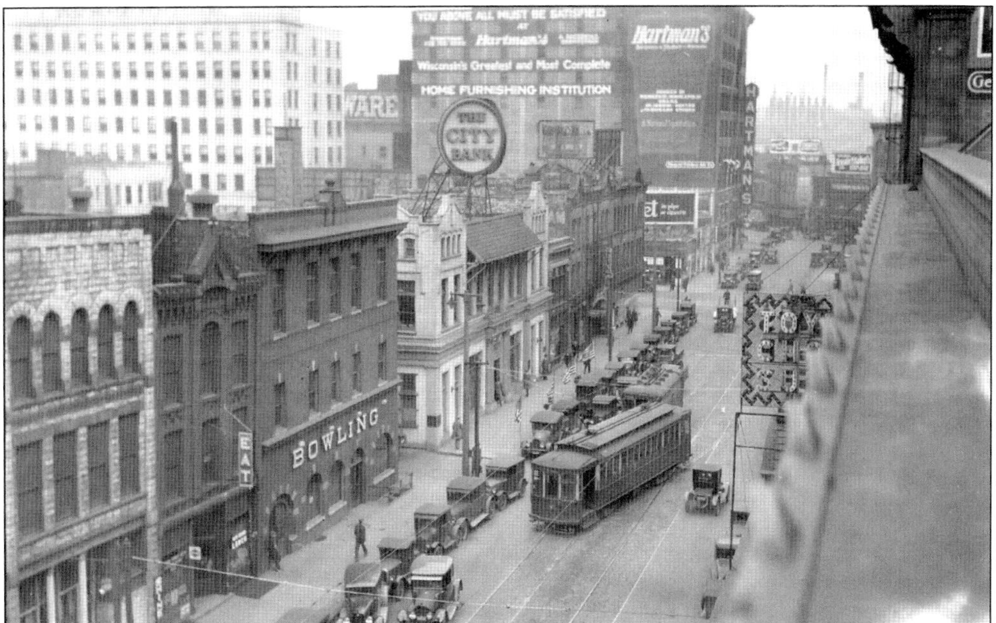

This 1920s photograph presents a view facing north along North Second Street from the roof of the building located directly south of the Toy Building at 172–174 North Second Street. The sign for Toys Chop Suey is visible on the right side of the photograph. (Courtesy of the Milwaukee Public Library.)

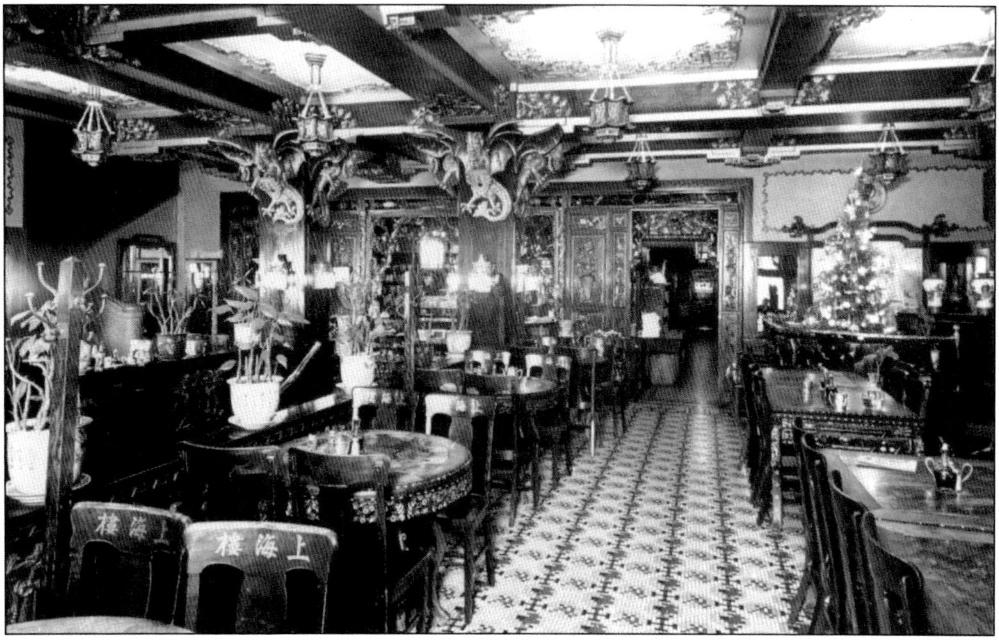

The interior of Toy's Restaurant on the second floor of the Toy Building, as shown on this photograph dated 1923, was the most elaborately decorated Chinese restaurant in Milwaukee, if not the United States. From its opening in 1913 through its closure in approximately 1937, the restaurant was a major center of social activity in the city of Milwaukee. A frequent visitor to the restaurant in the late 1920s and early 1930s reportedly was Walter Valentino Liberace (better known simply as Liberace), whose older brother George was a member of the house band. Some of the inlaid teakwood furniture from the restaurant remains in possession of members of the Toy family, and several pieces are on display in the Streets of Old Milwaukee exhibit at the Milwaukee Public Museum. (Courtesy of David Toy.)

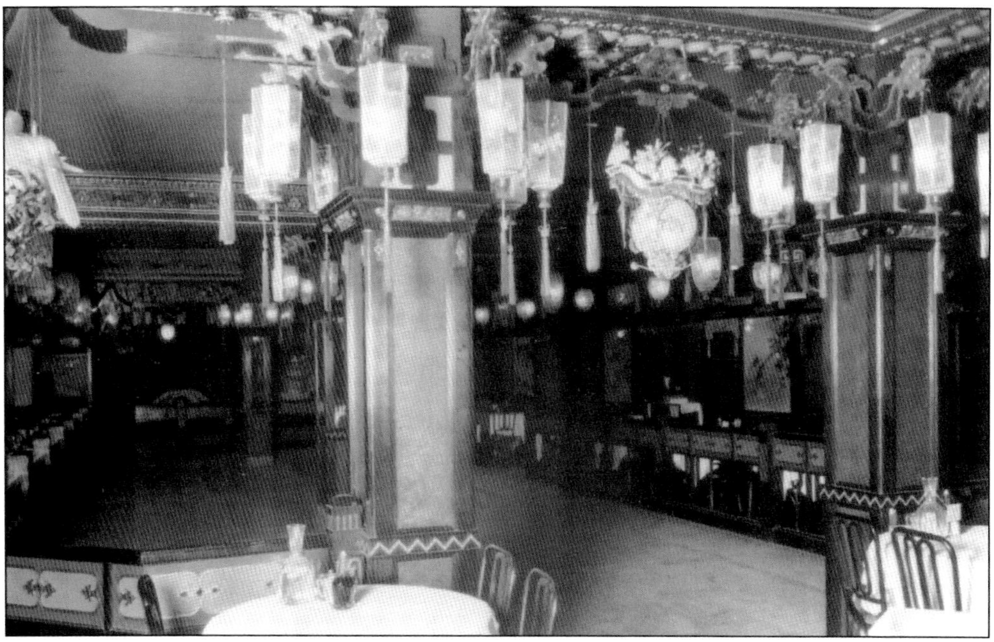

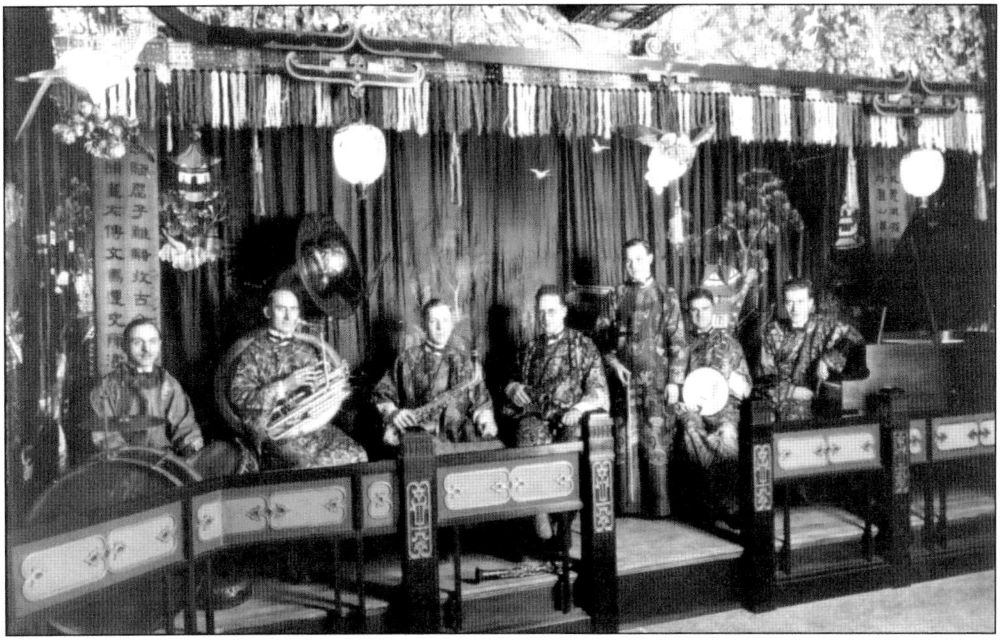

These photographs, dated December 27, 1923, are of Wing Toy and His Orientals, a band that performed in the dance hall area of the Toy's Restaurant located on the second floor of the Toy Building. Wing Toy reportedly was a relative of Charlie Toy, although the nature of the relationship is uncertain. The band reportedly recorded at least one album at the New York Recording Laboratories studio in Grafton, Wisconsin, in 1931, under the studio's Broadway label. The restaurant reportedly was one of three main venues for jazz and big band acts during the 1920s and 1930s, the others being the Wisconsin Roof and the Eagle's Club. Toy's Restaurant reportedly was the preferred venue for dancing. The lower photograph shows Charlie Toy (center), Moy B. Toy (right), and an unidentified relative (left) in front of the same stage in 1923. (Courtesy of the Toy family.)

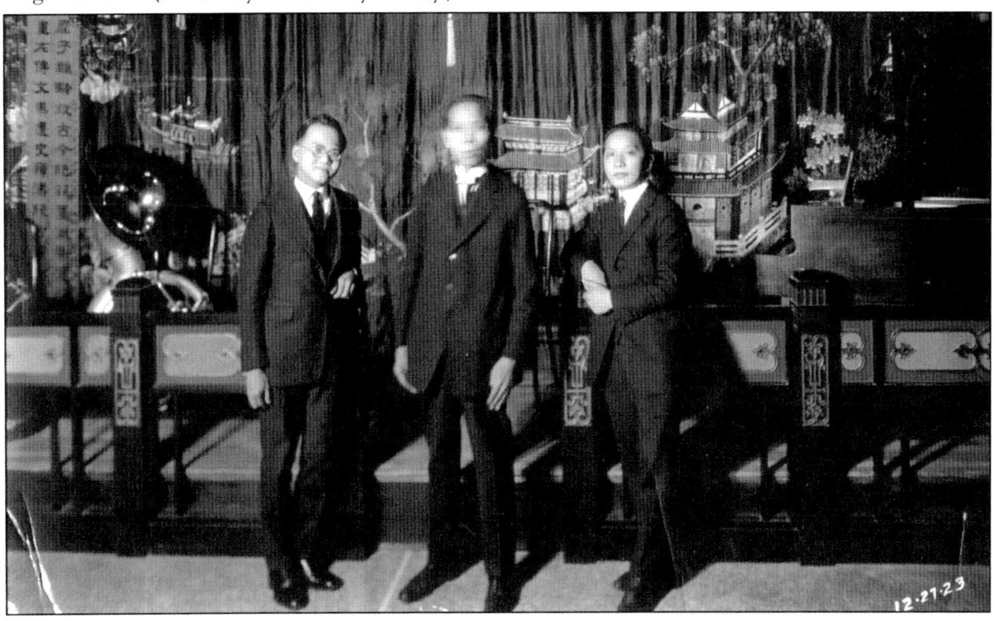

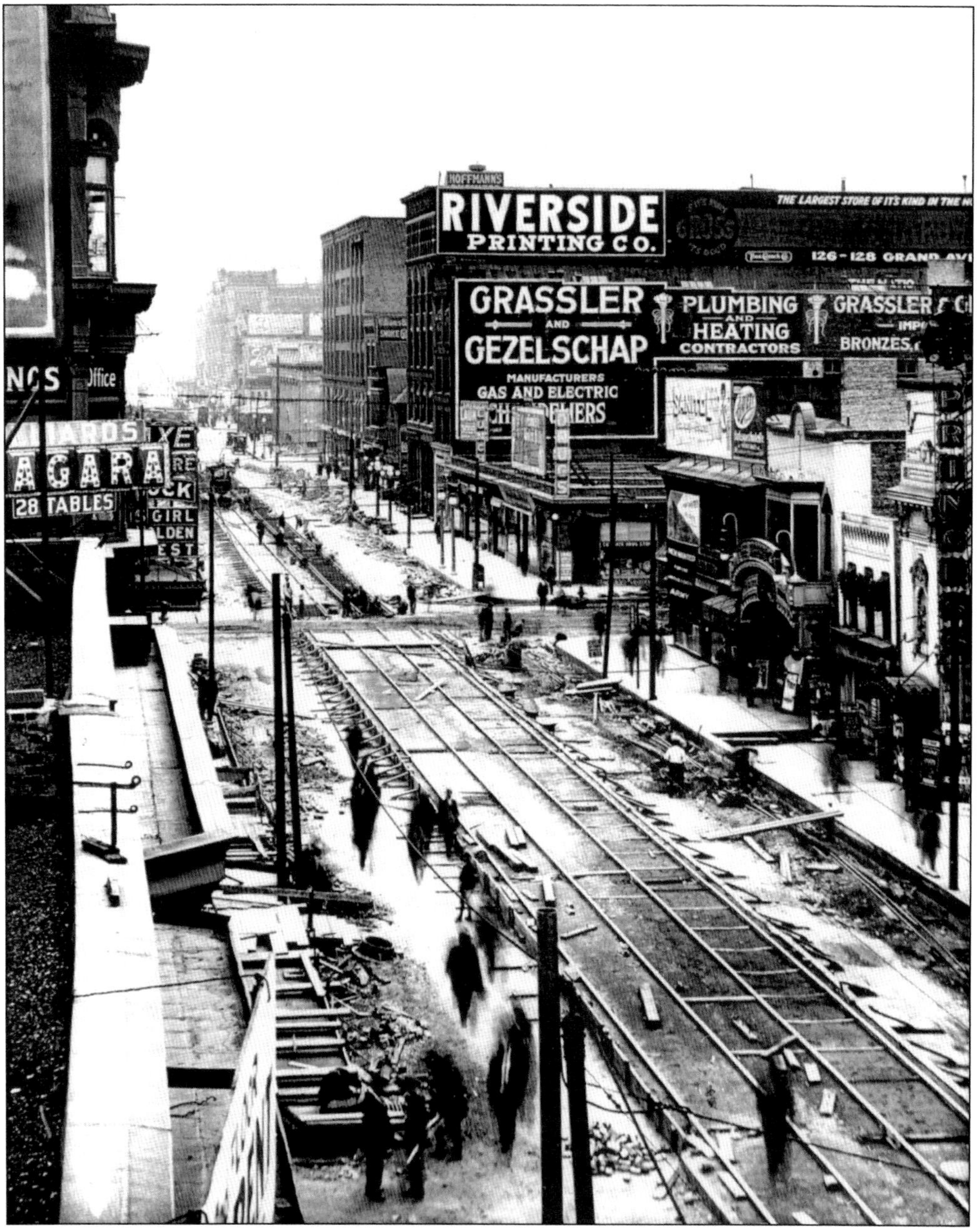

This 1913 photograph shows a view facing north of North Third Street from the intersection of West Wells Street. The signs on the buildings on the left side of the photograph include those for the King Yen Lo Restaurant located at 191–193 North Third Street, which was partially owned by Charlie Toy, and the Saxe Theatre at 197 North Third Street, which was managed at the time by Toy's brother. The Toy's Restaurant (also known for a period as the New Shanghai Mandarin Restaurant) was located one block to the east. This area was a major theater district in Milwaukee, with 9 of 48 theaters listed in the 1915 Milwaukee City Directory located within an approximately one-block radius. The streetcar lines shown being installed at the time of this photograph further added to the area's desirability for Chinese and other restaurant operators. (Courtesy of the Milwaukee Public Library.)

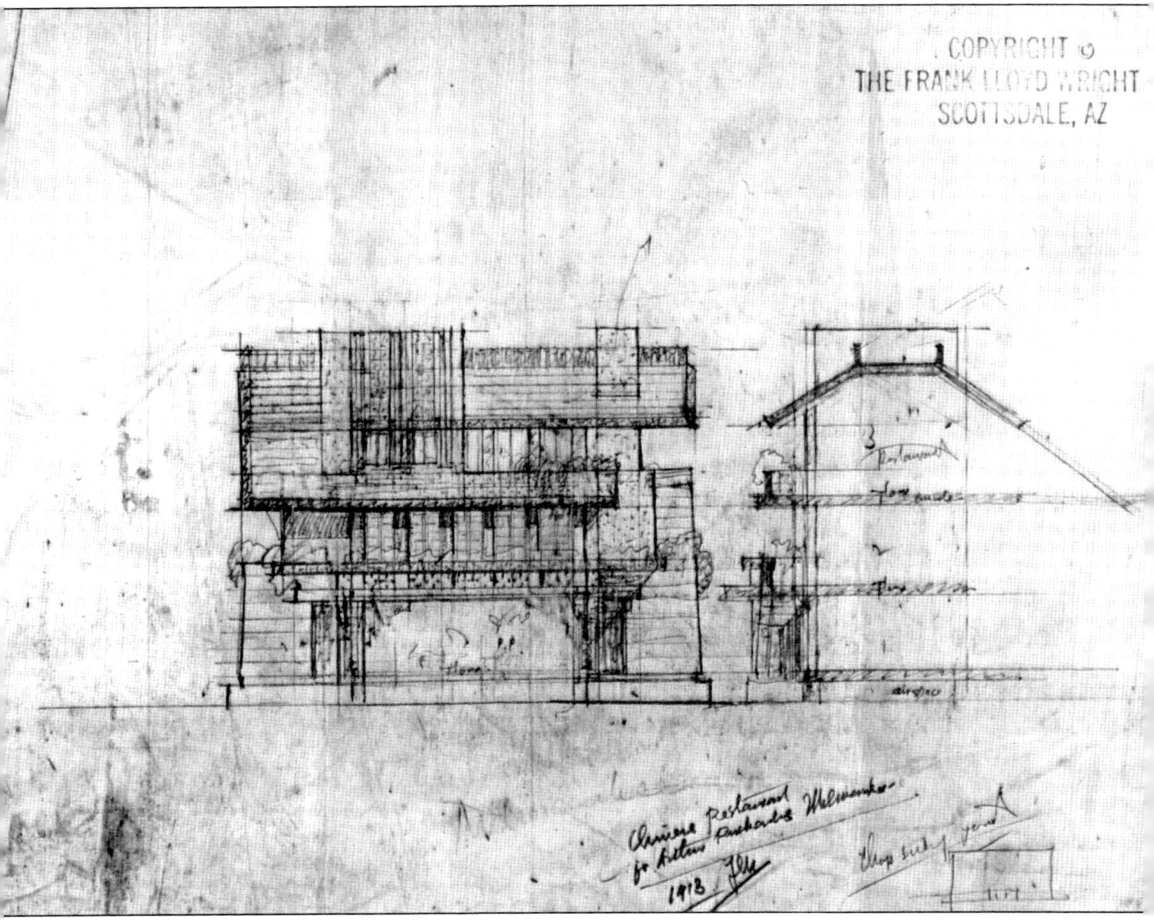

In 1918, Frank Lloyd Wright completed this conceptual design of a Chinese restaurant building for Charlie Toy. The name Arthur Richards on the drawing refers to a noted Milwaukee real estate developer who partnered in Toy's wholesale business, the Wing Lung Company. The extent of Charlie Toy's relationship with Frank Lloyd Wright is uncertain, but Richards was involved with at least 13 Wright projects for Wisconsin clients. Wright, perhaps Wisconsin's most renowned resident, was significantly influenced in his thinking by Chinese philosophy and made a trip to China in 1918, the same year as this design for Charlie Toy. The fact that the design was never executed may be a tribute to Charlie Toy's business acumen, given the cost overruns that were common to many of Wright's designs. (Drawing of Frank Lloyd Wright, copyright © 2008, the Frank Lloyd Wright Foundation, Taliesin West, Scottsdale, Arizona.)

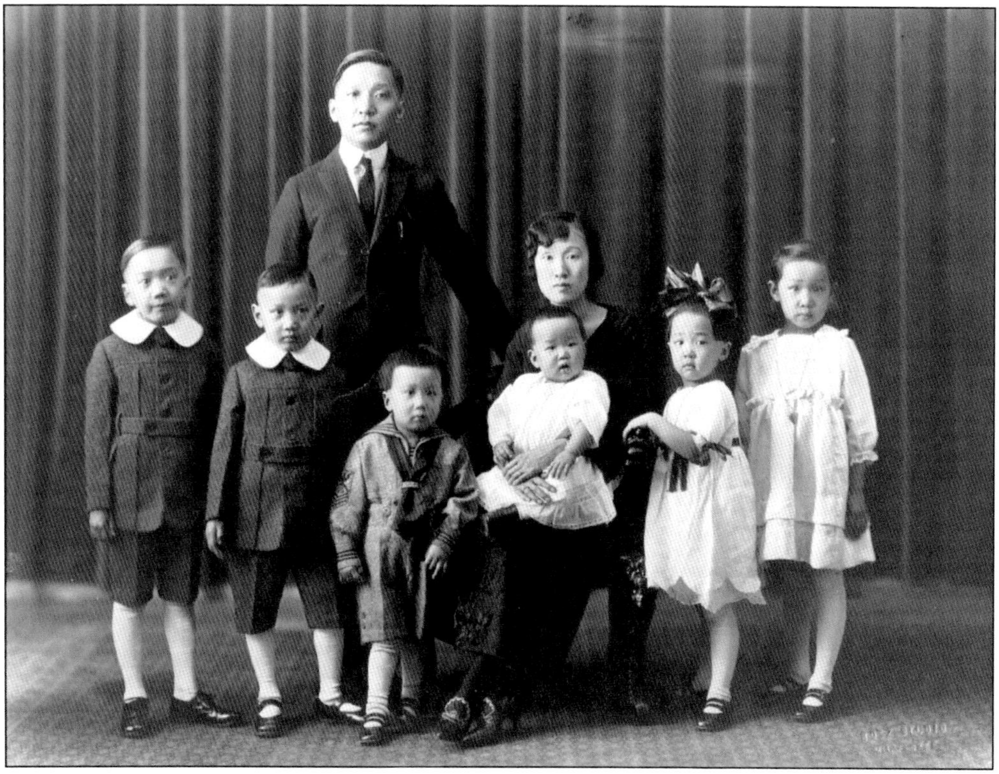

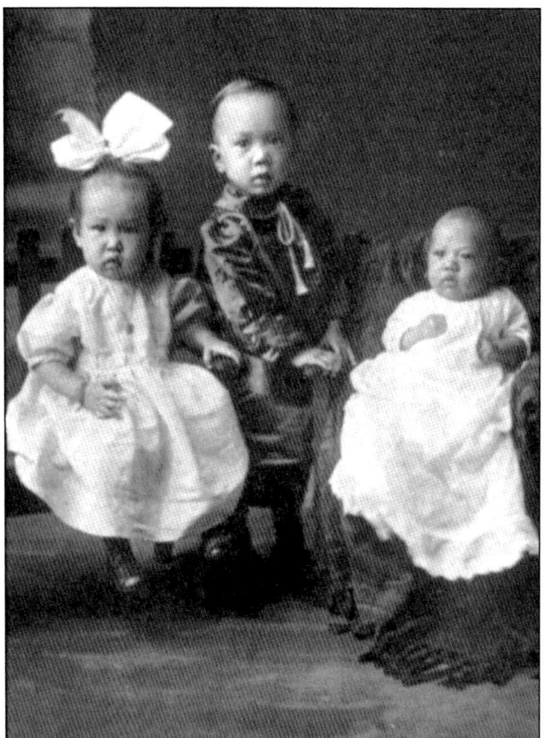

Moy B. Toy, Charlie Toy's second-oldest son, left for China on August 15, 1913, for the purpose of marrying Leung Yuey King. At the time of the wedding, Moy B. Toy was a student in electrical engineering at the University of Wisconsin. In January 1914, the couple returned to Milwaukee. On February 12, 1914, a reception was held by Charlie Toy at the New Shanghai Restaurant to honor the couple as well as another son, Moy Bock Quong, who had also traveled to China, married, and returned to Milwaukee at the same time as Moy B. Toy. Mayor Gerhard Bading of Milwaukee, among many distinguished guests, delivered a speech half in Chinese. Moy B. Toy and Leung Yuey King had nine children together, eight of whom lived to adulthood; all but one were born in Milwaukee. The above photograph shows the couple with six of their children in approximately 1921. The lower photograph shows the three oldest children in approximately 1918. (Courtesy of the Toy family.)

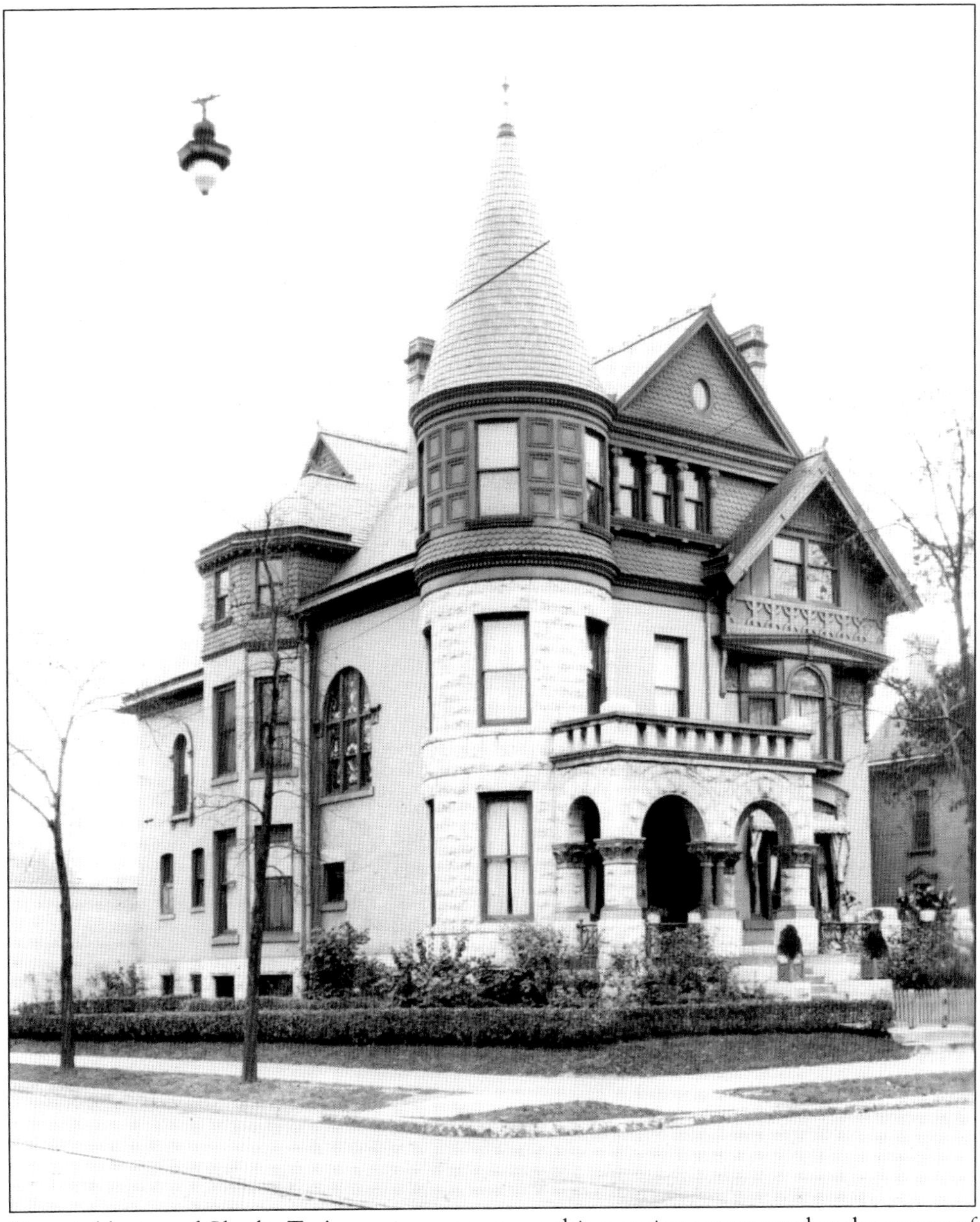

One visible sign of Charlie Toy's growing success was this mansion constructed at the corner of North Fourteenth Street and West Wells Street. In 1920, the house was listed as the residence for 16 members of the Toy family, including Charlie Toy (age 60), his sons Moy Bock Ton and Moy Bock Quong, their wives, his youngest daughter May, four grandsons, five granddaughters, and one nephew. The house was acquired by Marquette University in 1957 and later demolished. This photograph was taken by Kuhli Photo Service in 1914. Although the Toy residence was by no means typical for Milwaukee Chinese residents of this era, the move to a residential neighborhood was consistent with a larger trend in residential living patterns. Whereas in 1900, 12 of 13 Milwaukee Chinese residents identified in the Milwaukee City Directory were listed as living at the same address as their place of business, by 1930, this was true for only 48 of 112 residents. (Courtesy of the Toy family.)

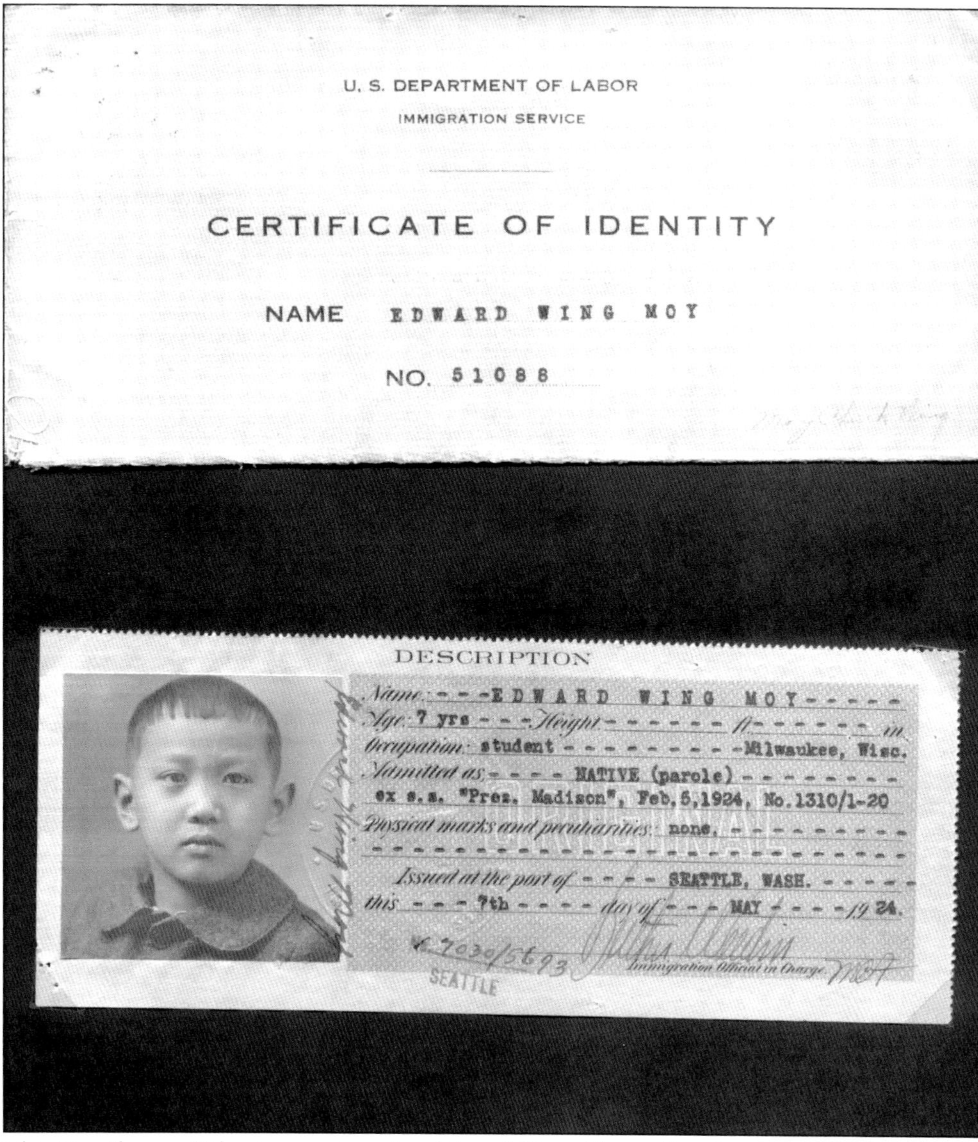
U. S. DEPARTMENT OF LABOR

IMMIGRATION SERVICE

CERTIFICATE OF IDENTITY

NAME EDWARD WING MOY

NO. 51088

DESCRIPTION

Name - - -EDWARD WING MOY- - - - -

Age 7 yrs - - -Height - - - - - - ft - - - - - - in.

Occupation: student - - - - - - - - -Milwaukee, Wisc.

Admitted as - - - - NATIVE (parole) - - - - - - - -

ex s.s. "Pres. Madison", Feb.5,1924, No.1310/1-20

Physical marks and peculiarities: none, - - - - - - - -

Issued at the port of - - - - SEATTLE, WASH. - - - - -

this - - - 7th - - - - day of - - - MAY - - - - 1924.

7030/5693

Immigration Official in Charge

SEATTLE

This Certificate of Identity was issued to Edward Wing Toy in Seattle on May 7, 1924, on his return to the United States from China. Edward was one of 11 grandchildren who accompanied Charlie Toy on a trip to China a year earlier. Charlie Toy traveled to China several times during the 1920s and 1930s, combining both business and family duties. The large family traveling group was often composed of grandchildren that Toy desired to have educated in China as well as the United States. The year 1924 was to mark the passage of perhaps the harshest of all anti-Chinese legislation, the Immigration Act of 1924, which even prohibited Chinese-born wives and children of American citizens from entering the United States. (Courtesy of the Toy family.)

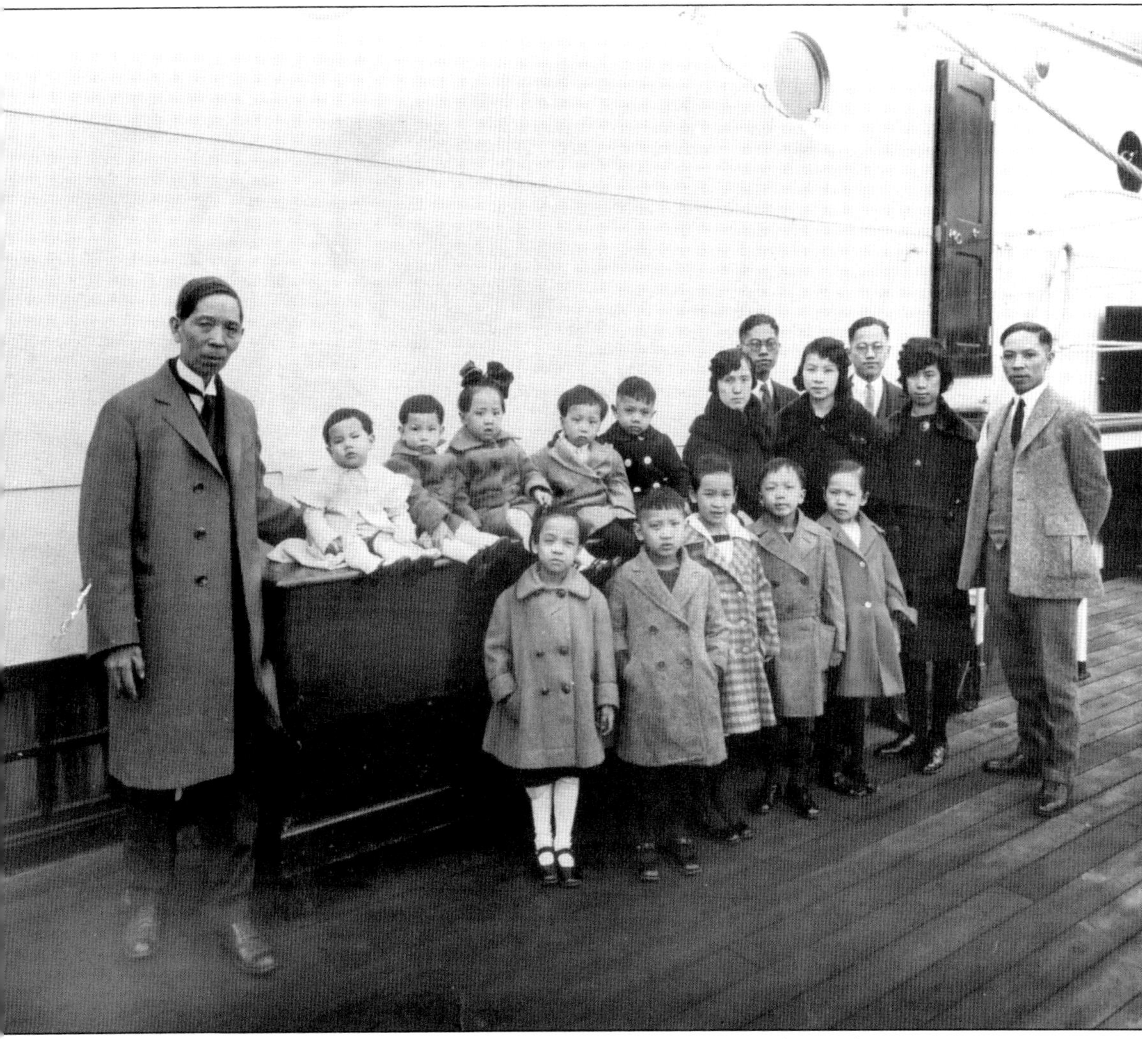

This photograph, dated 1923, is of Charlie Toy (left) with 15 of 18 family members accompanying him on a trip to China. The photograph was likely taken aboard the Canadian Pacific steamship *Empress of Canada*, on which the group traveled from Vancouver to Canton, via Hong Kong. An article in the Oshkosh newspaper reported that the purpose for the trip was for his grandchildren to learn the Chinese language and culture, as well as to enjoy the summer home that Charlie was planning to build on a hill overlooking the Pearl River in Canton. The group left Milwaukee on April 27, 1923, traveling first to Vancouver by first-class railcar, and then to China via the *Empress of Canada*, one of the biggest and fastest ships on the Pacific Ocean. Such a trip by a Chinese American family during this era was in many ways extraordinary and received front-page coverage in newspapers throughout the United States as well as Japan. (Courtesy of the Toy family.)

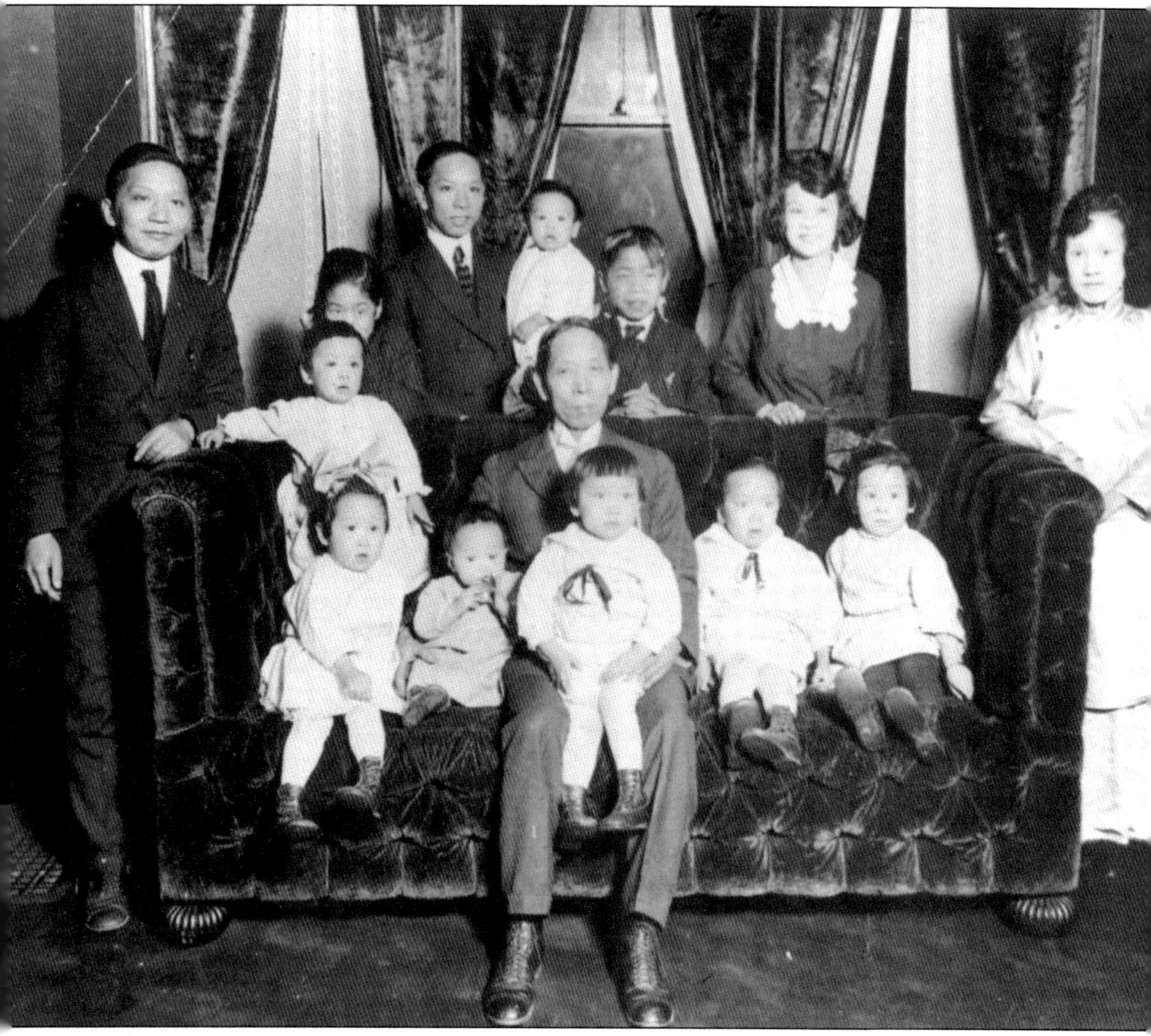

This photograph, dated approximately 1921, shows Charlie Toy (seated at center), with son Moy B. Toy (standing left), son Donald Toy (standing left center), two daughter-in-laws, and nine grandchildren. At the time of this photograph, the extended family was living in the mansion at 200 North Fourteenth Street shown in the photograph on page 43. (Courtesy of the Toy family.)

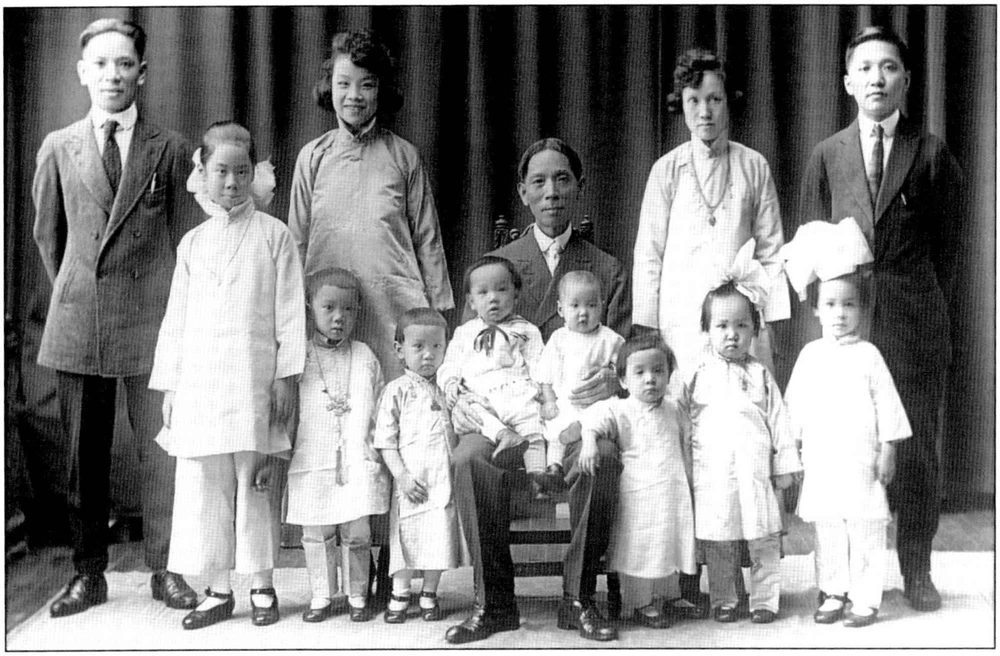

The photograph above, taken in approximately 1924, shows Charlie Toy (seated center), together with his second-oldest son, Moy (far right), his third-oldest son, Donald (far left), his sons' wives (standing back row), his youngest daughter May (second from left), and seven of his grandchildren in Milwaukee. The lower photograph is a version of the same photograph that has been modified to include a separate photograph of the family of Dung Lan Toy, Charlie Toy's oldest son. Dung Lan Toy was in charge of his father's export business in China and appears to have remained in China throughout his life. Dun Lan Toy had five children by two wives, all of whom appear in the lower photograph. Toy, like many immigrants, struggled to maintain ties between family members located on separate continents. (Above, courtesy of Katherine Toy; below, courtesy of the Toy family.)

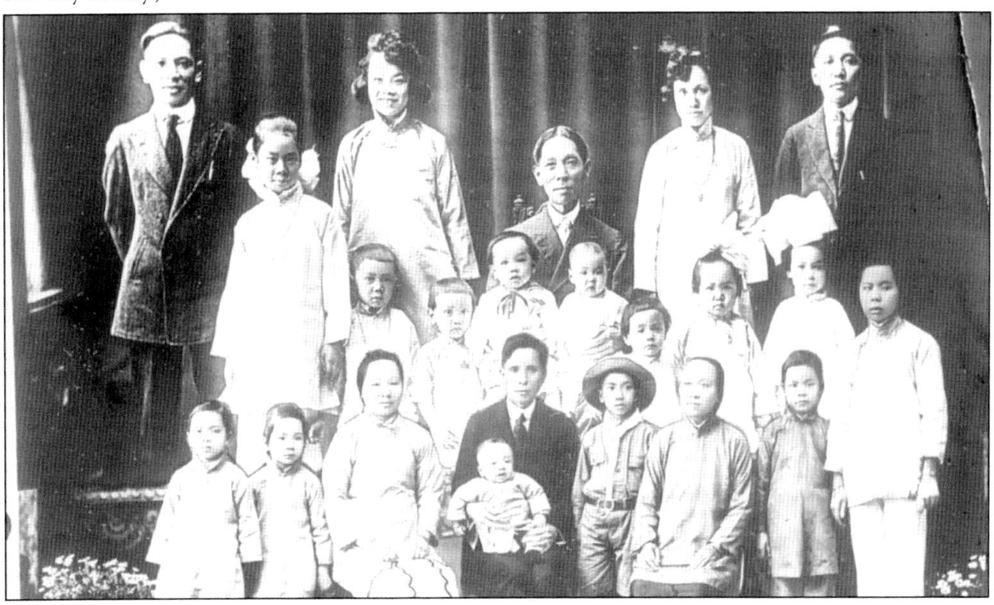

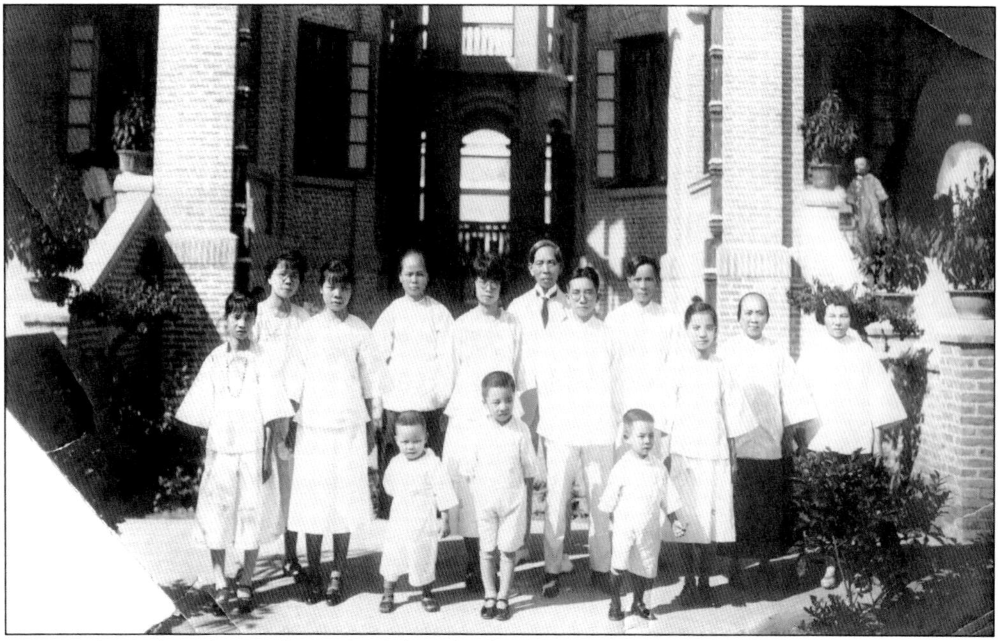

Toy Gardens, the Chinese home built by Charlie Toy, was located approximately 10 miles from Canton, on a hill overlooking the Pearl River, from which the red-tile roofs and twin pagoda towers in Canton were still visible in the distance. Nearby residences were owned by fellow Milwaukee Chinese from the Wong and Moy families, creating in effect a small Milwaukee neighborhood in China. The Chinese writing at the top of the original photographs identified the date of the photographs as October 10 of the Year 14 (above) and December 1 of the Year 19 (below). Based on a traditional Chinese method for referencing dates, Year 1 represents the first year of a new dynasty. In this instance, Year 1 references the founding of the Republic of China in 1912. Therefore, the dates of the photographs are October 10, 1925, and December 1, 1930. (Courtesy of the Toy family.)

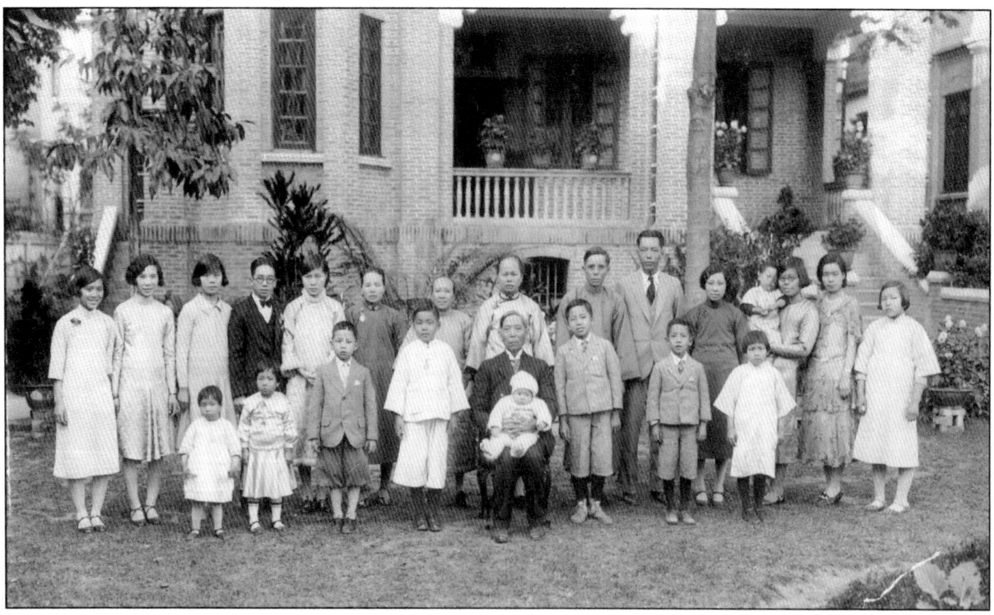

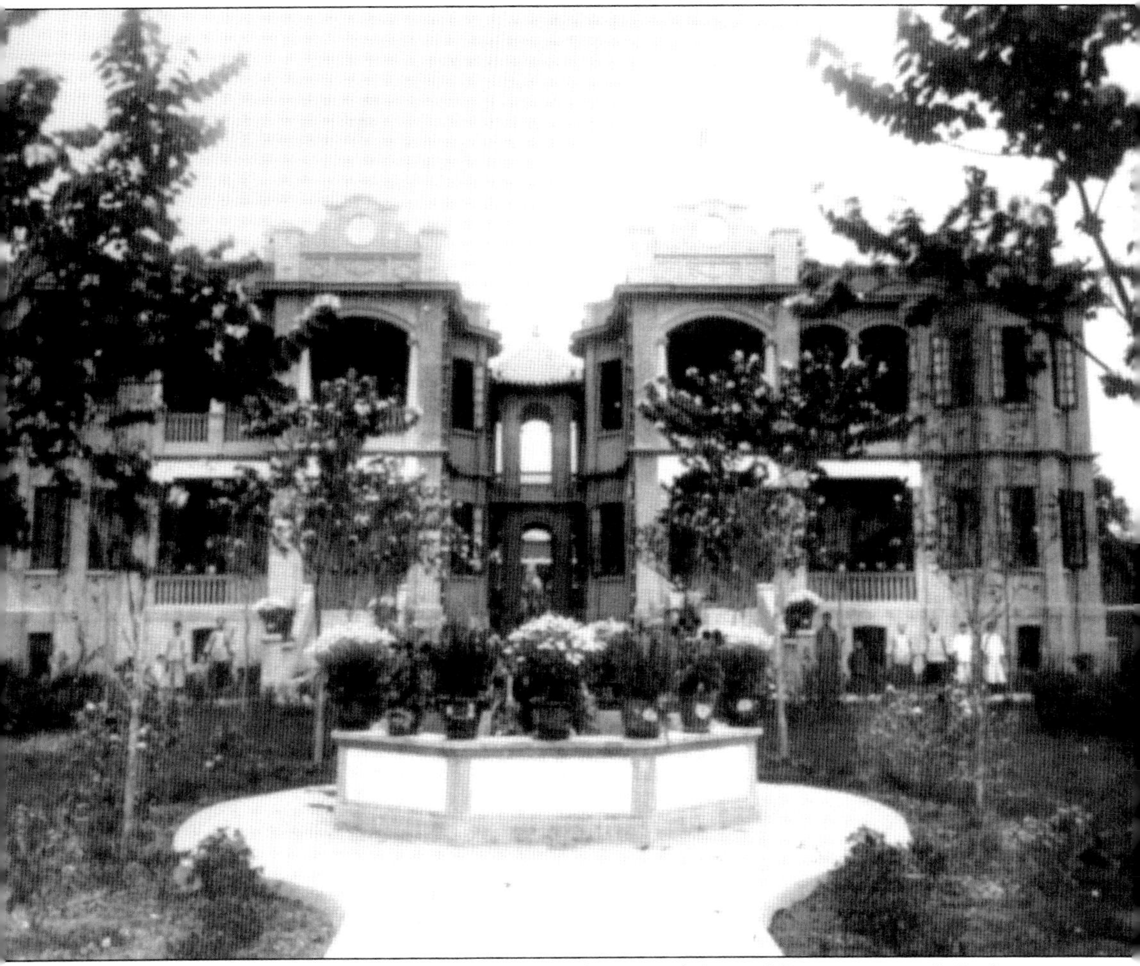

In 1922, Charlie Toy retained the Milwaukee architectural firm of Buemming and Guth to design a summer residence, Toy Gardens, for his family in Canton, China. Alexander Guth, one of the principals of the firm, had previously been the architect for the six-story Toy Building in downtown Milwaukee. While the earlier building was constructed in a Chinese architectural style, the residence in China was designed in an American architectural style, with separate towers or wings: for the family of Charlie Toy's oldest son, for the family from America when visiting China, and for American guests. The 25-room residence was completed in 1925. Toy retired to this residence in the mid-1930s but was forced to flee in 1938 as a result of the Japanese invasion and takeover of Canton. The house reportedly was occupied by Japanese soldiers for the remainder of World War II. Toy again retired to the residence in 1947 where he lived until his death in 1955. (Courtesy of the Toy family.)

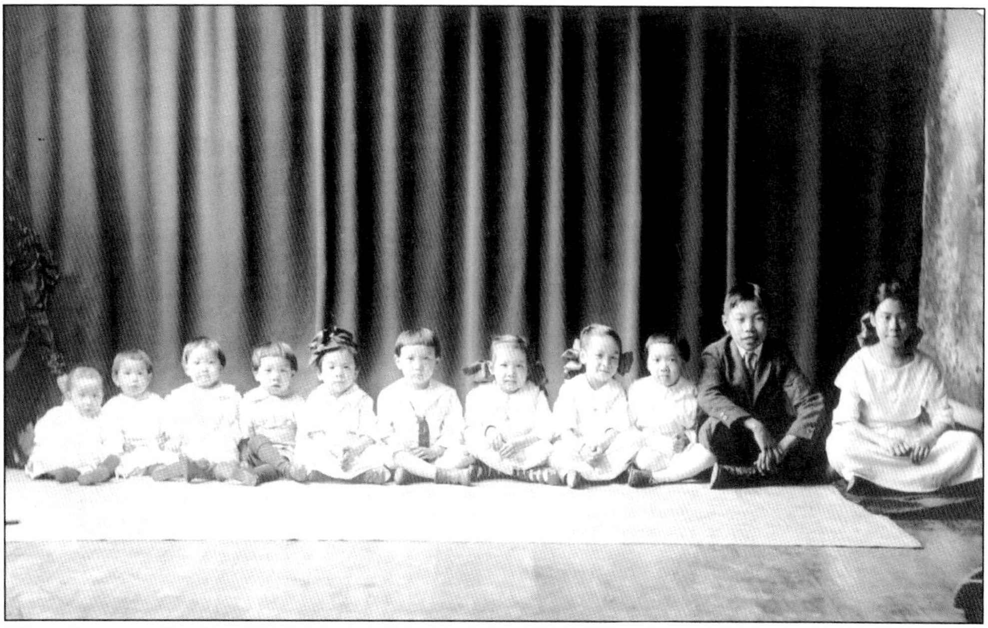

This photograph, dated approximately 1920, shows 10 children of Charlie Toy's second- and third-oldest sons, Moy B. and Donald, as well as May Toy, Charlie Toy's youngest daughter (far right). The photograph was taken on a stage in the Toy Theatre, where the children reportedly performed on a regular basis. (Courtesy of the Toy family.)

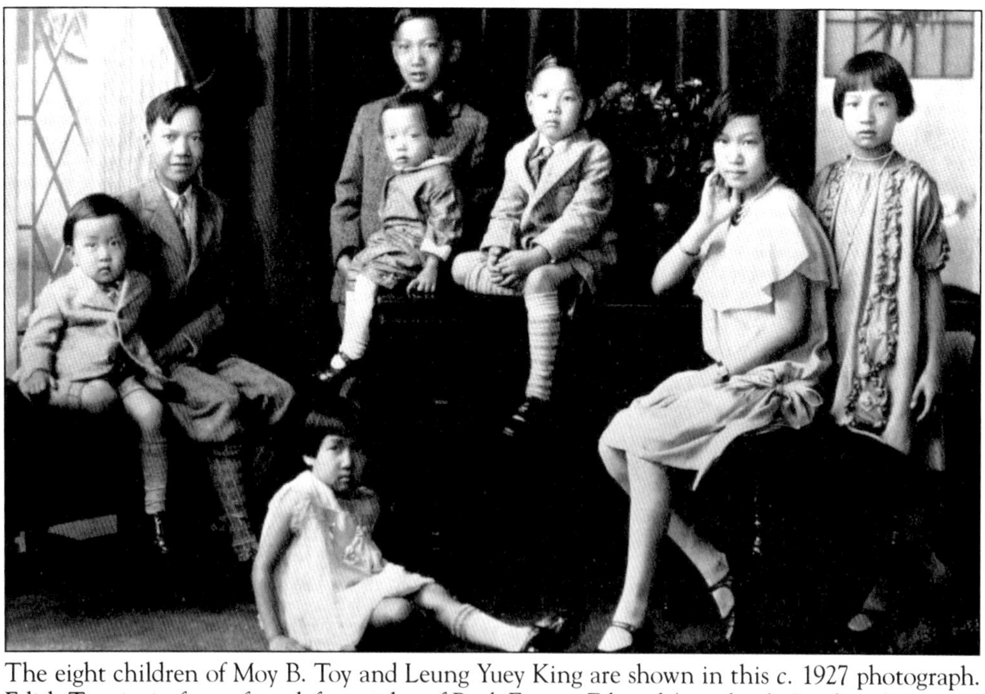

The eight children of Moy B. Toy and Leung Yuey King are shown in this *c.* 1927 photograph. Edith Toy sits in front, from left to right, of Paul, Ernest, Edward (standing), Stephen (sitting in front of Edward), David, Elizabeth, and Marjorie. In an era when only approximately 6 percent of women and 12 percent of men born in the United States obtained college degrees, it is remarkable that all eight children obtained college degrees. (Courtesy of Katherine Toy.)

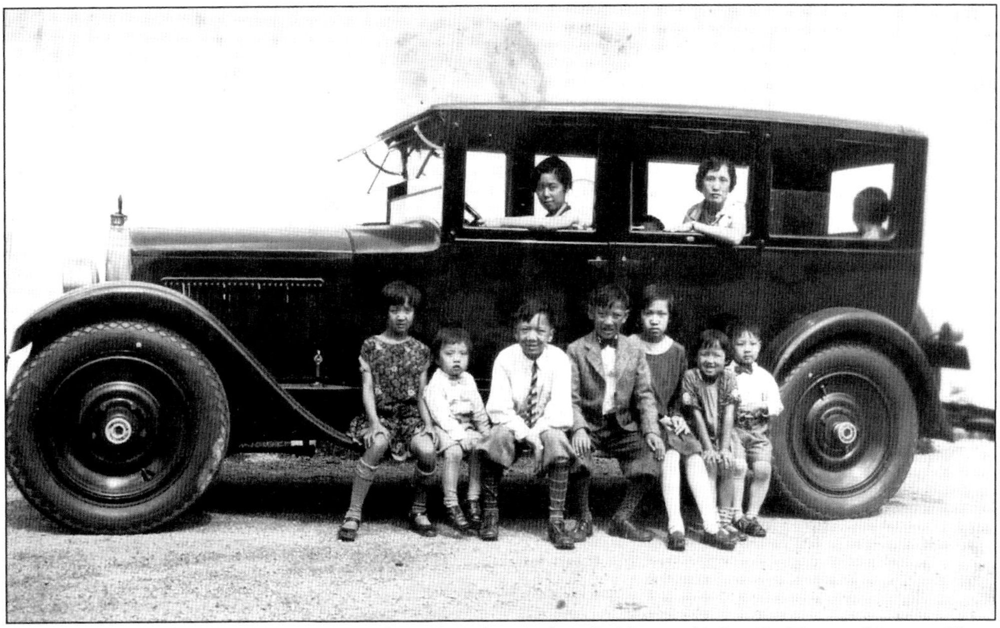

This photograph, dated approximately 1930, shows the children of Moy B. Toy and Leung Yuey King on an outing in the family car. Seated from left to right on the car's running board are Marjorie, Paul, Ernest, Edward, Elizabeth, Edith, and David. The children's aunt (May Toy) is seated in the driver's seat, and their mother, Leung, is visible in the middle window of the car. (Courtesy of Katherine Toy.)

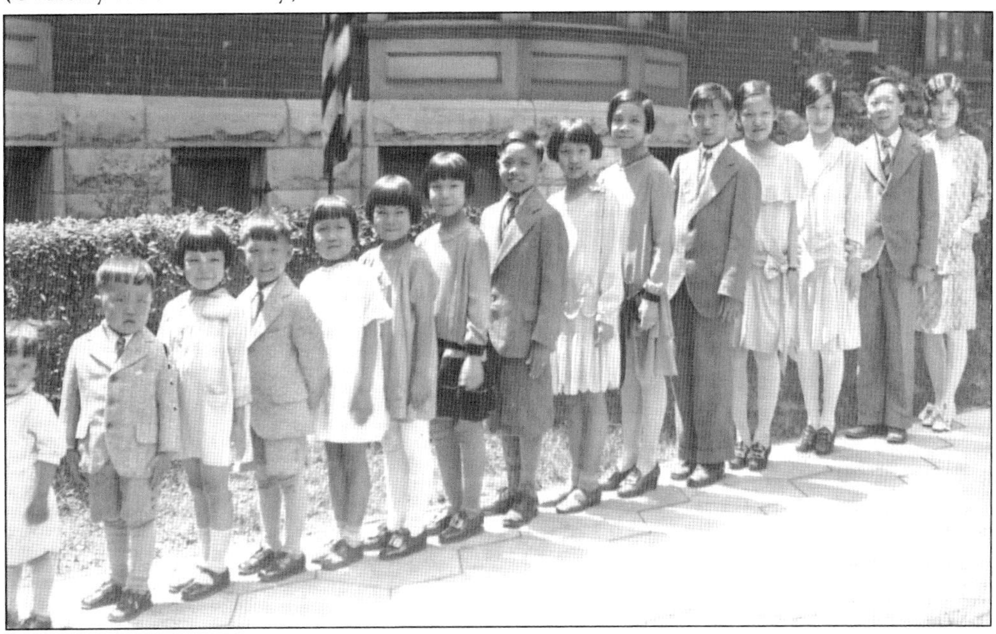

This photograph, taken on July 4, 1929, shows 14 of Charlie Toy's grandchildren and his youngest daughter May (far right) in front of the family home at 759 North Twenty-ninth Street. The children included the sons and daughters of Moy B. Toy and Donald Toy, Charlie Toy's second- and third-oldest sons. The two families shared a home together throughout much of the 1920s and 1930s. (Courtesy of the Toy family.)

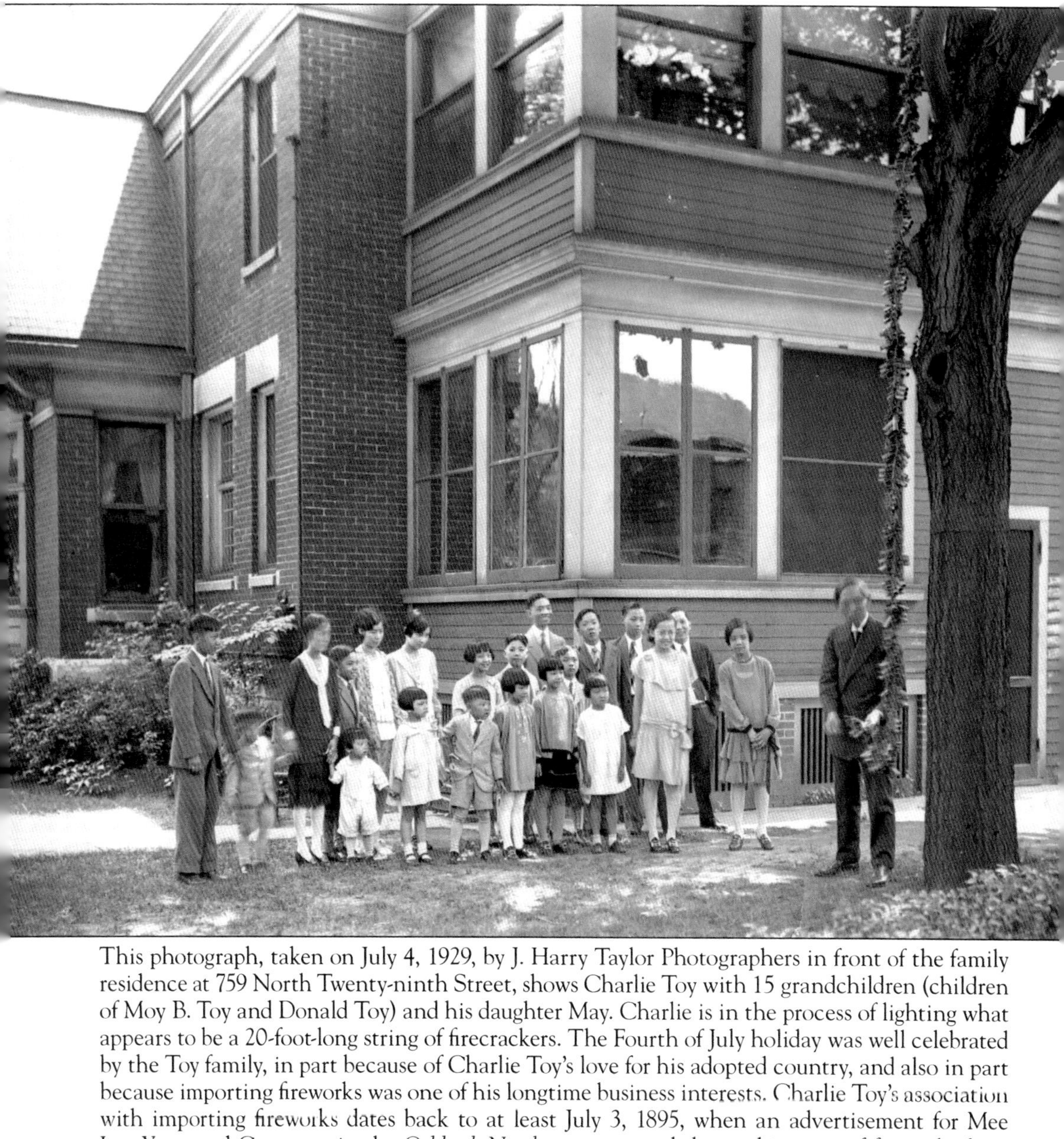

This photograph, taken on July 4, 1929, by J. Harry Taylor Photographers in front of the family residence at 759 North Twenty-ninth Street, shows Charlie Toy with 15 grandchildren (children of Moy B. Toy and Donald Toy) and his daughter May. Charlie is in the process of lighting what appears to be a 20-foot-long string of firecrackers. The Fourth of July holiday was well celebrated by the Toy family, in part because of Charlie Toy's love for his adopted country, and also in part because importing fireworks was one of his longtime business interests. Charlie Toy's association with importing fireworks dates back to at least July 3, 1895, when an advertisement for Mee Lee Yuen and Company in the *Oshkosh Northwestern* stated that a shipment of fireworks from Charlie Toy (who was on a trip to China) had just arrived and was available for sale. (Courtesy of the Toy family.)

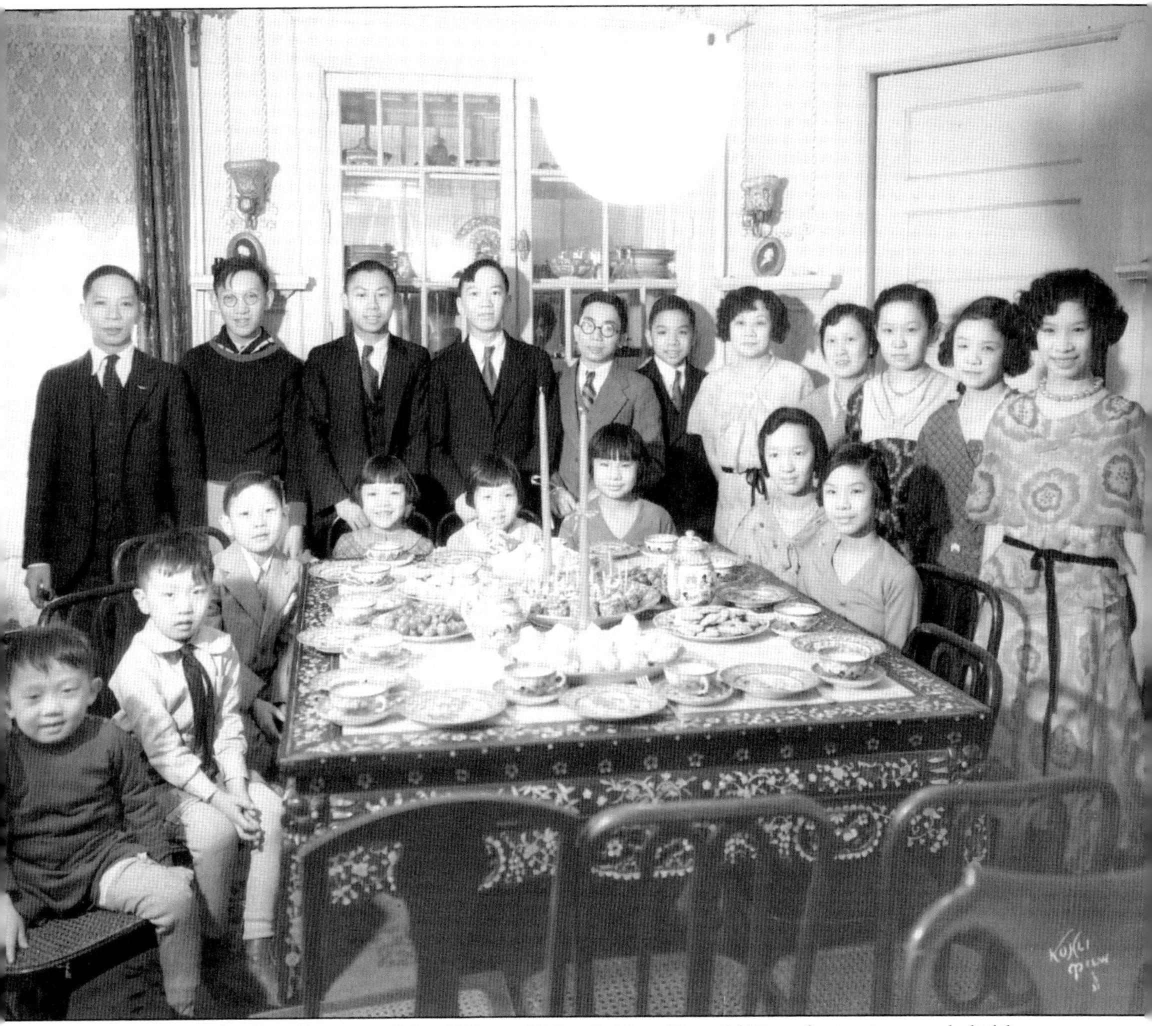

This photograph, dated January 28, 1930, is of Moy B. Toy, Donald Toy, their wives and children, and other relatives at a holiday dinner at the Toy residence at 759 North Twenty-ninth Street in Milwaukee. This is likely a traditional dinner served on New Year's Eve (January 28, 1930), which was typically the biggest event of the Chinese New Year. Food served at the New Year's Eve family dinner typically included a dish containing fish, as well as dumplings, which symbolized wealth due to their resemblance to the shape of gold nuggets. (Courtesy of the Toy family.)

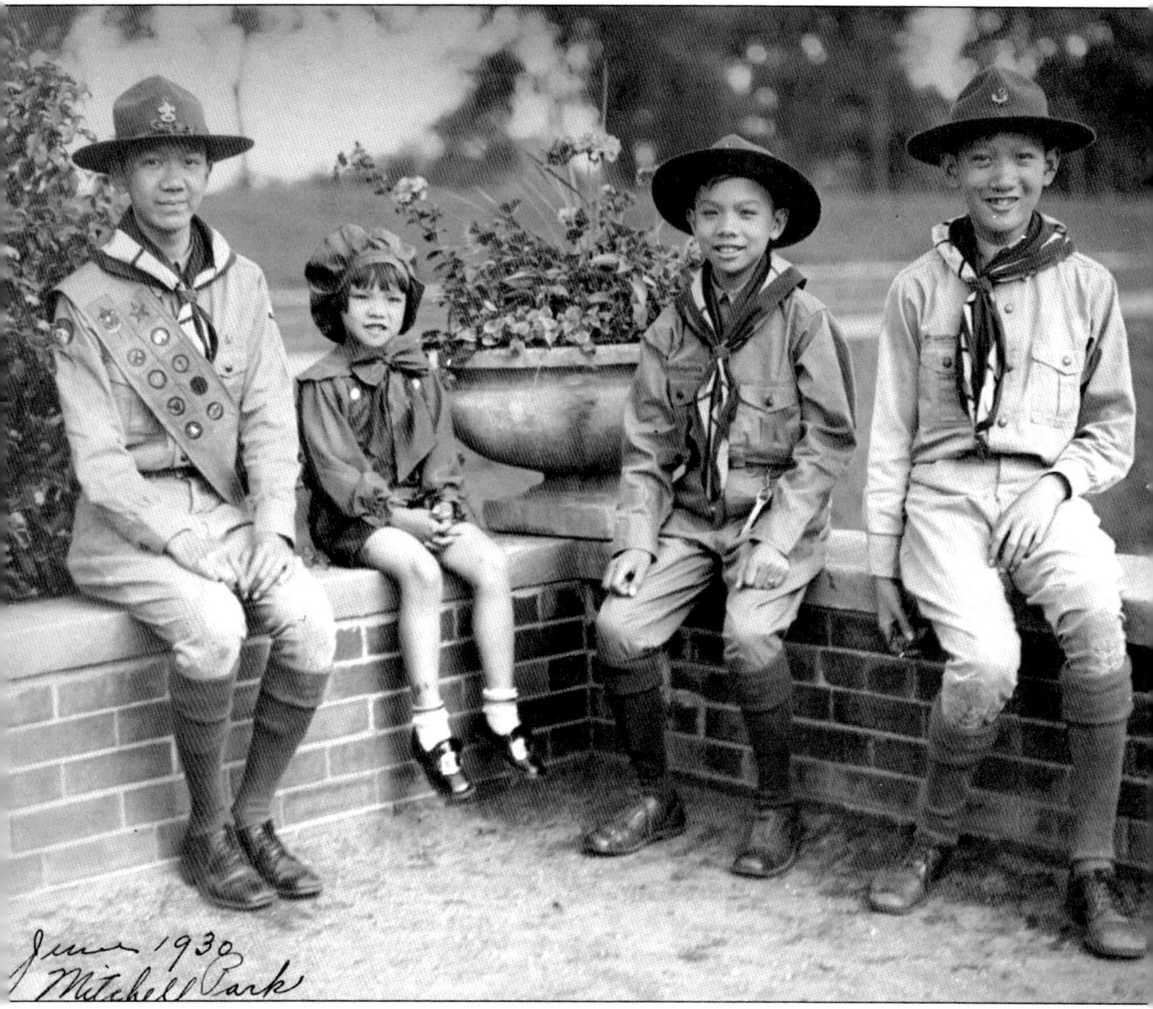

Scouting was a tradition shared by several generations of the Toy family in Milwaukee. This photograph, taken in Mitchell Park in Milwaukee in June 1930, shows several of the Toy children in their Scouting uniforms, including Ernest (on the left), Alfred (on the middle right), and Edward (on the far right). (Courtesy of Katherine Toy.)

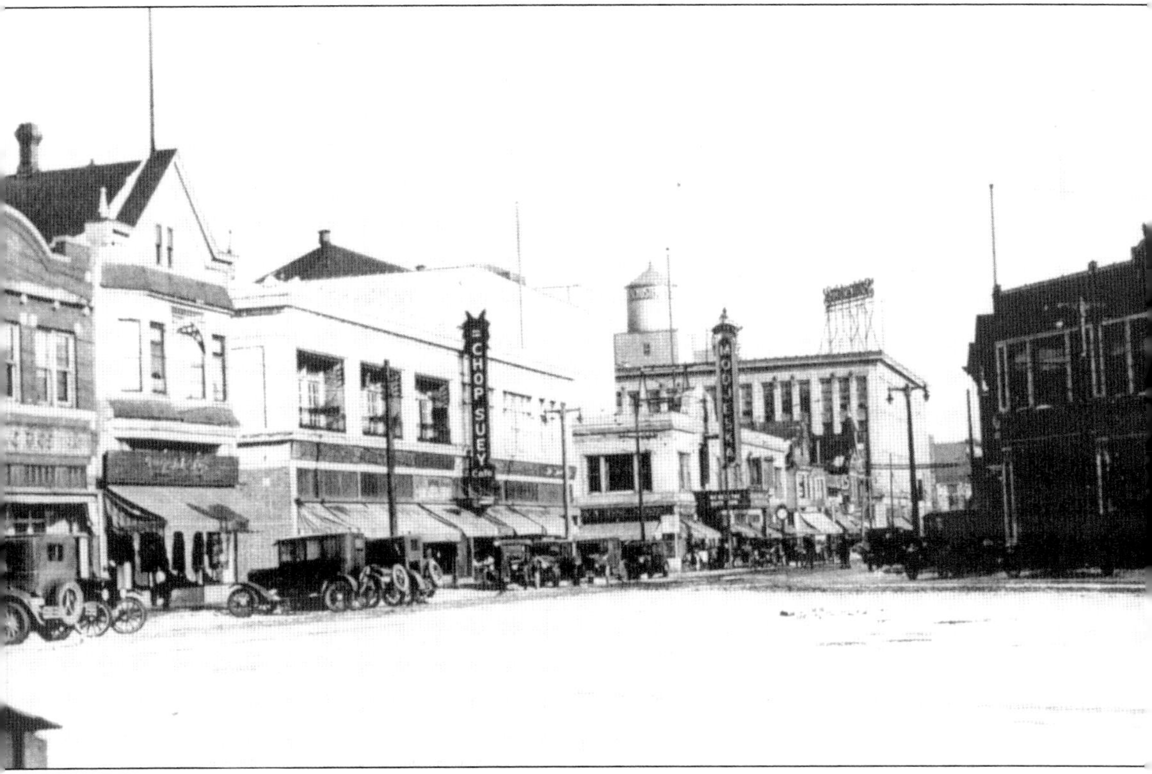

This is a photograph, dated January 11, 1927, of the Nan King Café located at 606 West Mitchell Street. The 1927 Milwaukee City Directory identifies Sam Wah as being the manager. The Nan King Café was one of the first Chinese restaurants located on the Milwaukee south side. However, other Chinese businesses had been located in this area much earlier, including the Sam Lee Chinese Laundry, which is listed in the 1888 Milwaukee City Directory as being located at 518 West Mitchell Street. Like many early Chinese restaurants in the city, the Nan King Café was located near a theater, in this instance, the Modjeska Theatre, located one-half block to the east at 596 West Mitchell Street. (Courtesy of the Milwaukee Public Library.)

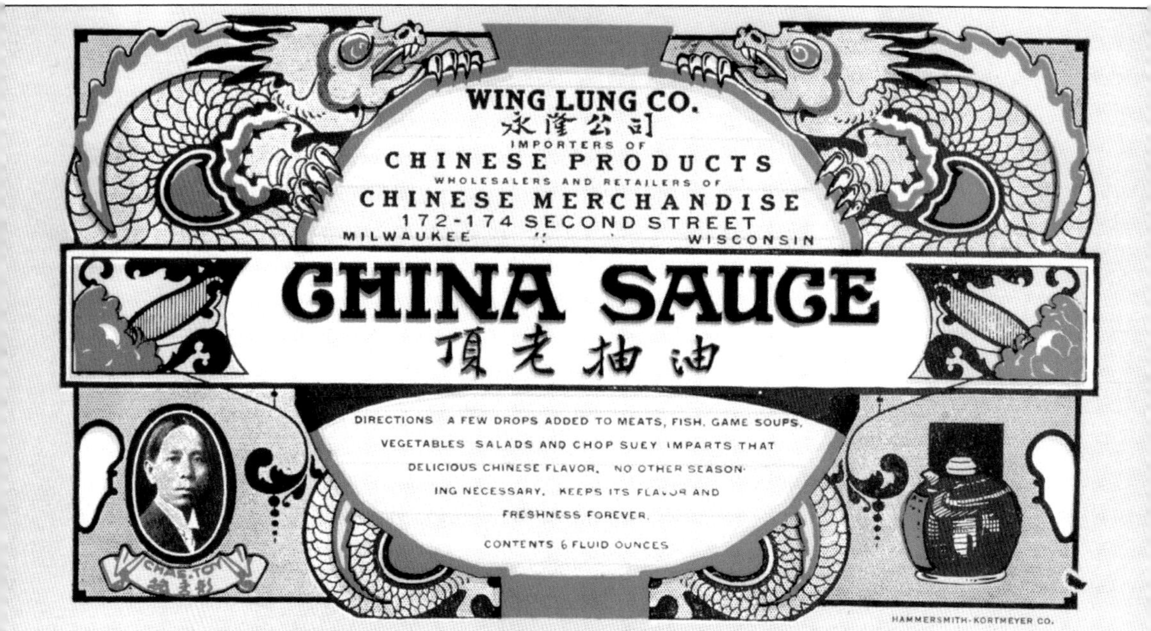

In 1901, Charlie Toy began to establish business interests in Milwaukee. Several years later, he moved to Milwaukee and opened the New Shanghai Restaurant and started the Wing Lung Company, which became one of the largest Chinese retail and wholesale mercantile establishments in the United States, with offices in Milwaukee, Seattle, and Hong Kong. The offices for the Wing Lung Company were initially located at 172–174–176 West Water Street and later moved to the Toy Building at 172–174 North Second Street. Among the many products imported or produced by the Wing Lung Company was China Sauce, a type of soy sauce. This label, dating from before 1931, provides an outstanding example of early-20th-century Chinese American advertising art. (Courtesy of Dr. Dennis Toy.)

Four

DEPRESSION AND WORLD WAR
1930–1949

By 1930, the Milwaukee Chinese community had taken on most of the characteristics of Chinese communities in other U.S. cities: a largely bachelor community relying almost exclusively on laundries and restaurants for employment, speaking little English, and controlled by family name associations and secret societies (tongs) with roots in southern China. The few import shops provided important social gathering places. In the early 1930s, a shop at North Fourth and West State Streets emerged as the most significant gathering place for Milwaukee Chinese. Its wealthy owner, a member of the On Leong Tong, became the unofficial mayor of Milwaukee's Chinese community.

The Milwaukee Chinese community never developed the concentrated residential neighborhoods that characterized Chinese communities in places like San Francisco and Chicago. Chinese business owners located their businesses, and therefore residences, near prospective customers. For laundries, this meant locating in residential areas. Restaurants sought out locations near Milwaukee's business community.

In the 1930s, with the Japanese invasion of China, the Milwaukee Chinese were repeatedly asked to contribute financially to the war effort. This was not voluntary; with almost no employment opportunities outside of Chinese-owned businesses, any Chinese who refused to comply found himself socially ostracized. By 1940, Milwaukee had reportedly donated more money to China's war effort than any Chinese community in the United States except San Francisco.

In 1934, a few young Chinese men approached the pastor of the First Baptist Church at 911 East Ogden Street, explaining that they wanted to spend their Sunday afternoons in Christian surroundings. The following Sunday, eight young Chinese men and eight teachers began organizing a Chinese Sunday school. One teacher, Eva Johnson, who had conducted Americanization work with other immigrant groups, eventually became the first Sunday school superintendent. The Chinese were eager to learn English, especially at no charge. This, rather than religious instruction, was the primary motivating factor for many of the students. The Sunday school gave the Chinese an alternative to the tong as a means of negotiating the intricacies of the larger society. This eventually marked the demise of the tong as a means of social control.

During World War II, with China a crucial ally in the war effort, the United States was forced to reexamine its exclusionary policies toward Chinese immigrants. In 1943, the Chinese Exclusion Act was repealed. This and related legislation resulted in dramatic changes in the size and demographic profile of Chinese throughout the United States and Milwaukee.

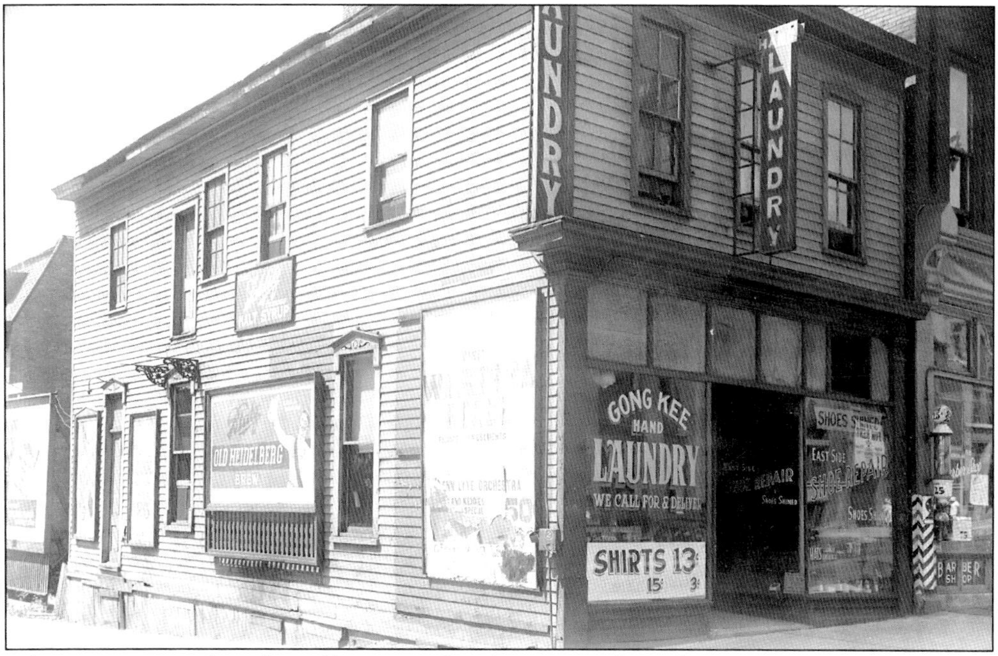

After remaining relatively stable in number from 1889 through 1920, Chinese laundries in Milwaukee increased dramatically, and by 1930, there were 58 listed in the Milwaukee City Directory. The photograph above, by Henry Hunter dated July 27, 1932, shows the outside of the Gong Kee Hand Laundry, which was located at 633 East Wisconsin Avenue. Although the Chinese dominated the laundry business in some respects, there were at least 52 steam laundries located in Milwaukee in 1932, as well as 20 hand laundries. An example of a non-Chinese hand laundry, owned by William Hammer at 712 West Wells Street, is shown in the lower photograph, dated August 17, 1932. Of 118 individuals with Chinese surnames listed in the 1930 Milwaukee City Directory, 72 (or 61 percent) are identified as having occupations associated with laundries. (Courtesy of the Milwaukee Public Library.)

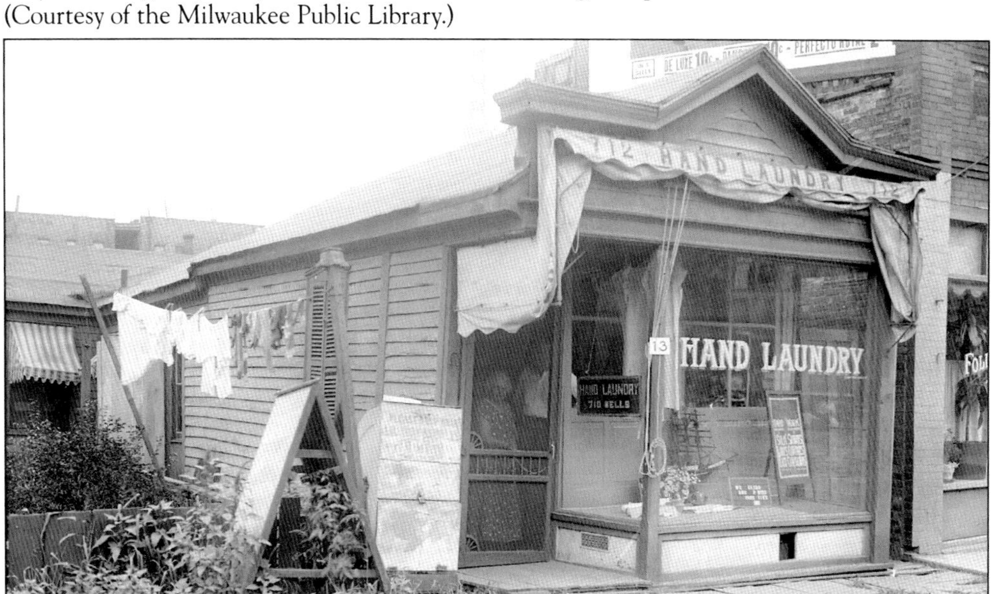

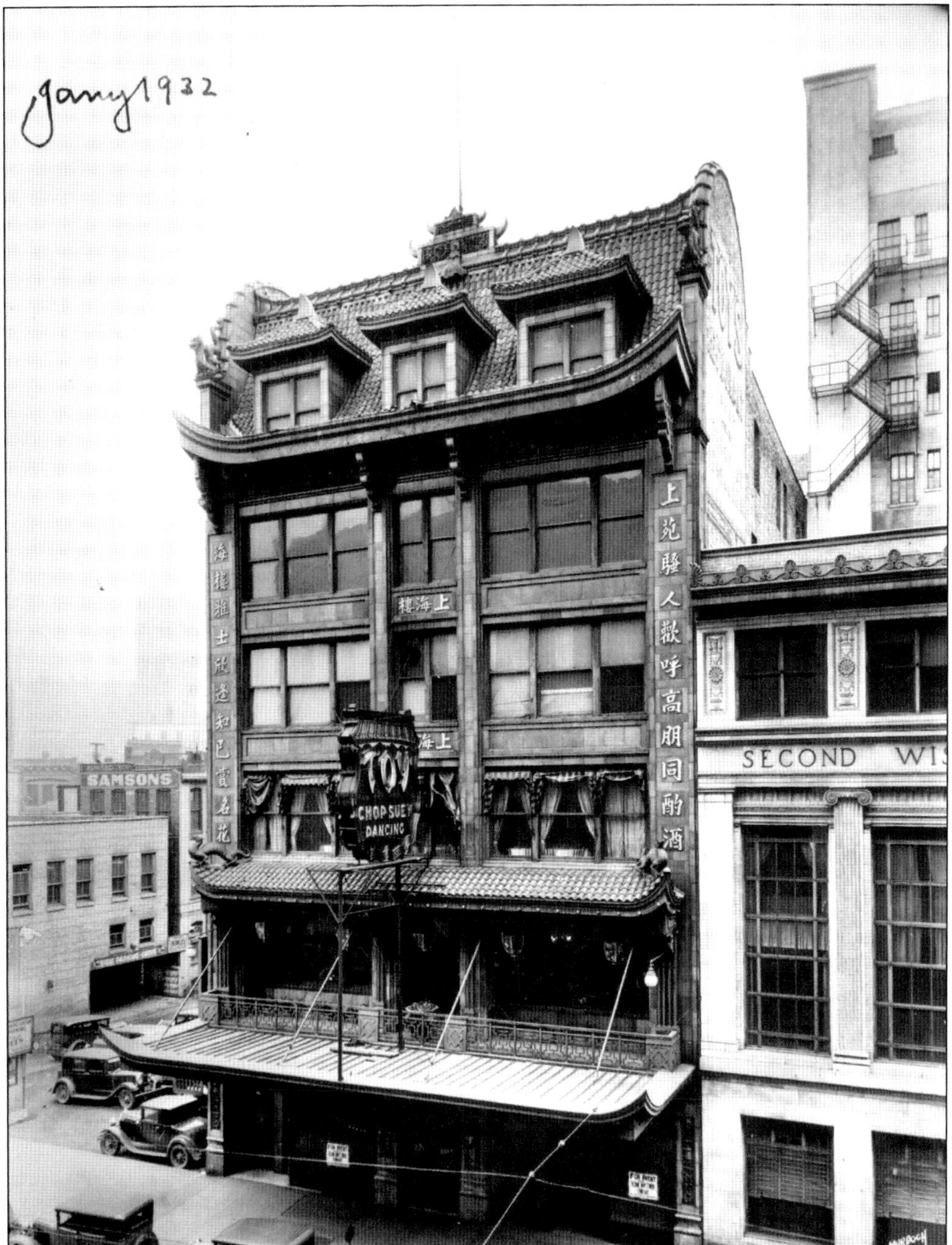

This photograph of the Toy Building was taken in January 1932. The Toy Theatre that had occupied the first floor had been closed for nearly eight years. The neighboring Crystal Theatre to the north had been demolished in 1927 to make way for a parking lot. The Toy Building itself was to be demolished by the City of Milwaukee approximately six years after this photograph, to make way for a parking structure, but thereby depriving future Milwaukeeans of a Chinese American landmark of possible national significance. (Courtesy of the Milwaukee Public Library.)

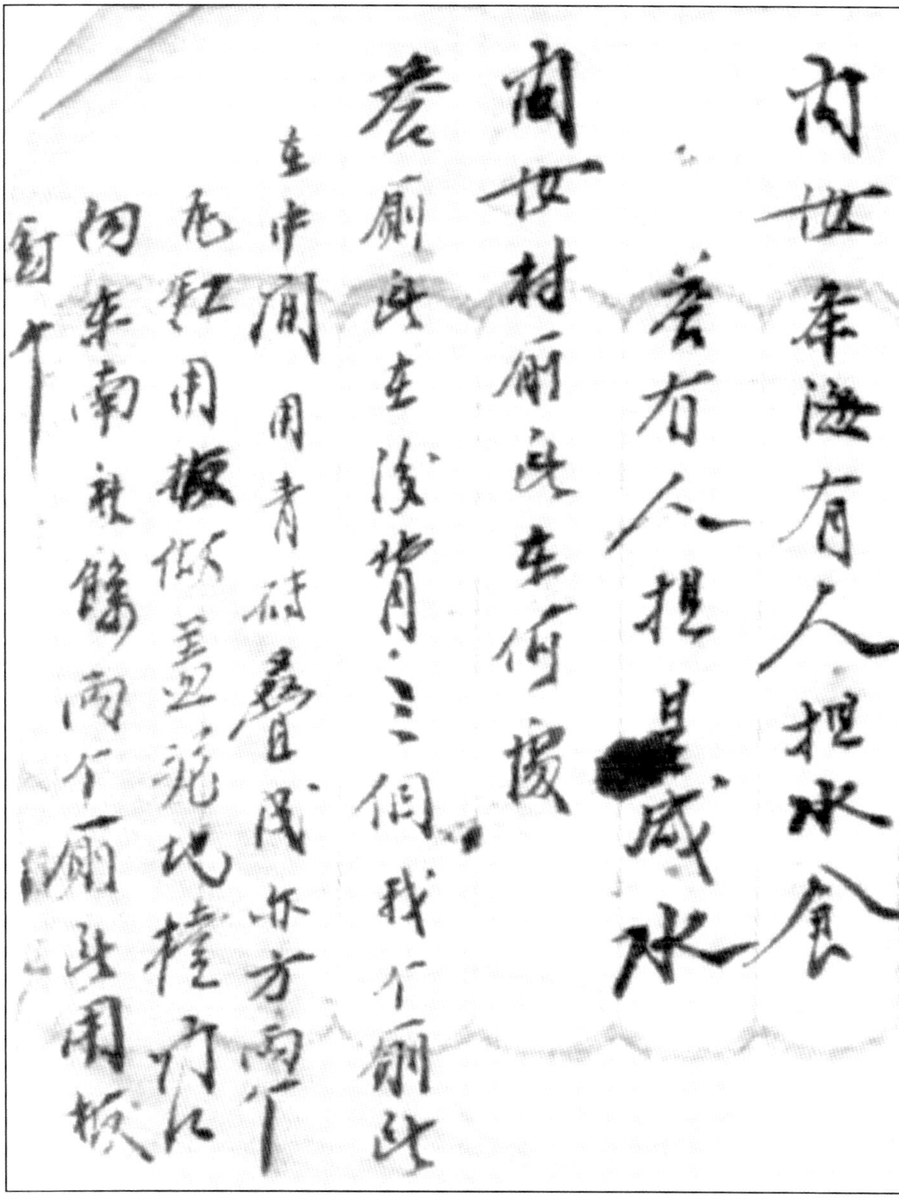

Prior to the repeal of the Chinese Exclusion Act in 1943, nearly all Chinese immigrants were subjected to grueling interrogations by immigration inspectors upon arrival in the United States. The interviews were performed in an attempt to identify applicants using false identities, and would last from several hours to several days. Applicants would be asked a series of questions related to minute details of their family history, village, and home. All testimony would be recorded by a stenographer and compared with the testimony of previous family members. Any deviations from previous testimony could result in a prolonged stay at a detention center and/or deportation (if the perceived inconsistencies could not be further collaborated). As a result, Chinese immigrants would typically spend months preparing for these interviews and committing hundreds of family details to memory. The document shown above contains details related to the number, location, and design of bathrooms in a home in China, and is one of 32 sheets used by a Milwaukee area Chinese man in preparation for an immigration interview in the early 1930s.

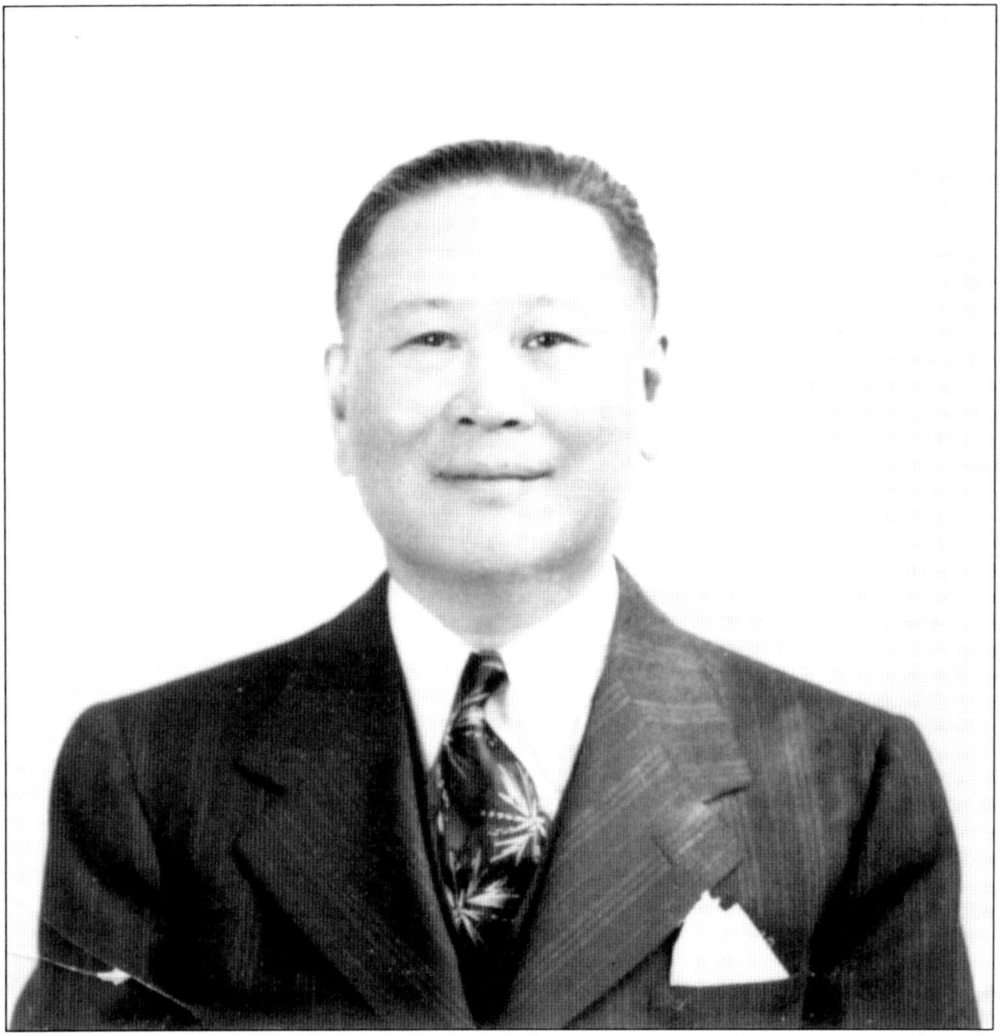

This photograph of John "Jack" Hing Wong was taken in the 1930s. Jack Hing Wong reportedly came to Milwaukee from China in 1902 and opened a restaurant in the 400 block of West Wisconsin Avenue. Jack Hing Wong was a longtime leader of the local Chinese community. In 1916, he opened an import-export shop and grocery store, which at the time of this photograph was located at 931 North Fourth Street. The store was located more or less at the geographic center of the Chinese community in Milwaukee, and in many ways, it served as a center of social activities, including traditional Chinese games of mah-jongg and fan-tan. Jack Hing Wong ran a successful import business with his son, John A. Wong, and was reported to have found employment for the jobless, adjudicated disputes, oversaw the buying and selling of businesses, and helped to lead several fund-raising drives for Chinese war efforts against the Japanese during the 1930s and 1940s. (Courtesy of Paul Wong.)

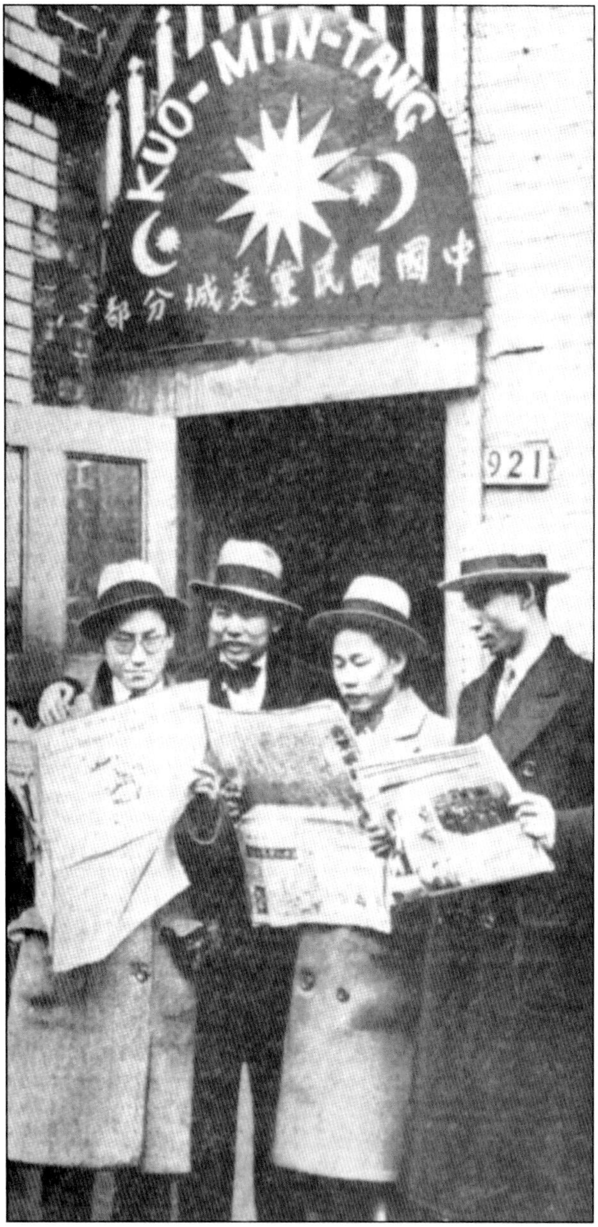

Stephen, Herbert, George, and Woy Wong (not related to each other) read the latest news about the war in China in this photograph from the February 10, 1932, edition of the *Milwaukee Journal*. The Wongs were members of the Chinese Nationalist Club, located at 921 North Fourth Street, where the Milwaukee Arena now stands. Beginning in 1937, the leader of the Chinese community directed each employed Chinese to donate a minimum of $10 per month to China's war effort. Anyone earning $200 or more per month was expected to donate at least $20 per month. In some instances, the assessment was equal to more than half an individual's wage. As a result, by 1940, Milwaukee had reportedly donated more money to fund China's war effort against Japan than any Chinese community in the United States except that of San Francisco (which at the time had a Chinese population at least 50 times greater than that of Milwaukee). (Courtesy of the Milwaukee Public Library.)

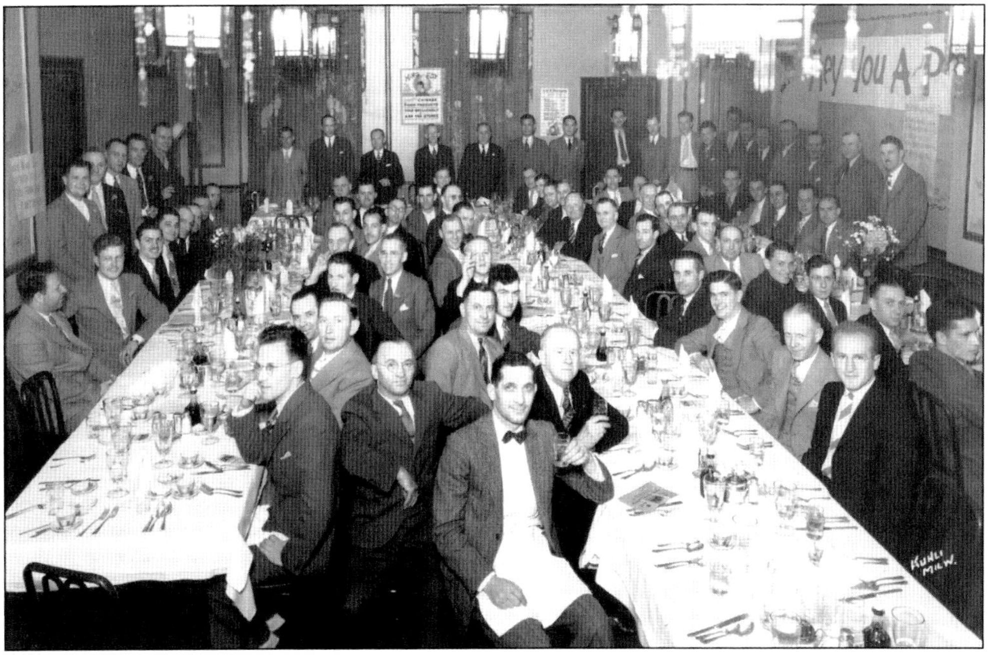

A banquet for supervisors and managers of the Great Atlantic and Pacific (A&P) Tea Company hosted by the Chinese Trading Company is shown in the photograph above, taken at Toy's Restaurant in downtown Milwaukee on June 12, 1935. Signs posted on the walls reference a brand of Chinese groceries named Ming Foy that was "Genuine Chinese food products sold exclusively at A&P stores." Although there is no listing for the Chinese Trading Company in the 1935 Milwaukee City Directory, it is possible that this company and the Ming Foy brand were connected with one of the Milwaukee area Chinese trading companies. The photograph below shows a street scene near North Twenty-seventh Street and West Vliet Street including, on the right-hand side, a store owned by A&P's main competitor, the National Tea Company. (Above, courtesy of the Toy family; below, courtesy of the Milwaukee Public Library.)

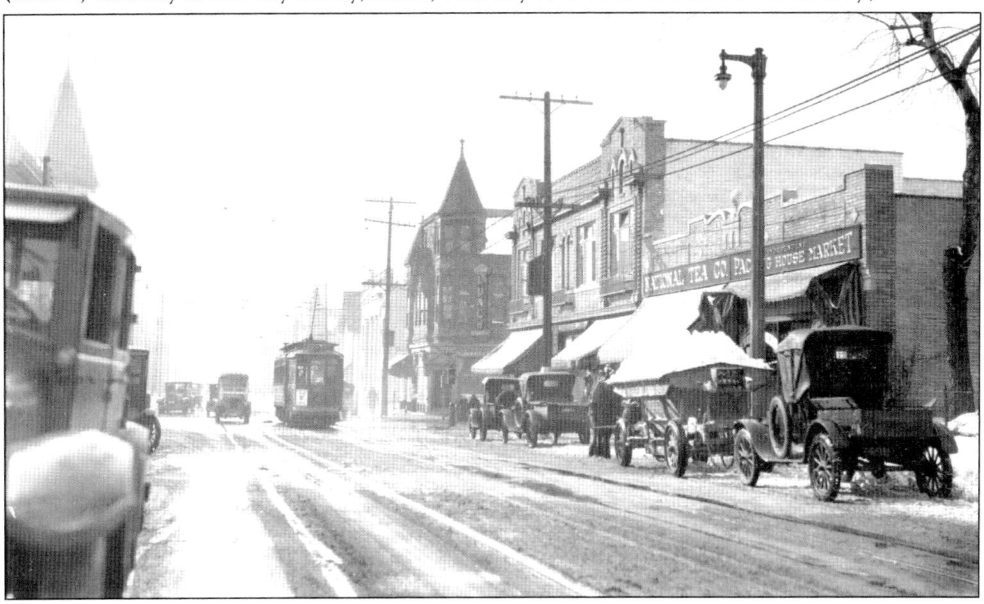

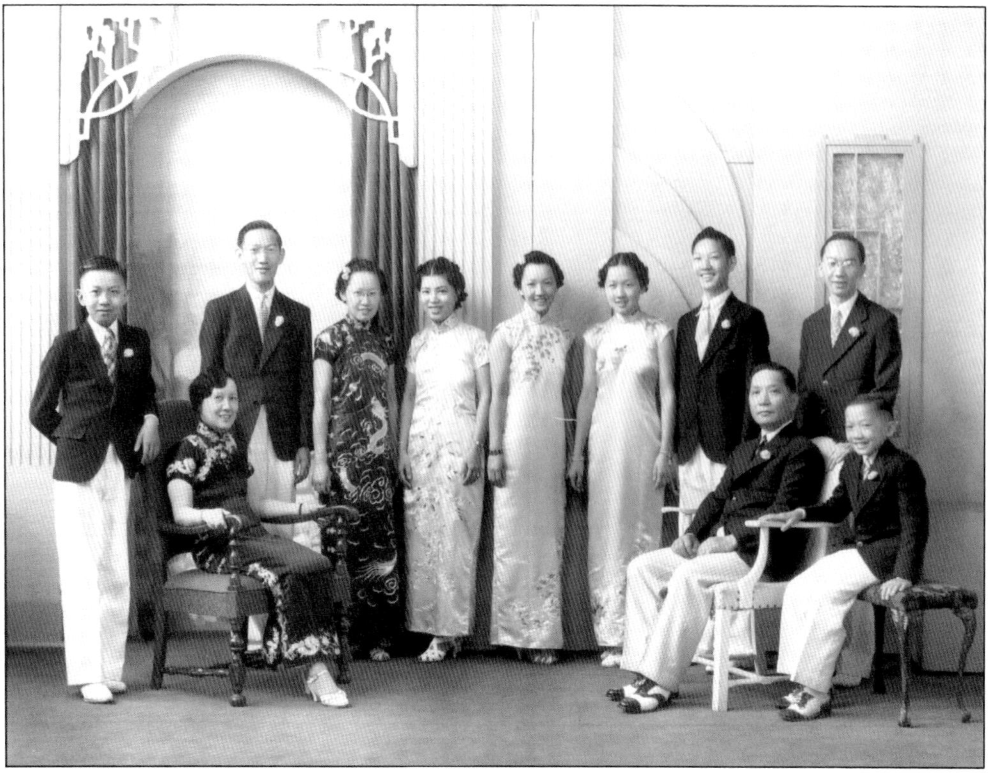

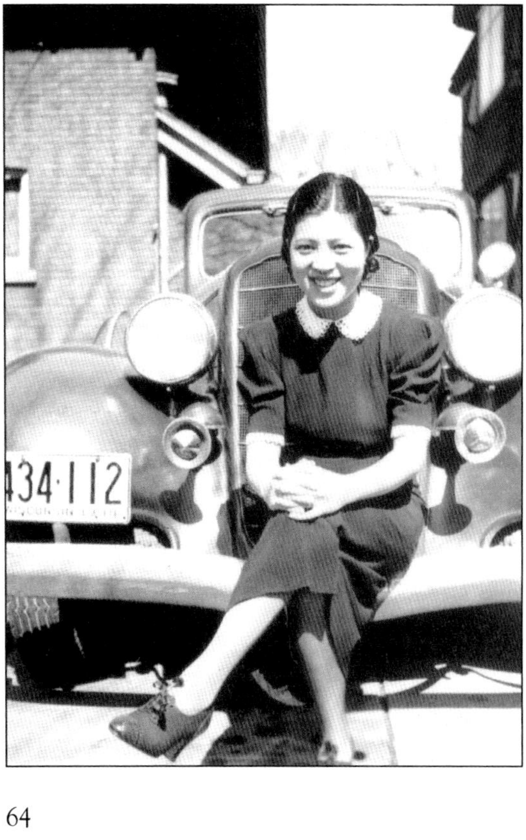

Ernest M. Toy and Peggy Yue were married in China in approximately 1937. The photograph above was taken during a reception held in Milwaukee following the return of the couple to Milwaukee. Ernest was the oldest son of Moy B. Toy and a grandson of Charlie Toy. In 1942, Ernest was listed in the Milwaukee City Directory as being an economist working for the United States Department of Agriculture. Although the men are all dressed in American-style formal clothing, the women are dressed elegantly in Chinese-style dresses. The lower photograph shows Peggy Yue Toy in 1938 in a more relaxed setting at the home she and Ernest shared with her in-laws at 3107 West Kilbourn Avenue. (Courtesy of Dennis Toy.)

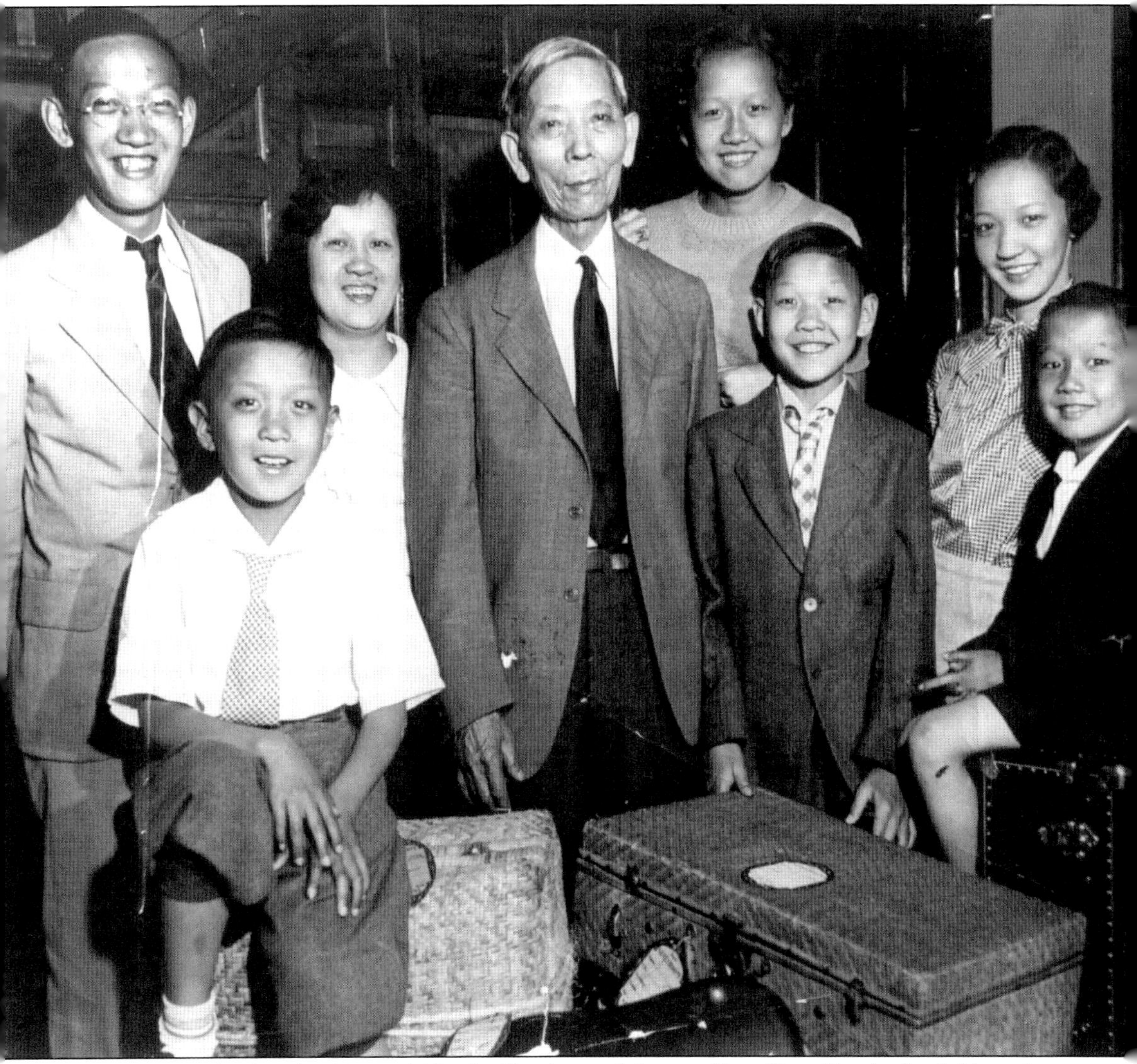

This photograph, dated 1933, is of Charlie Toy (center), Leung Yuey King Toy (to his left), and six of his grandchildren, with luggage packed for Charlie and several of the grandchildren who were planning to obtain university educations in China. Four years later, in 1937, an article in a Milwaukee newspaper reported on the return of three of Charlie Toy's grandchildren to Milwaukee. Elizabeth, 21, the oldest of the three, had just completed four years at Ling Nan University in Canton, China. Edward, 19, and Marjorie, 18, had both completed two years of university study in Canton. With a Japanese attack reported as being imminent, all three had evacuated to Hong Kong. Elizabeth returned to Canton a few days later, only to be present for a Japanese bombing attack that demolished the airport, a half mile from where she had been staying. (Courtesy of the Toy family.)

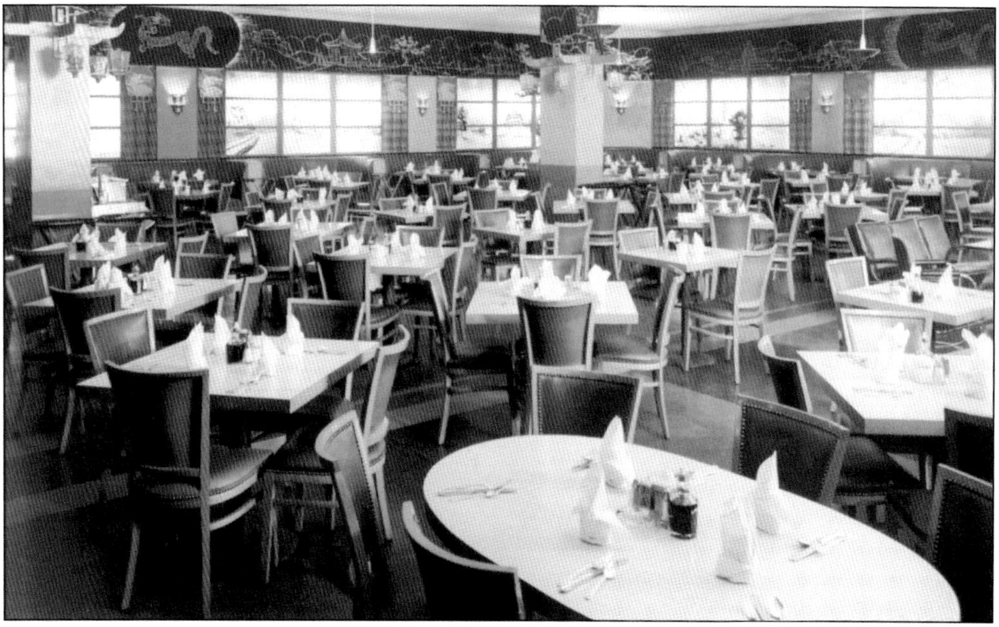

Toy's Chinatown Restaurant was a popular restaurant in downtown Milwaukee for 30 years (from 1938 to 1968). The restaurant was located on the second floor of a building on the northwest corner of the intersection of North Third Street and West Wisconsin Avenue, above Walgreen's drugstore. This photograph was reportedly taken by Kuhli Photo Service at approximately the time of the restaurant's opening in 1938. (Courtesy of the Toy family.)

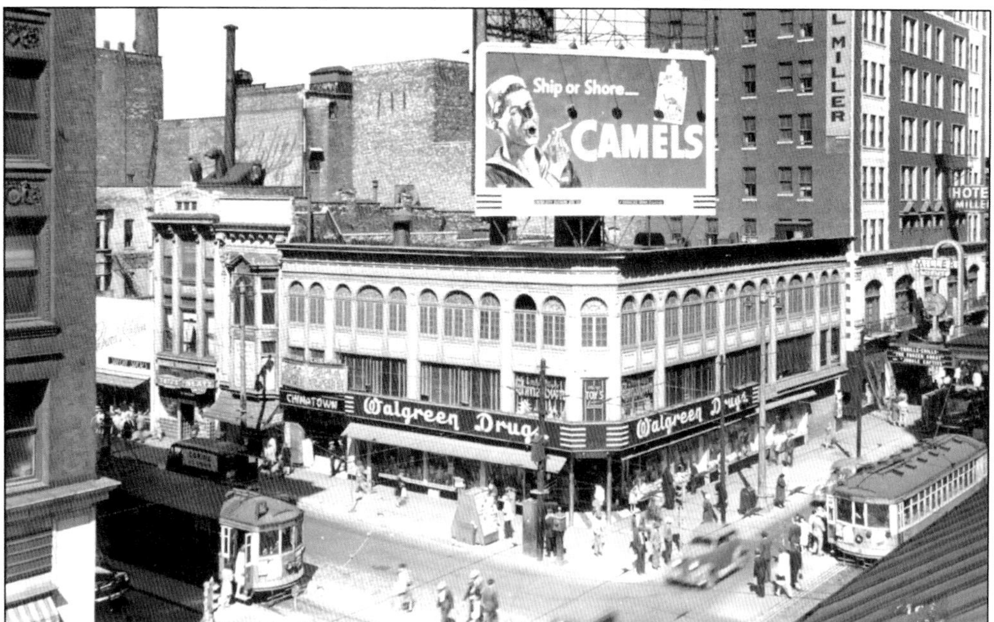

Toy's Chinatown Restaurant at 316 West Wisconsin Avenue is visible at the center of this photograph taken in 1945 of the northwest corner of the intersection of North Third Street and West Wisconsin Avenue. Moy B. Toy operated the restaurant at this location for approximately 30 years (from 1938 to 1968). (Courtesy of the Milwaukee Public Library.)

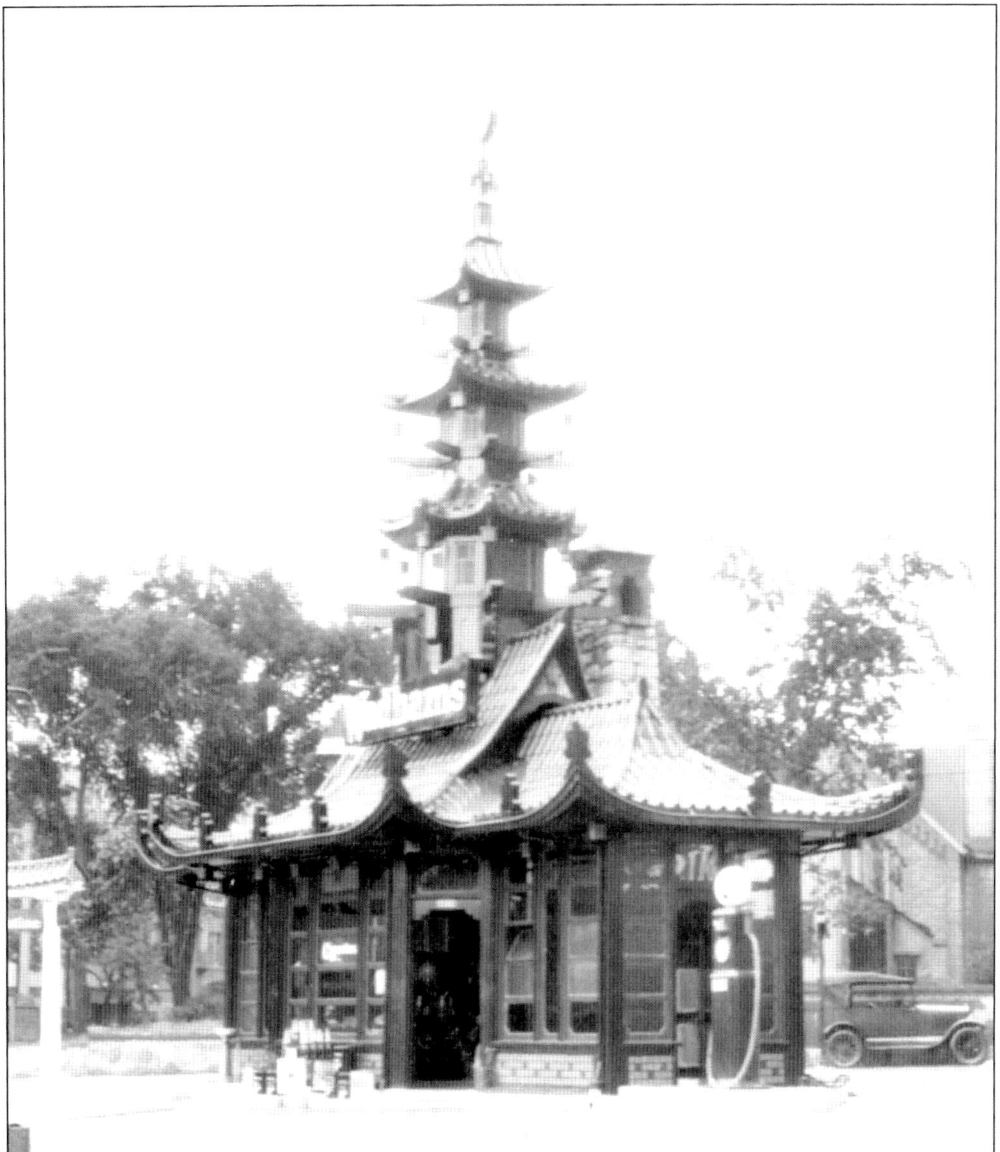

The pagoda-style gas station in this 1931 photograph was one of approximately 100 similarly designed gas stations built between 1917 and 1930 for the Wadham's Oil Company, which was based in Milwaukee. The gas station in this photograph was located at the corner of North Twenty-seventh Street and West Wisconsin Avenue. The design of the gas stations by prominent Milwaukee architect Alexander Eschweiler is considered by many scholars to be one of the most successful iconic designs in gas retailing history. The prototype for the gas stations was built in 1917 at Fifth Street and Wisconsin Avenue in downtown Milwaukee, less than four years after the completion of the Toy Building in downtown Milwaukee. The Wadham's pagoda-style gas stations may represent one of the many unexpected ways in which the small Chinese population of Milwaukee and Chinese culture influenced the cultural fabric of Milwaukee. (Courtesy of the Milwaukee Public Library.)

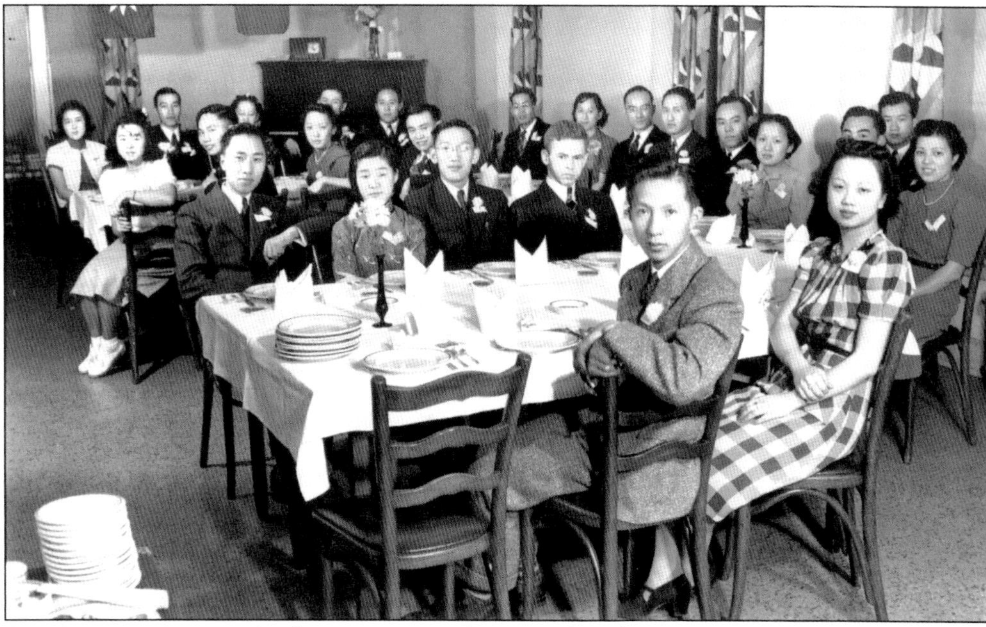

Seen here is a photograph of a joint meeting between the Chinese Student Association and the Wisconsin Student Association held on December 2, 1939. One of the students is Edward M. Toy, seated third from the left on the far side of the nearest table. At the time of this photograph, Edward was 22 years old and had just received an engineering degree from the University of Wisconsin in Madison. (Courtesy of the Toy family.)

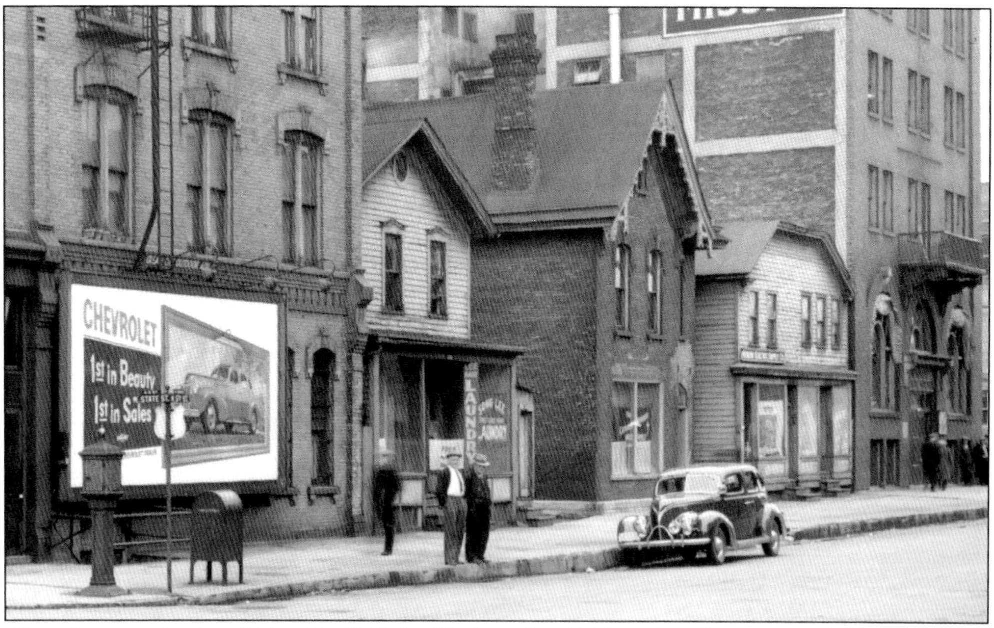

This photograph, dated May 19, 1940, by Herb Zeck of Milwaukee Commercial Photographers, shows the west side of North Fifth Street, between West State Street and West Highland Avenue, including the Lee Song Chinese Laundry at 1007 North Fifth Street. This laundry was one of a total of 79 Chinese laundries listed in the 1940 Milwaukee City Directory. (Courtesy of the Milwaukee Public Library.)

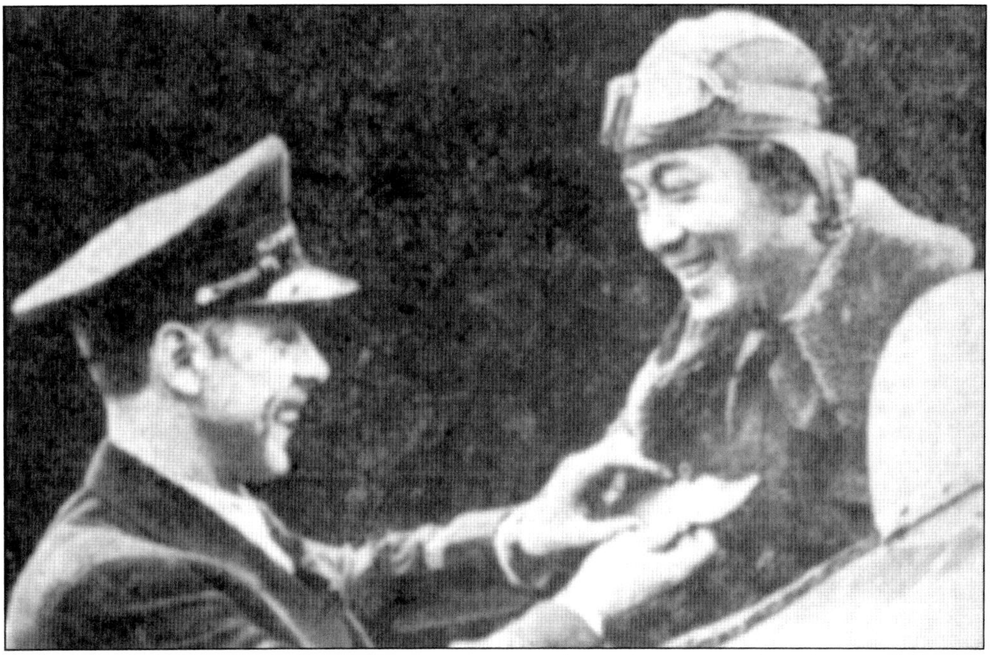

Frank Wong, a waiter in a West Allis restaurant, is shown being pinned with a pair of paper wings by his instructor, Jim Knaup, following completion of his first solo flight. Wong was one of at least 10 Milwaukee area Chinese who began training as pilots following the Japanese invasion of Manchuria in 1931. This photograph appeared in the January 23, 1932, edition of the *Milwaukee Journal*. (Courtesy of the Milwaukee Public Library.)

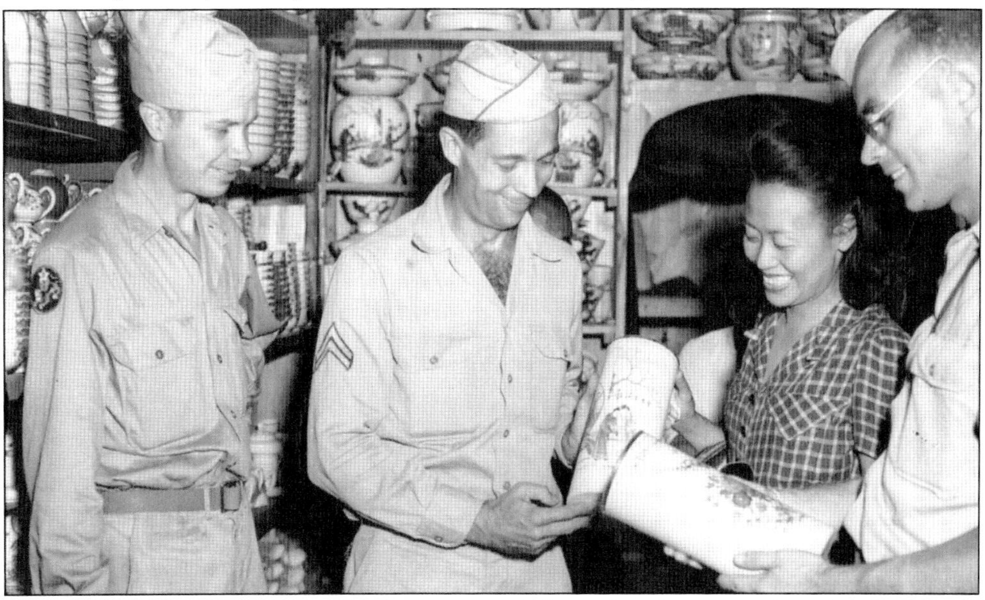

This photograph appeared on the front page of the *Milwaukee Sentinel* on November 15, 1945, and shows Milwaukeean Jennie Chan, a member of the Red Cross staff, helping several servicemen from Wisconsin shop for Christmas presents. Many Milwaukee Chinese, including women, served in the United States military and support organizations during World War II. (Courtesy of Jennie Chan.)

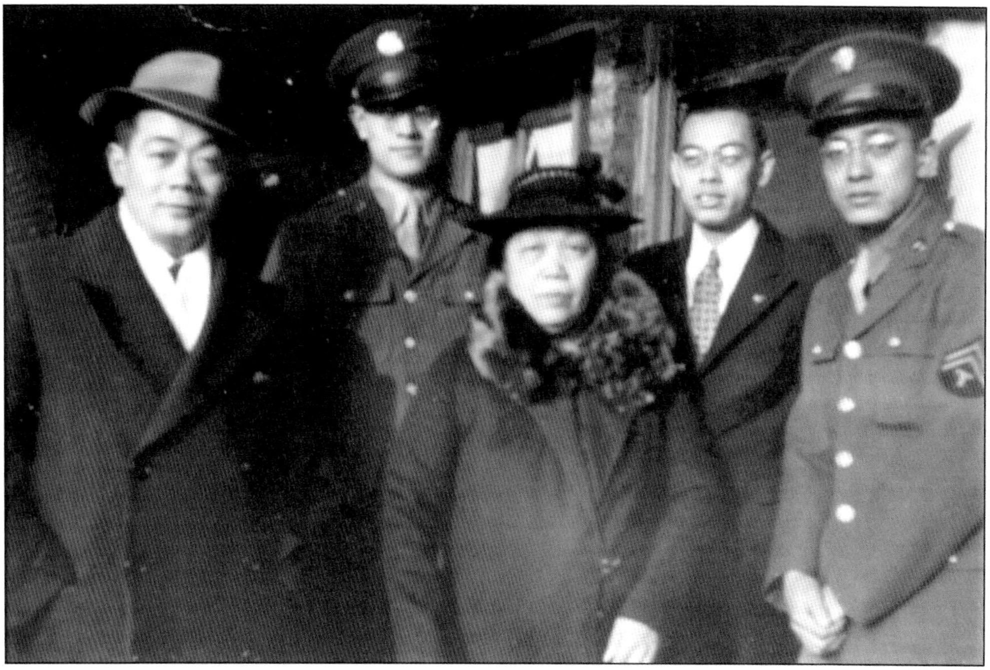

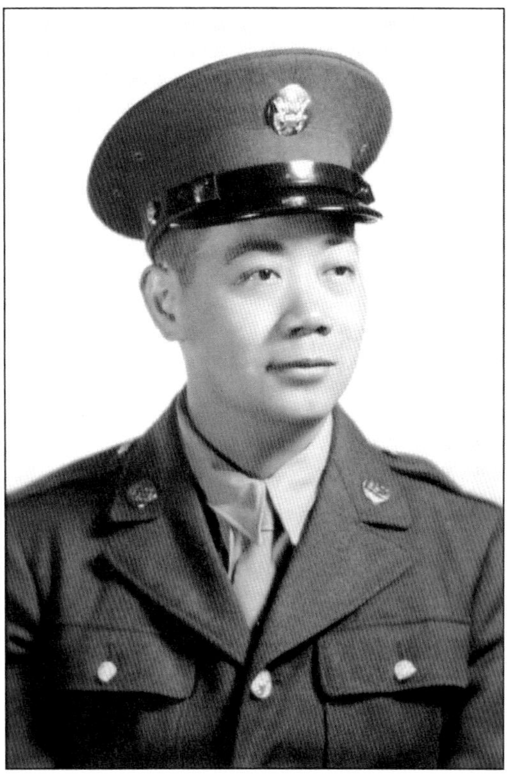

Many Milwaukee Chinese served in the United States military during World War II. Both the Toy and Wong families reportedly had at least five members serving in the military. Unlike other Milwaukeeans, for whom World War II lasted four years, the beginning of the war for many of the Chinese dated back to as early as the Japanese invasion of Manchuria in 1931. In 1932, newspapers reported that at least 10 Milwaukee area Chinese were training to be pilots to help with the war effort against Japan. Great financial sacrifices were made by the Milwaukee Chinese community from 1937 to 1940, at which time the community raised and donated more funds to the Chinese war effort against Japan than any other Chinese community in the United State besides San Francisco. Brothers Daniel, Warren, Ben, and Wallace Wong (three of whom served in the United States military) are shown with their mother, Ginger Wong, in this early-1940s photograph. Daniel Wong is also shown in the lower photograph. (Courtesy of Jennie Chan.)

This photograph of Rose Sun, a granddaughter of Sun Yat-sen (founder of the Chinese Republic), was taken on July 6, 1945, at which time she was a student at the University of Wisconsin in Madison. Rose Sun reportedly came to the University of Wisconsin to study English as part of a summer school program. (Courtesy of the Wisconsin Historical Society, image No. 43405.)

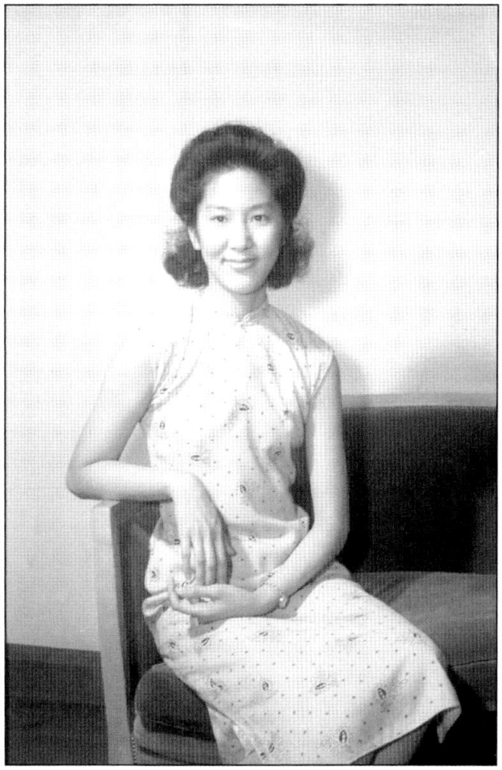

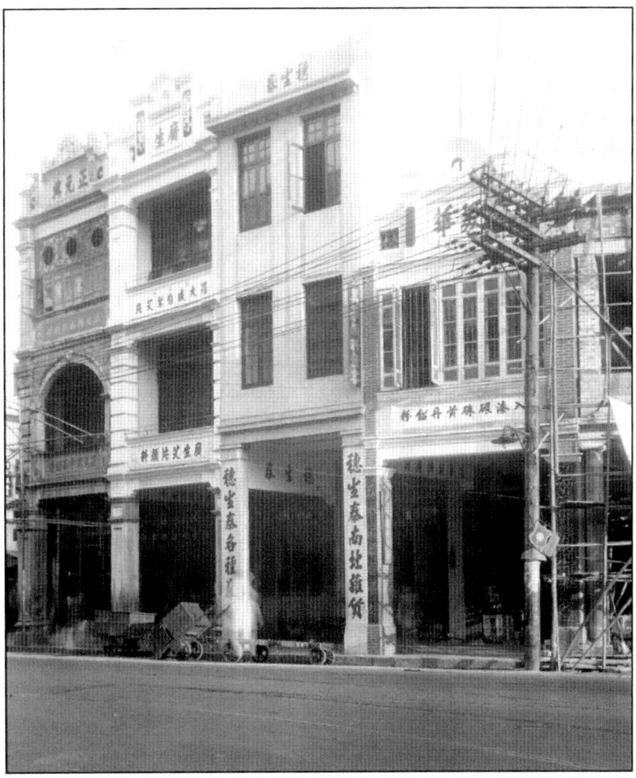

Many successful Chinese in the Milwaukee area maintained political and business interests in China as well as the United States (see page 62). The buildings shown in this photograph are commercial properties owned by Charlie Toy in Canton, China (now called Guangzhou). This photograph was taken in 1947, approximately two years before the Communist takeover of China's mainland. (Courtesy of the Toy family.)

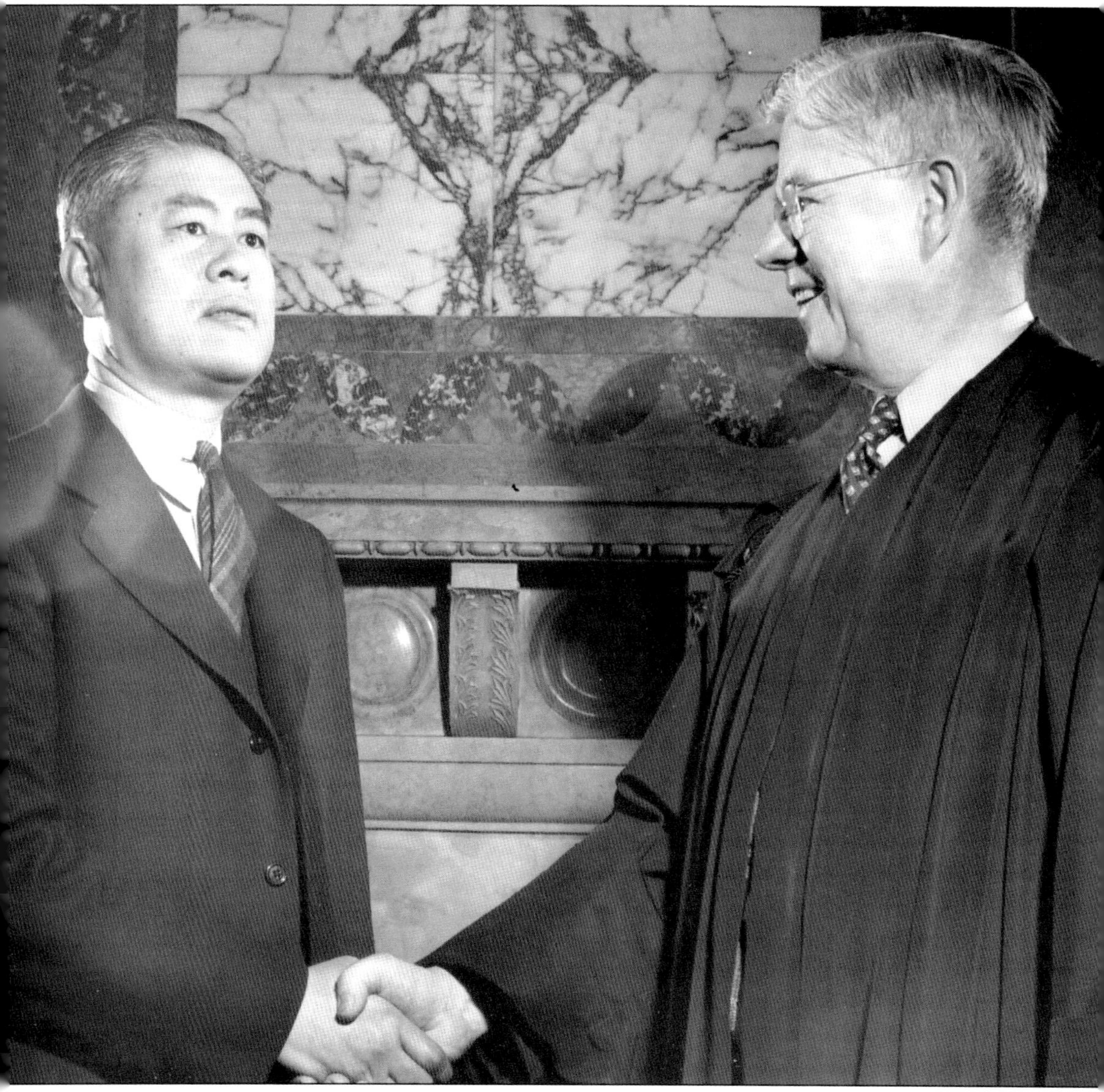

Joseph H. (Joe) Wong, born Jue Him near Canton, China, in approximately 1895, was a longtime leader of Milwaukee's Chinese community. Around 1911, Wong immigrated to Madison, where he graduated from Madison Central High School. After studying mining and engineering at the University of Wisconsin–Madison, Wong moved to Milwaukee to work in his father's restaurant on North Second Street. In 1925, he opened Sun Chop Suey Restaurant at the southeast corner of North Third Street and West North Avenue. In 1933, he opened a second restaurant, La Joy Restaurant, at 4720 West Lisbon Avenue, which remained open for nearly 60 years. Joe Wong was reported to have been the first Milwaukee area Chinese resident to apply for citizenship following the repeal of the Chinese Exclusion Act in 1943. This photograph is believed to have been taken in 1944, and to show Joe being congratulated following the ceremony at which he became naturalized as a United States citizen. (Courtesy of Paul Wong.)

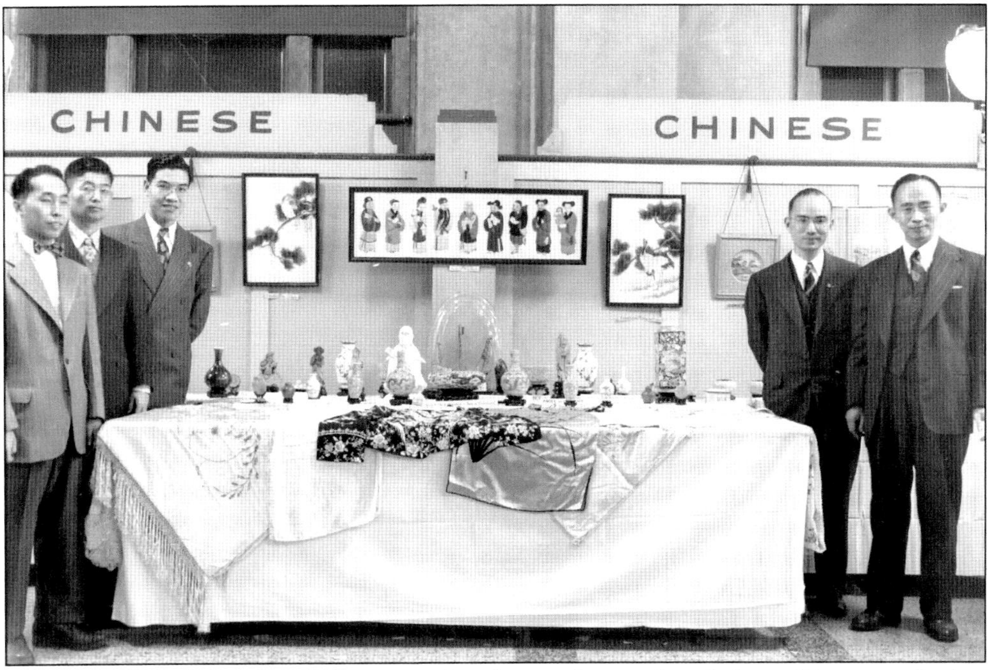

The International Institute of Wisconsin played a significant role in helping Chinese and other immigrants adjust to life in Milwaukee. In addition to helping with immigration paperwork, one of the annual activities sponsored by the International Institute was the Holiday Folk Fair. These photographs show the Chinese exhibit at the Holiday Folk Fair in the years 1946 and 1947, respectively. (Courtesy of the International Institute of Wisconsin.)

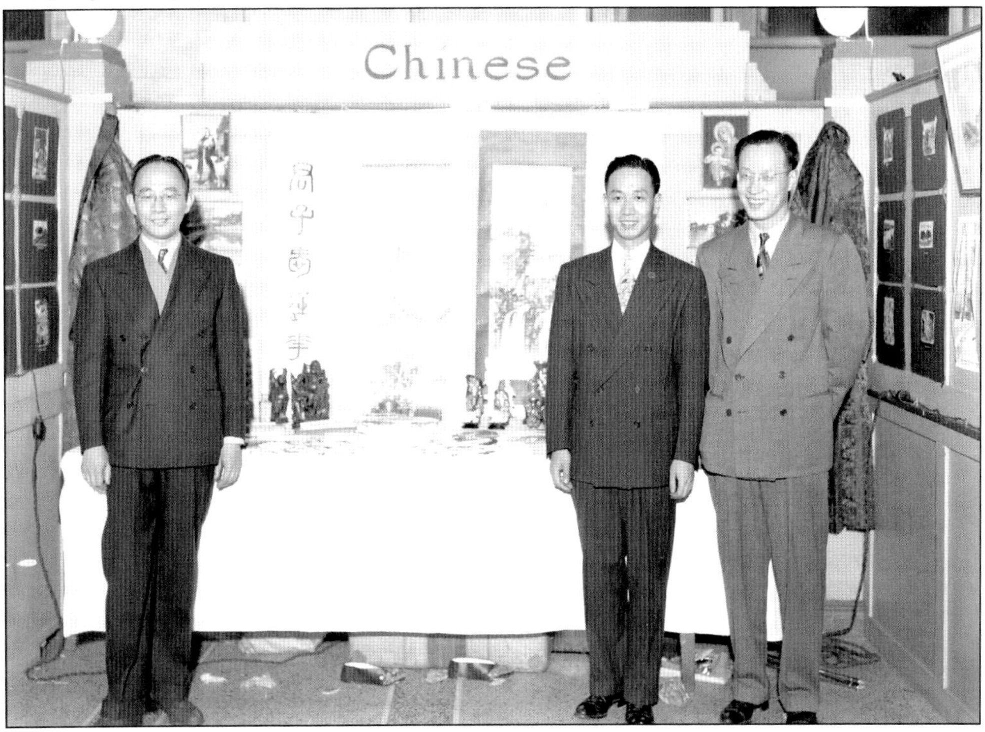

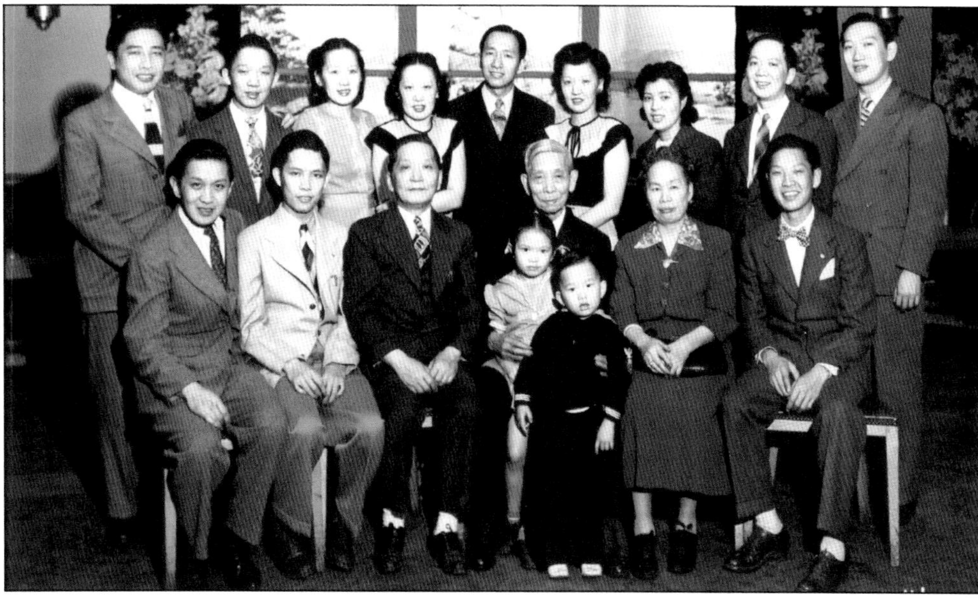

This photograph, dated March 17, 1946, of Charlie Toy with his family was taken at Toy's Chinatown Restaurant at 316 West Wisconsin Avenue on the occasion of a farewell reception held for Charlie Toy by his family on the eve of his departure for Canton, China, where he was to live out the remainder of his life. At the time of the photograph, Charlie was 86 years old. An earlier retirement during the 1930s was interrupted by the Japanese invasion of China and World War II. (Courtesy of the Toy family.)

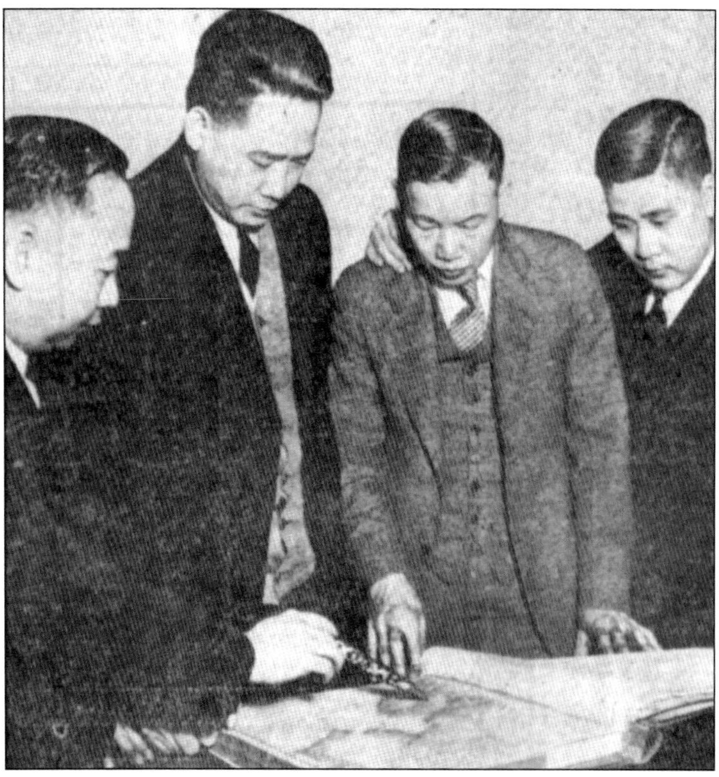

Jack Hing Wong (left) and brothers Robert, Frank, and Chester Wong are shown in reviewing a map of China's war district in this photograph, which appeared in the January 31, 1932, edition of the *Milwaukee Journal*. Jack Hing Wong was identified in the caption for the photograph as being chairman of the Milwaukee area branch of the Kuomintang, or Chinese Nationalist Party. The men were reported as excited at news of armed resistance by the Chinese to attacks by the Japanese. (Courtesy of the Milwaukee Public Library.)

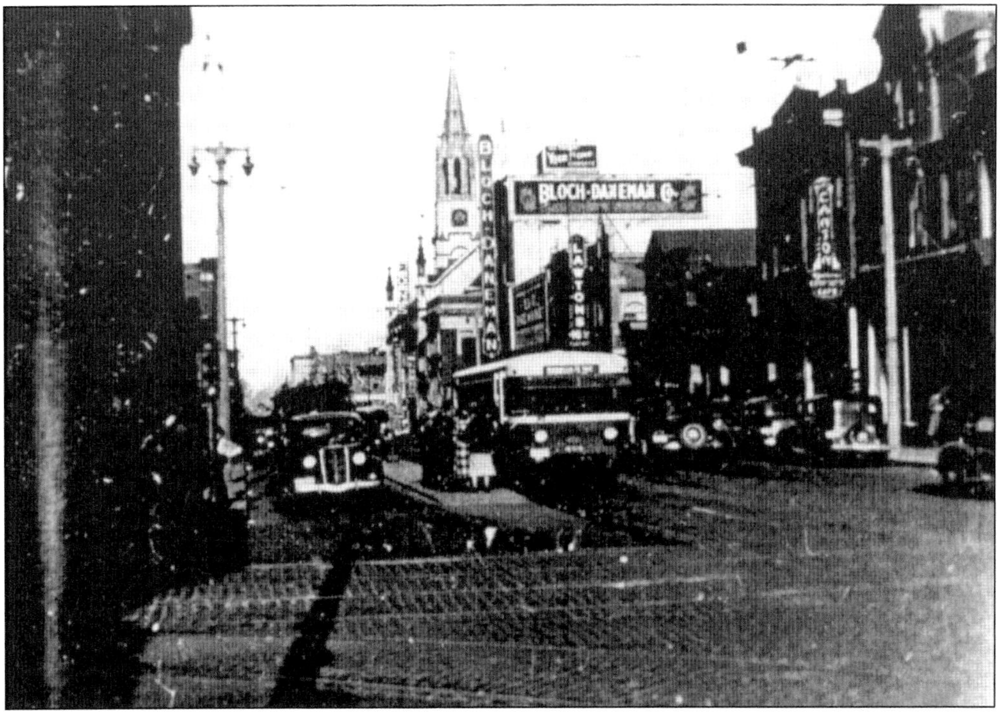

A sign for the New Canton Café, located at 1033 West Mitchell Street, is visible on the right-hand side of this photograph taken in 1937 facing east along West Mitchell Street from a vantage point near the intersection with South Eleventh Street. The restaurant was one of only a few Chinese restaurants located on the south side of Milwaukee at this early date. (Courtesy of the Milwaukee Public Library.)

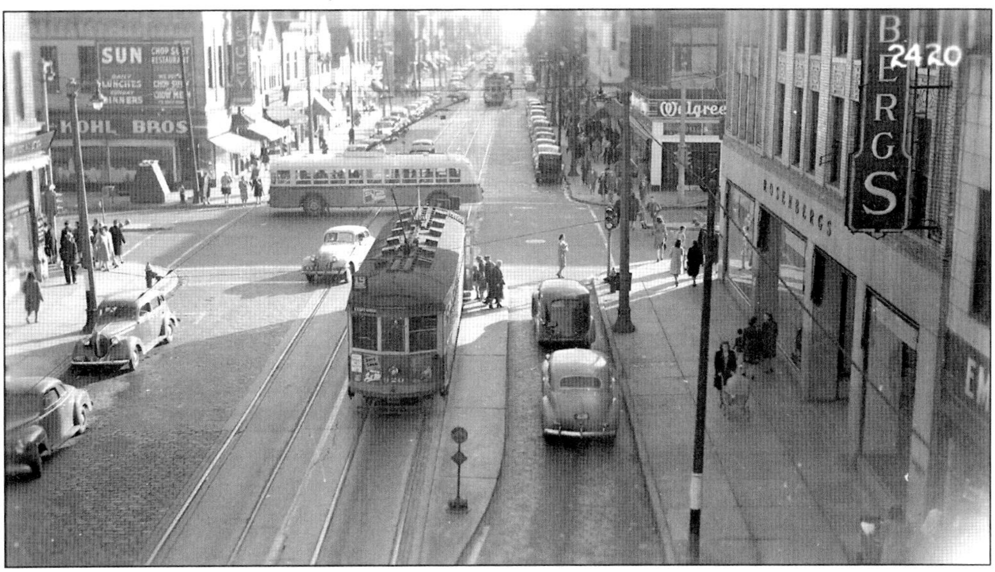

A sign for Sun Chop Suey Restaurant, at 2242 North Third Street, is visible in the upper left-hand corner of this 1937 photograph taken near the intersection of North Third Street with West North Avenue. Sun Chop Suey Restaurant was opened by Joe Wong in 1925. (Courtesy of the Milwaukee Public Library.)

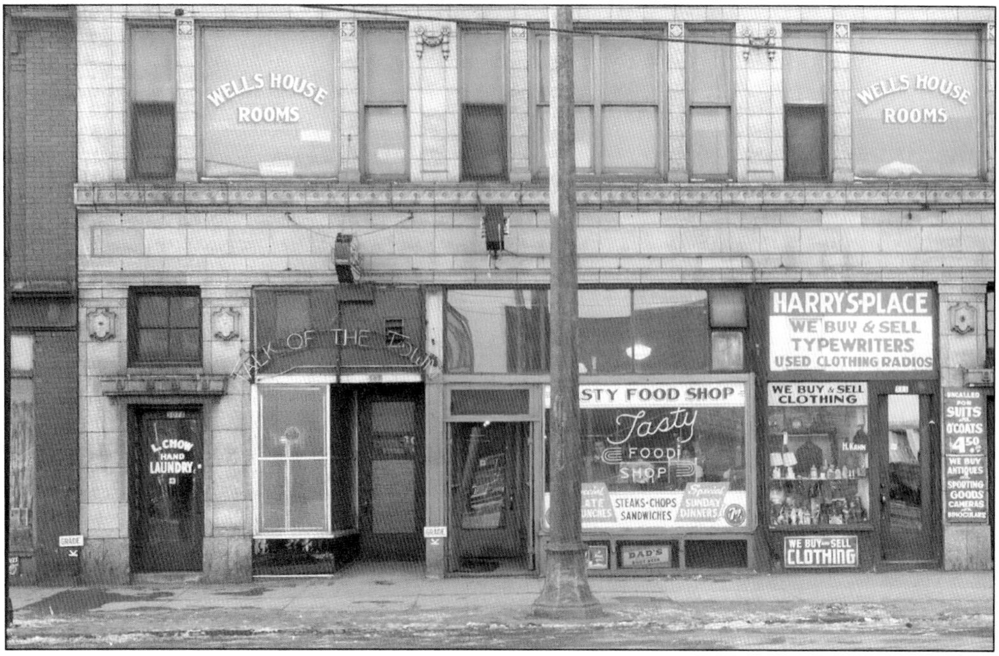

This photograph, taken by Milwaukee Commercial Photographers and dated March 8, 1949, shows the L. Chow Hand Laundry, located at 507A West Wells Street, owned by Lin G. Chow. By this date, the number of Chinese laundries and other hand laundries in the city was already beginning to decline in response to the availability of coin-operated Laundromats, home laundry equipment, and permanent-press clothing. (Courtesy of the Milwaukee Public Library.)

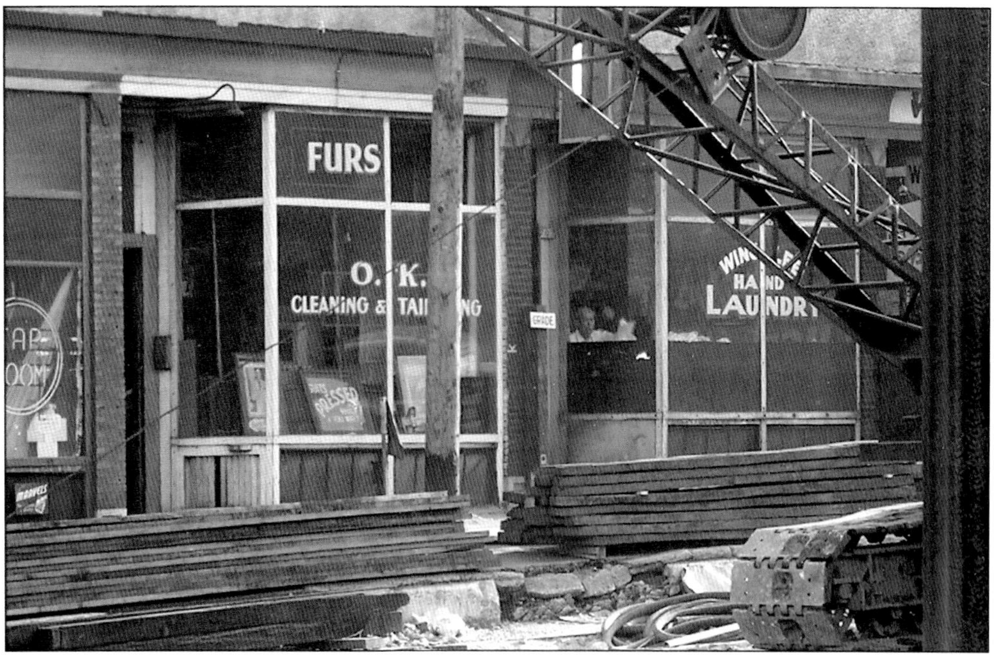

This photograph, taken by Milwaukee Commercial Photographers and dated April 21, 1949, shows the front of the Wing Lee Hand Laundry at 705 West Wells Street. Wing Lee at work is visible through the front window of the building. (Courtesy of the Milwaukee Public Library.)

Five

Family Reunification 1950–1959

The 1943 repeal of the Chinese Exclusion Act of 1882 and passage of the quota system and other legislation, combined with international events, resulted in enormous changes in the demography of Chinese communities nationwide. Three distinct groups, previously excluded, were now able to enter the country legally with the intent of staying permanently: wives and children of the Toishanese who had heretofore formed the bulk of the Chinese community, educated Chinese and students from elsewhere in China stranded in the United States because of the Communist revolution, and members of the "brain drain" coming from Taiwan and Hong Kong as students.

The most immediately noticeable change in Milwaukee was the arrival in the late 1940s and 1950s of large numbers of wives and children of the Toishanese men. This had a tremendous impact on the community. Accommodations appropriate for de facto bachelors were not suitable for women and children, so housing had to be found away from the place of work. With intact families, the men were less inclined to socialize in the import store at Fourth and State Streets, which resulted in a decline in the power of the tong and greater influences by local Christian churches. Shifting demographics throughout the Milwaukee area changed residential patterns throughout the region, resulting in the relocation of many Chinese businesses.

The Chinese laundry plummeted in importance with the introduction of Laundromats, home laundry equipment, and permanent-press clothing. This coincided roughly with the return to the United States of American military personnel who had developed a liking for Chinese food and resulted in the widening of the market for Chinese restaurants. Many laundry owners, seeing their businesses dwindle, opted to open restaurants.

The impact on the Sunday school was immediate and noticeable; it almost tripled in size between 1943 and 1950. In 1951, the First Baptist Church brought in a former missionary as a full-time staff member, Charlotte Cobb, to work with the Chinese, and two years later changed the status of the Sunday school to that of mission. She not only taught English and saw to her congregants' spiritual lives, but also instituted programs and classes to acquaint the Chinese with American customs. She also extended herself by helping families on an individual basis.

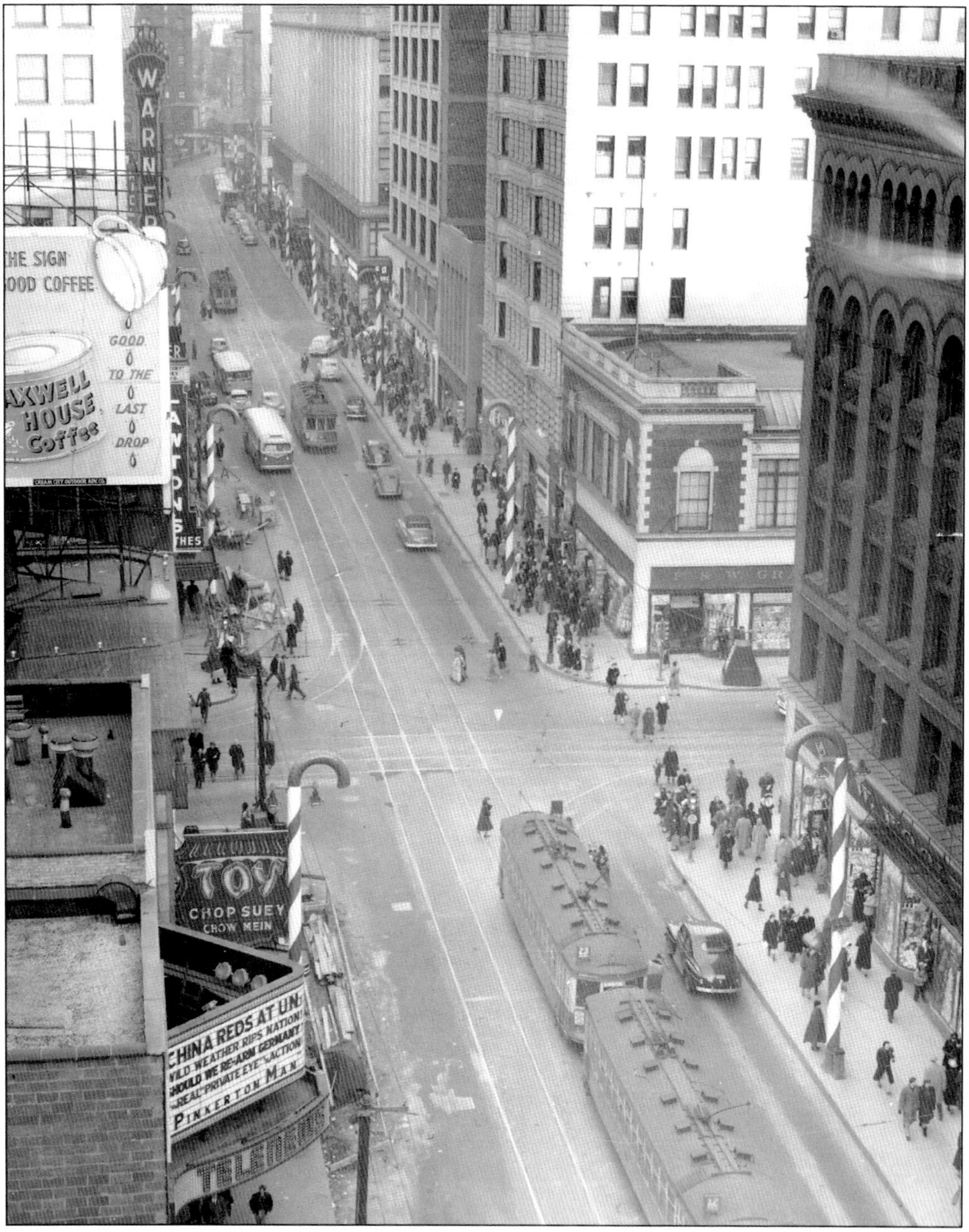

Seen here is a photograph, dated December 29, 1950, with a view facing east down Wisconsin Avenue across from the Woolworth building. The sign for Toy's Chinatown Restaurant, at 316 West Wisconsin Avenue, is visible on the north side of West Wisconsin Avenue. Restaurants remained a significant source of employment for the Milwaukee Chinese community during the 1950s. Approximate 30 percent of the Chinese residents listed in the 1950 and 1960 Milwaukee City Directories were identified as being employed in restaurants. The official Chinese population of the city grew rapidly during the 1950s, nearly doubling from 234 to 464 residents. (Courtesy of the Milwaukee Public Library.)

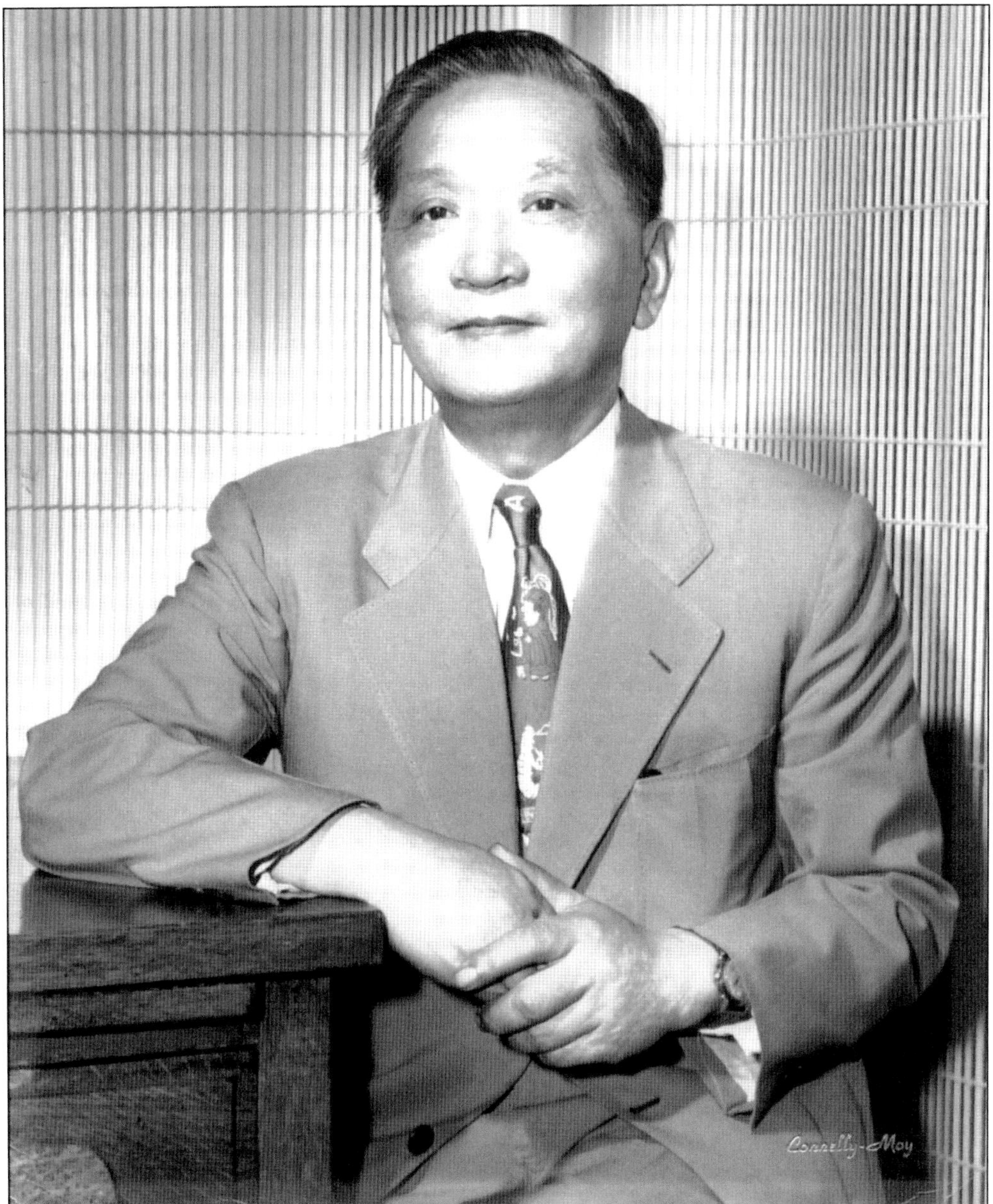

Moy B. Toy (Moy Bock Toon), shown here in 1953, was born in 1891 in Taishan, in Guangdong, China. He was Charlie Toy's second son. At age 10, Moy B. Toy left his homeland to join his father in Oshkosh. He attended the University of Wisconsin-Milwaukee for two years, studying English, German, and mathematics, before studying civil engineering at the Armour Institute of Technology in Chicago. Moy B. Toy married in China in 1913 and returned with his wife, Leung Yuey King, to Milwaukee in 1914. They had nine children, eight living to adulthood. Toy was his father's business partner in both a restaurant and trading company. In 1938, Moy B. Toy opened his own restaurant, Toy's Chinatown Restaurant at 306 West Wisconsin Avenue. In 1944, after Chinese were finally allowed to become naturalized citizens, both Moy B. Toy and his wife applied for and were granted citizenship. He often went to work wearing a pin-striped suit and his favorite Adidas tennis shoes. (Courtesy of the Toy family.)

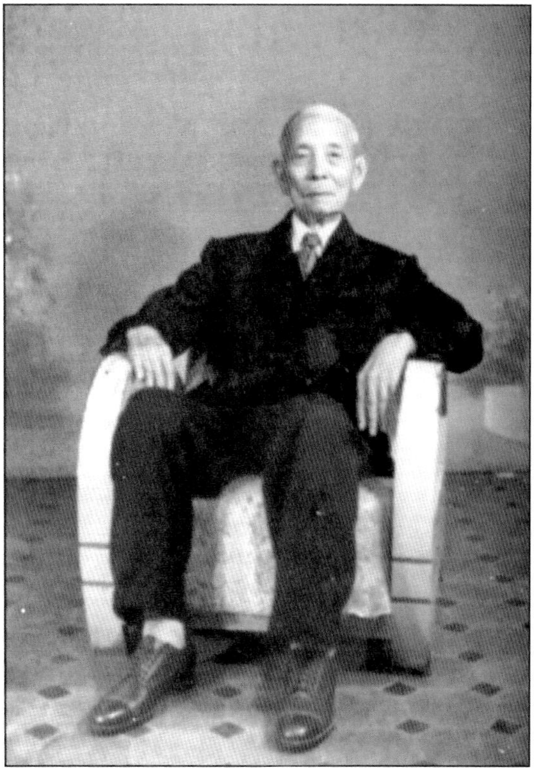

This photograph of Charlie Toy is believed to be the last image taken prior to his death in China in 1955 at age 95. He had retired to China in 1946, during the Chinese civil war period that followed the end of World War II. (Courtesy of the Toy family.)

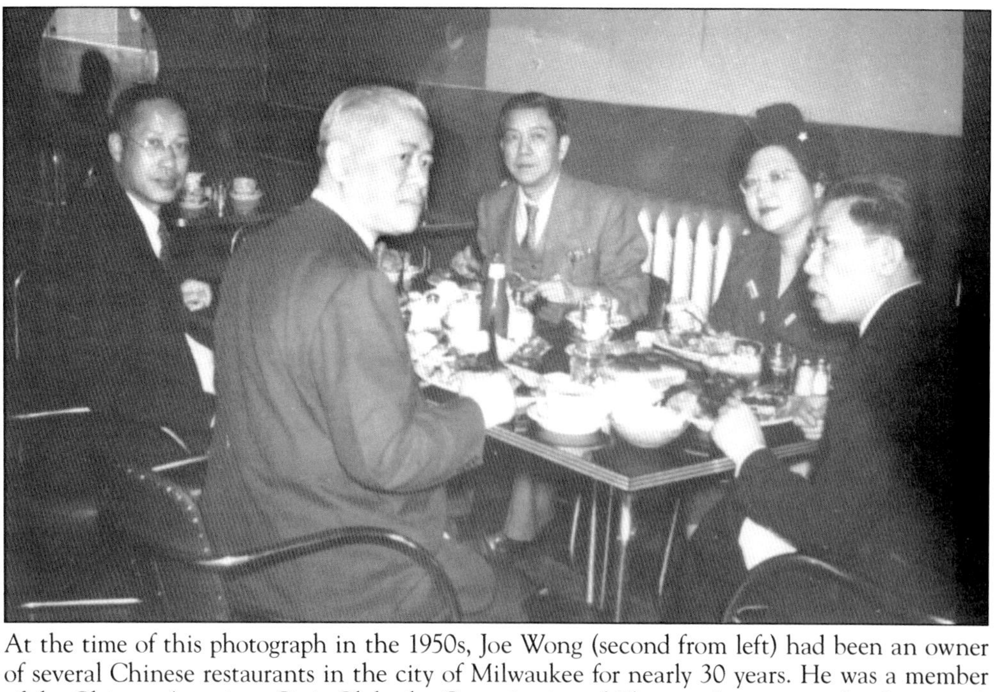

At the time of this photograph in the 1950s, Joe Wong (second from left) had been an owner of several Chinese restaurants in the city of Milwaukee for nearly 30 years. He was a member of the Chinese American Civic Club, the Organization of Chinese Americans, the Governor's Commission on Human Rights, and a president of the Chinese-American Welfare Association. (Courtesy of Paul Wong.)

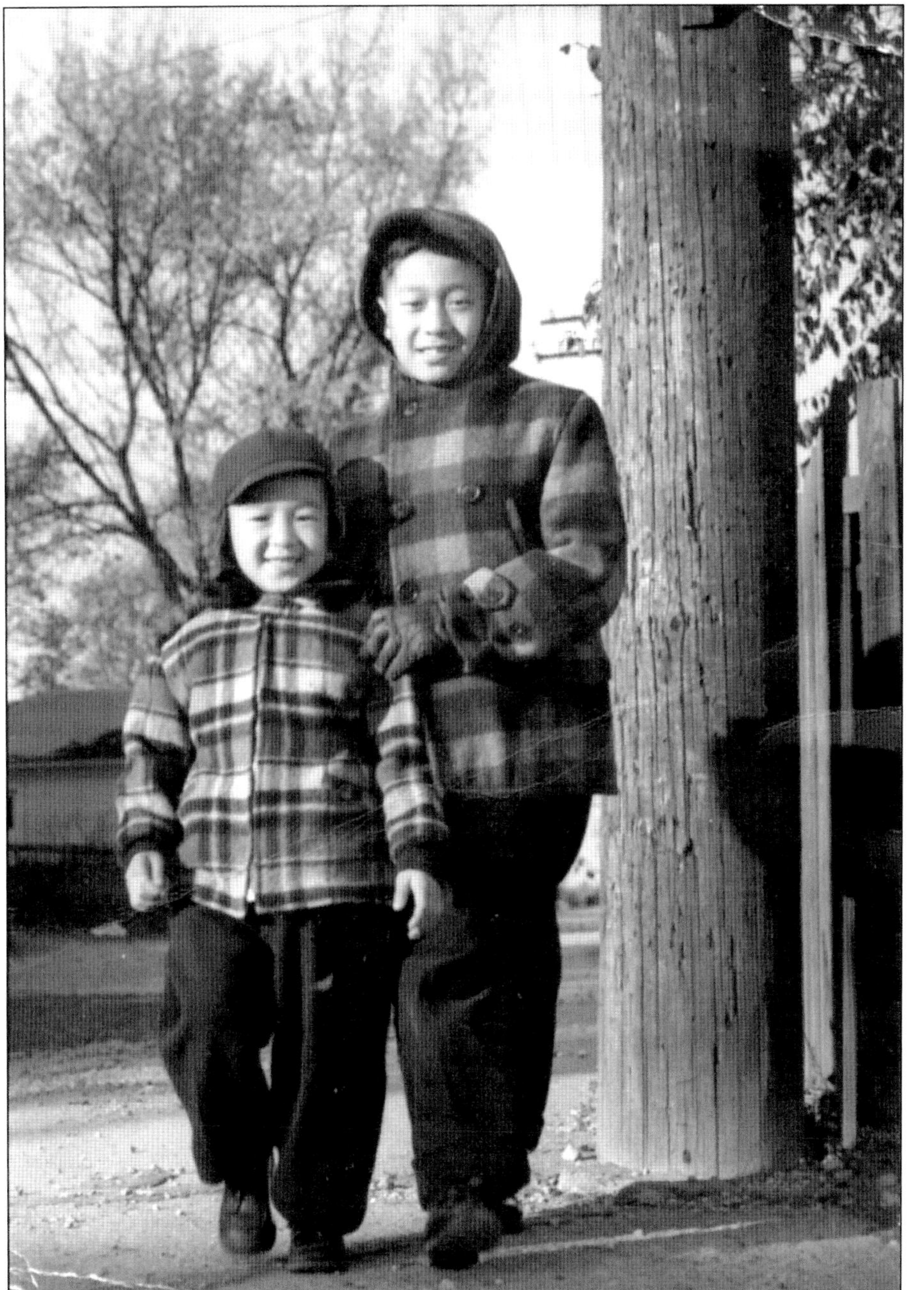

This photograph, dating from the early 1950s, shows Paul Wong (left) with his cousin Edward Chin (right). The two cousins were grandchildren of longtime Chinese community leader and restaurateur Joe Wong. After graduating from the University of Wisconsin–Madison with majors in business and history, Paul Wong managed several restaurants and bars before deciding in 1979 to team up with Edward to start a local Chinese fast-food restaurant chain (Wong's Wok). In addition to a chain of 11 Wong's Wok outlets, the cousins also operated Toy's Chinatown Restaurant for approximately 14 years and La Joy Restaurant for 20 years. (Courtesy of Paul Wong.)

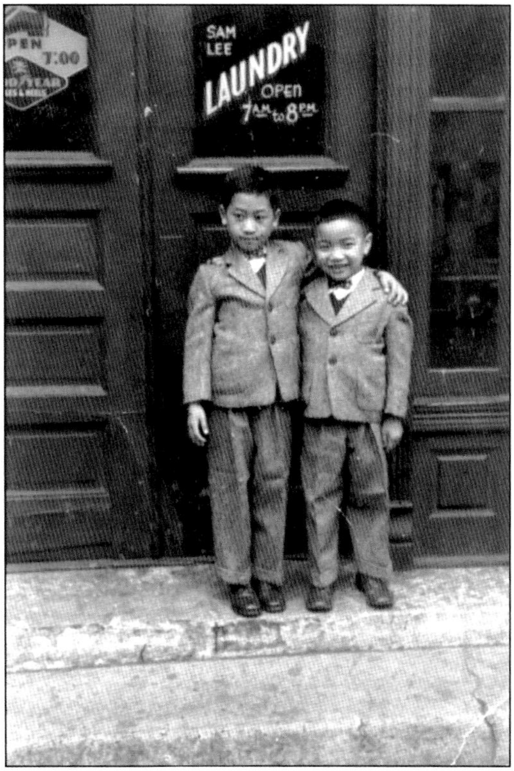

Kenny Moy (left) and Sam Moy (right) are shown in this 1952 photograph in front of the Sam Lee Laundry owned by their grandfather Fong Moy at 612 North Fifth Street in downtown Milwaukee. A second Sam Lee Laundry was located at this time at 1404 North Marshall Street. (Courtesy of Sally Moy Klatt.)

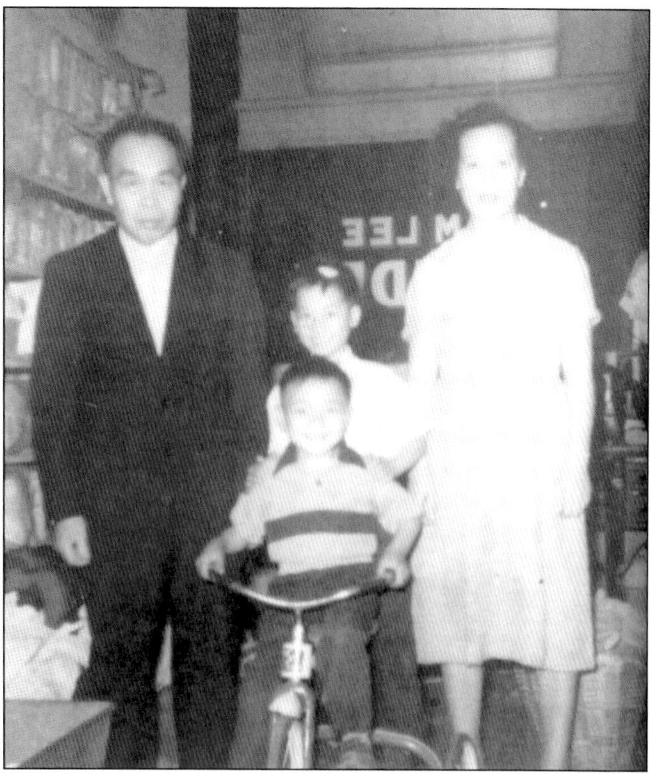

The interior of the Sam Lee Laundry at 612 North Fifth Street is shown in this early-1950s photograph. Laundry neatly wrapped in brown kraft paper and waiting for pickup by customers is visible on the shelves. Fong Moy (left), the laundry owner, is shown with his daughter-in-law Nancy Chan Moy and two grandchildren, Sam Moy (front center) and Kenny Moy (rear center). (Courtesy of Sally Moy Klatt.)

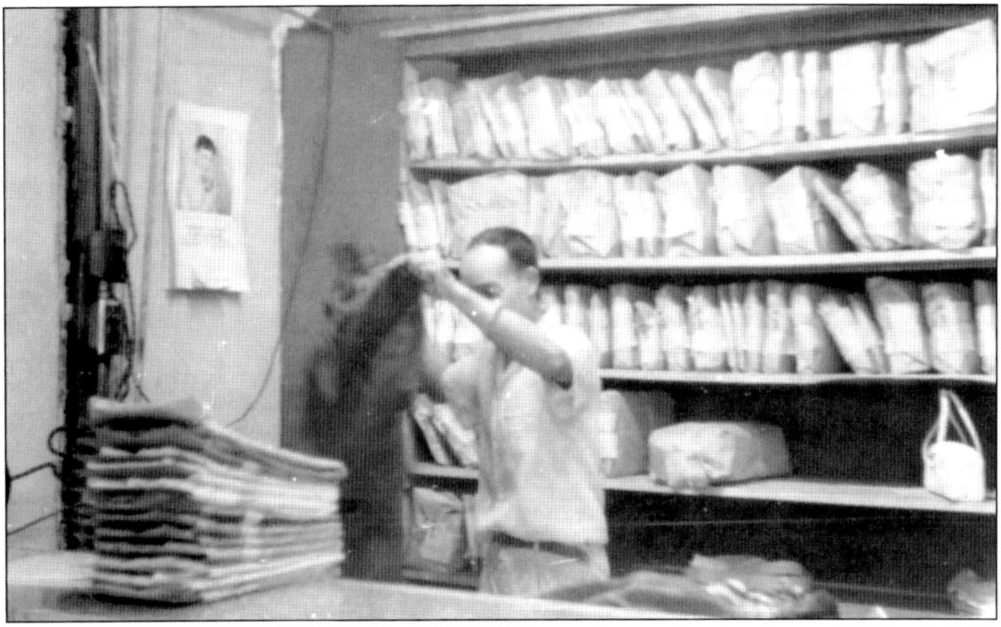

This mid-1950s photograph shows Geng Wing Moy working in his laundry at 612 North Fifth Street. A stack of clean shirts that have been pressed, ironed, and folded are visible on the counter, ready to be wrapped in kraft paper. Geng Moy worked a full-time job at Johnson Service Company from 7:00 a.m. to 3:30 p.m. each weekday, after which he would spend an additional four hours working at the laundry. (Courtesy of Sally Moy Klatt.)

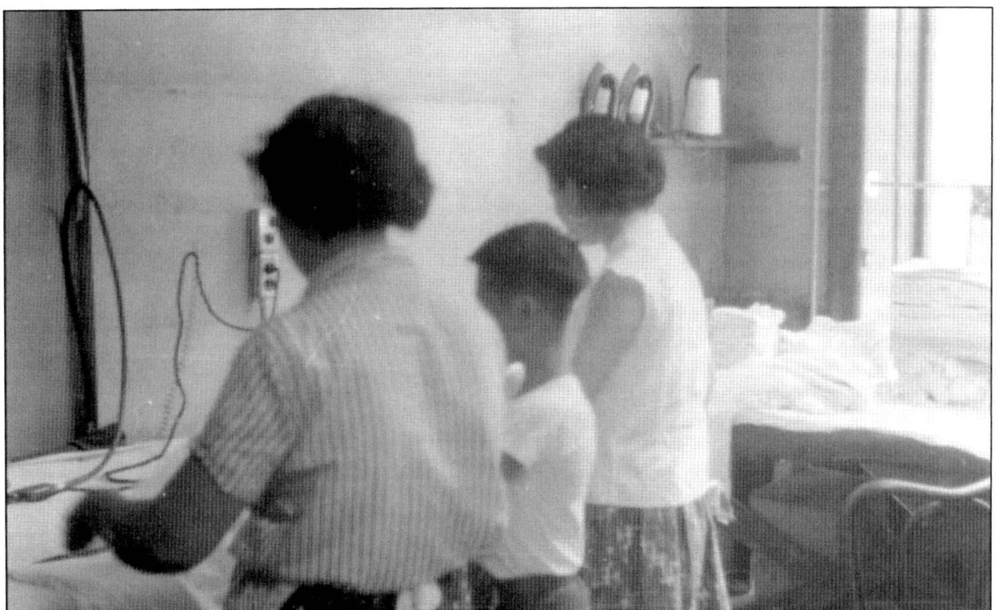

This photograph, dated approximately 1957 or 1958, shows the interior of a Chinese laundry located on North Twenty-seventh Street between West North Avenue and West Garfield Avenue. Nancy Moy (left) is showing Kenny Moy (center) how to iron clothes. (Courtesy of Sally Moy Klatt.)

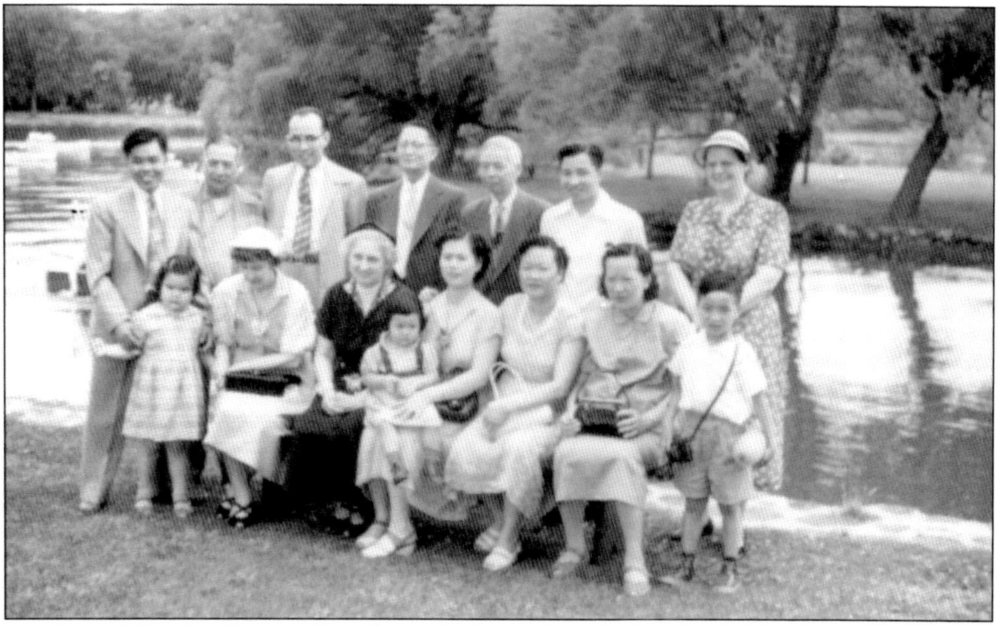

Members of the First Baptist Church are shown in this 1950s photograph at a park outing. Eva Johnson (front row, third from left) began ministering to Milwaukee's Chinese community in 1934, teaching Sunday school classes at 911 East Ogden Avenue. Also shown is Charlotte Cobb (back row, far right), who had previously been a missionary in China but returned to Milwaukee after being forced to leave after the Communist takeover. (Courtesy of Sally Moy Klatt.)

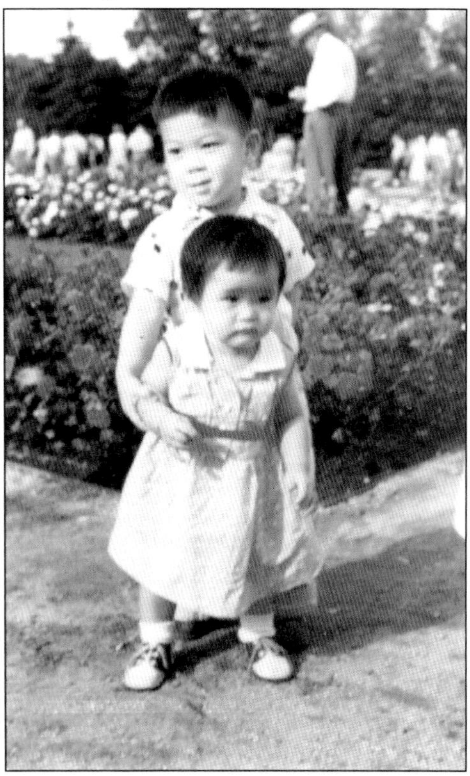

Sally Moy (front) and Henry Lee (back) are shown in this 1954 photograph taken in Whitnall Park in Milwaukee, a favorite place for outings by the Moy and other Chinese laundry families. Sally was the first Milwaukee-born child of eight children born to Geng and Nancy Moy. (Courtesy of Sally Moy Klatt.)

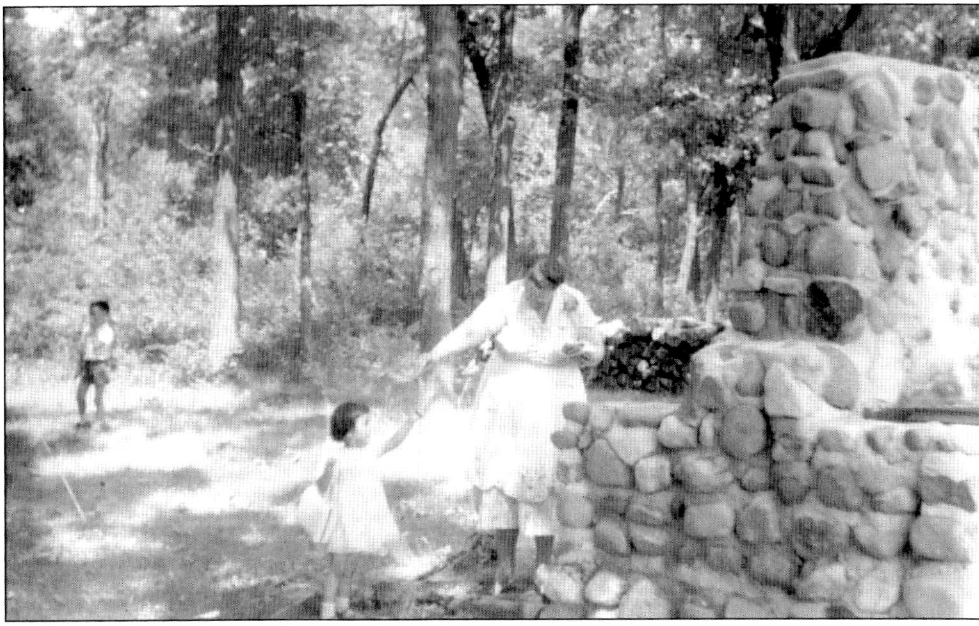

Sally Moy and her brother Sam are shown with Charlotte Cobb in this 1957 photograph of a church outing. Cobb was hired by the Wisconsin State Baptist Convention to serve as a full-time paid staff person attending to the Chinese community. Cobb played an important role in the Chinese community and devoted herself not only to the spiritual needs of the community but also to the adjustment of newcomers to American society. (Courtesy of Sally Moy Klatt.)

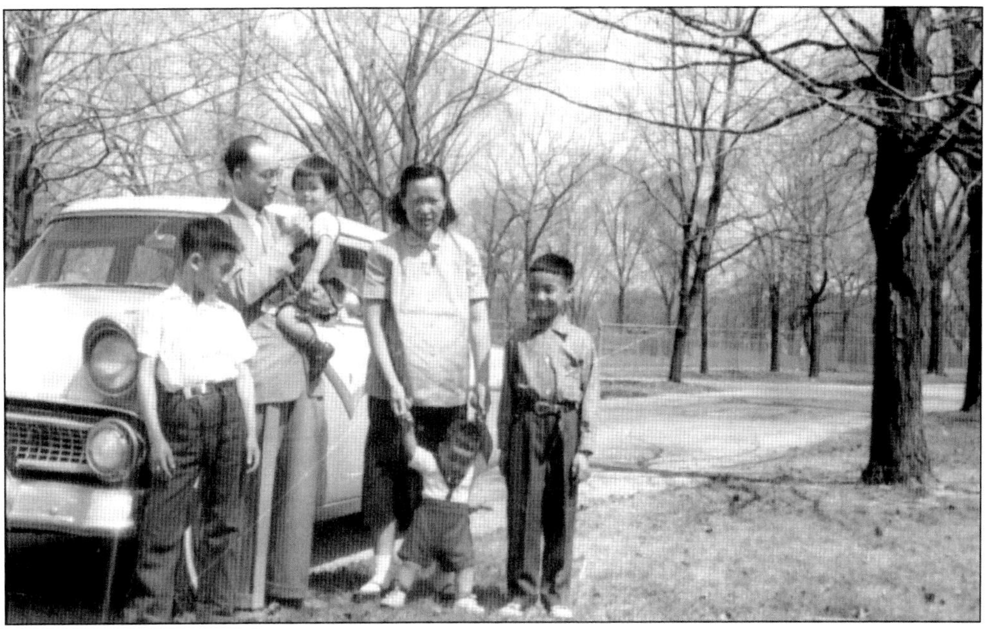

Geng and Nancy Moy, with four of their children (Kenny, Sally, Ronny, and Sam), visit Forest Home Cemetery and the grave of Geng Moy's father, Fong Moy, in 1955. Before 1945, most Chinese in Milwaukee were buried in Evergreen Cemetery. Every 15 years, bones were disinterred and shipped back to China for burial. After 1945, due to civil war in China, all Chinese were buried at Forest Home and other cemeteries and no longer disinterred. (Courtesy of Sally Moy Klatt.)

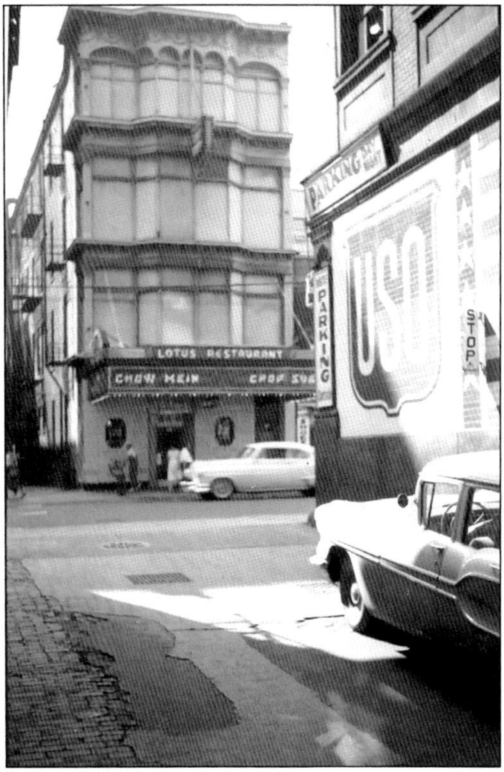

The exterior of Lotus Restaurant, a popular Chinese restaurant located at 731–733 North Third Street, is shown in this photograph taken in August 1959. (Courtesy of the Milwaukee Public Library.)

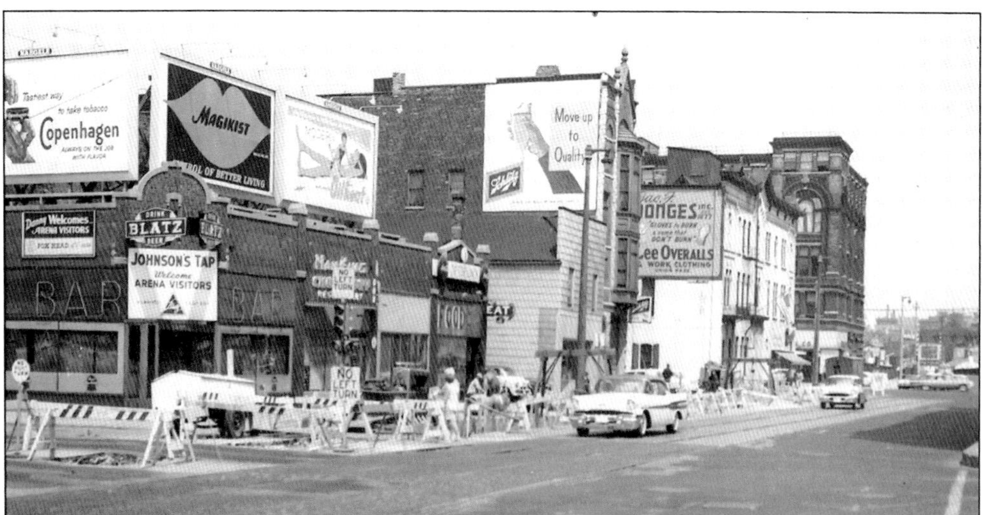

Nan King Chop Suey Restaurant is visible on West State Street in this photograph dated 1959. The photograph provides a view facing east of the block located between North Third Street and North Fourth Street. (Courtesy of the Milwaukee Public Library.)

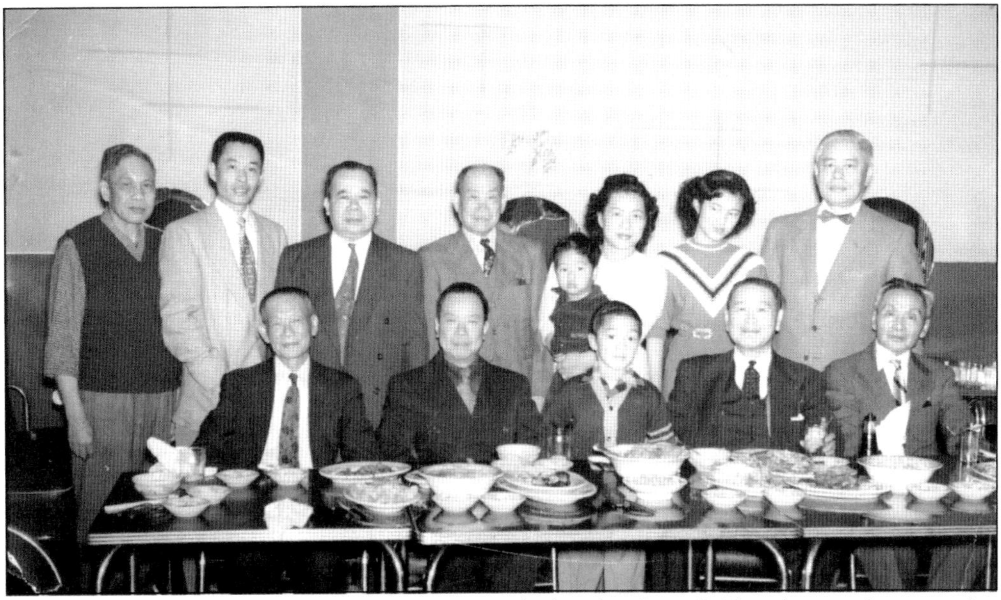

Several generations and members of the Wong and Chin families of Milwaukee are shown in this photograph dated approximately 1952, which includes Joe Wong (back row, far right), Jack Wong (first row, second from right), and Paul Wong (first row, center), as well as other unidentified family members. (Courtesy of Paul Wong.)

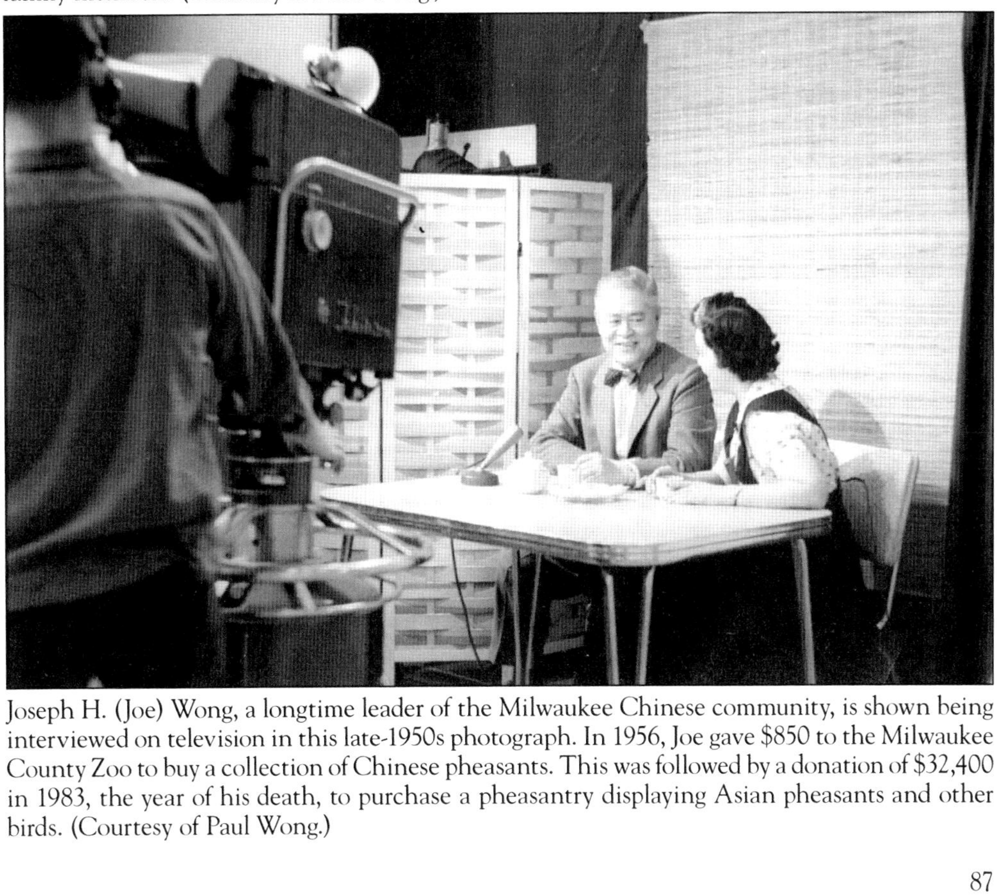

Joseph H. (Joe) Wong, a longtime leader of the Milwaukee Chinese community, is shown being interviewed on television in this late-1950s photograph. In 1956, Joe gave $850 to the Milwaukee County Zoo to buy a collection of Chinese pheasants. This was followed by a donation of $32,400 in 1983, the year of his death, to purchase a pheasantry displaying Asian pheasants and other birds. (Courtesy of Paul Wong.)

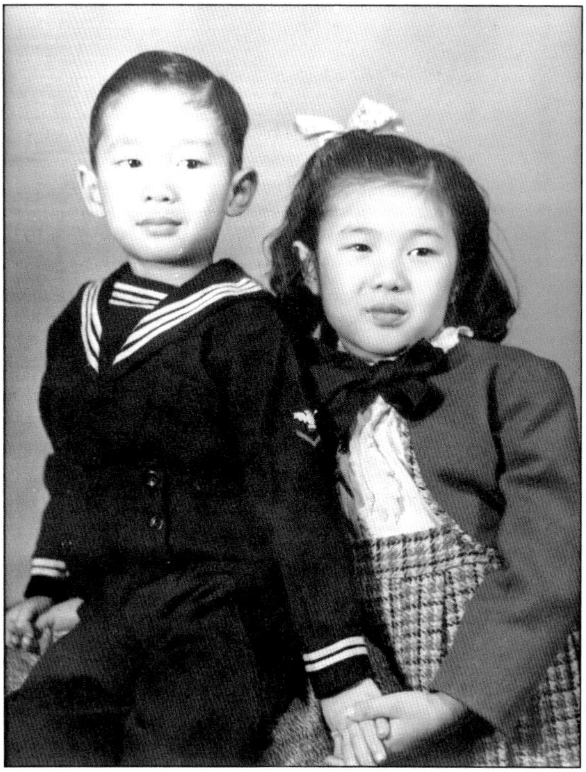

Edward Chin and his sister, Francis Chin, are shown in this photograph dating from the mid-1940s. They were grandchildren of longtime Chinese community leader and restaurateur Joe Wong. Edward, together with his cousin Paul Wong, would eventually take over their grandfather's restaurant, and then the two would go on to develop a well-known Chinese fast-food restaurant chain in the Milwaukee area named Wong's Wok. (Courtesy of Paul Wong.)

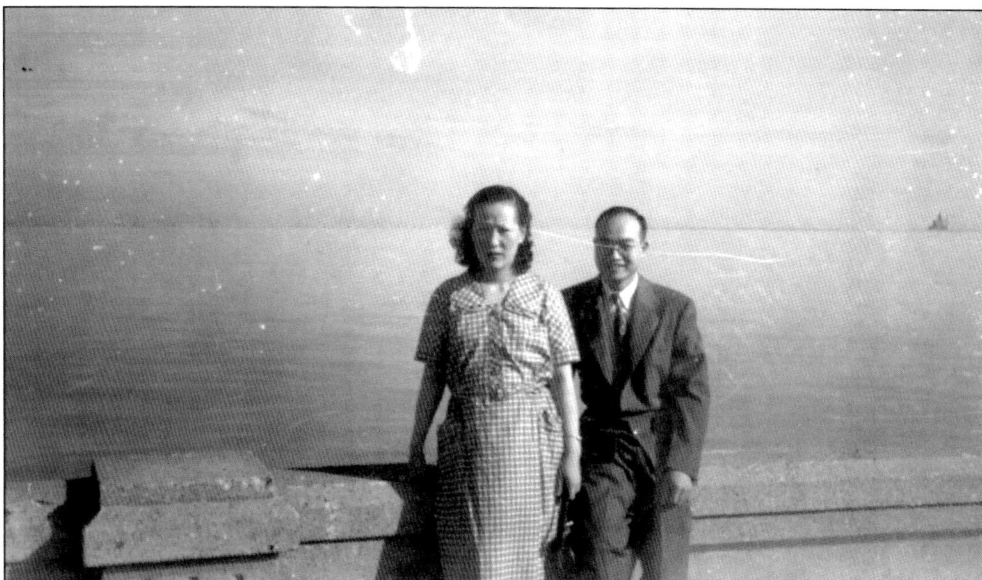

This 1952 photograph shows Geng and Nancy Moy at Milwaukee's lakefront. Geng Moy first immigrated to Milwaukee as a young boy in the early 1930s to live with his father, Fong Moy, and attend school. He returned to China in the late 1930s, where he married and had a daughter before his first wife died (around 1943). Within a year, he had met Nancy and remarried. In 1945 or 1946, Geng was able to return to Milwaukee. Unfortunately, Nancy and their three children were unable to join Geng in Milwaukee until 1952. (Courtesy of Sally Moy Klatt.)

Six

Changing Patterns 1960–1975

In 1966, Charlotte Cobb, who had headed the First Baptist Church Chinese mission since 1951, was replaced by a Shanghai-born minister, Rev. Charles Ho. He relocated the church to a different building, changed the name to the Community Baptist Church and Asian–American Community Center, and recruited professional Chinese as members, a move which prompted some resentment from restaurant families.

The few stranded Chinese developed a community of professionals with few ties with the Toishanese laundry/restaurant families. Despite their high educational achievements, many encountered difficulties finding jobs. Most professionals who settled in greater Milwaukee did so primarily because of economic opportunities, a love for the city developing only afterward.

Racial prejudice also impacted housing choices. Professional Chinese developed a pattern of living first in rental units, then purchasing modest homes, frequently in blue-collar neighborhoods on Milwaukee's South Side. These served as starter homes for families that eventually moved into more prestigious housing elsewhere in the suburbs.

They were joined in the 1960s by members of the "brain drain" from Taiwan and Hong Kong. United by advanced educations and professional careers, they organized the Chinese American Civic Club in the early 1950s, as well as student clubs at Milwaukee's universities. Affiliated with the International Institute of Wisconsin, the Chinese American Civic Club participated in the annual Holiday Folk Fair, took part in the City of Festivals Parade, and provided a means by which schools and civic organizations could locate a Chinese individual to speak about Chinese culture or demonstrate Chinese folk arts.

Among the professionals, one group maintained a distinct identity. Those from Taiwan included both people whose predecessors had migrated from China's Fujian Province in the 19th century and others who had accompanied the Nationalist government to Taiwan following the Communist takeover of mainland China. Some of the former identified themselves not as Chinese but as Taiwanese and formed their own association.

The passage in 1965 of the Immigration and Nationality Act abolished the quota system and replaced it with a system of preferences based on family relationships and professional occupations. This enabled Chinese to change their visa status from student to immigrant and/or to bring in family members, resulting in large numbers of Chinese arrivals. The 1975 fall of Saigon resulted in an influx of Indochinese refugees, including the Hmong, which further altered the Chinese community.

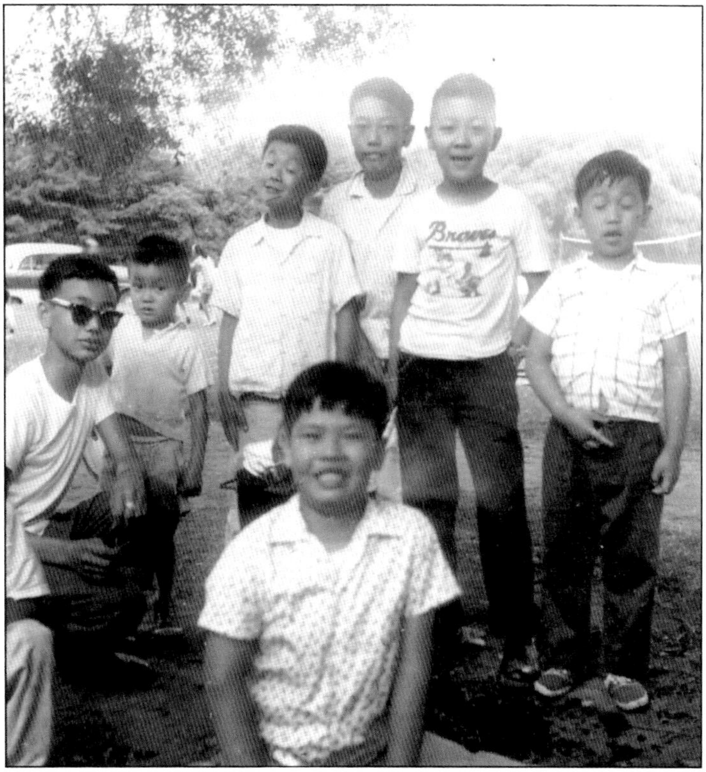

Cleveland Fong (front), and Sam Moy, Gary Moy, Eddie Chow, Franklin Fong, Victor Wong, and Tommy Moy (rear, from left to right) are shown having fun in this 1960 photograph from a five-family outing to a Milwaukee park. (Courtesy of Elinor Lee Cheung.)

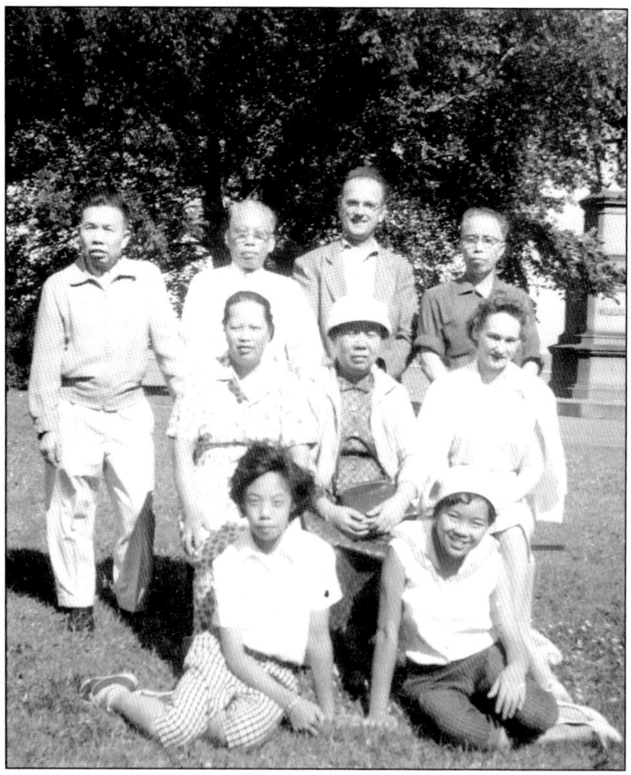

Elinor Lee Cheung (first row, left), Lily Chow (first row, right), Mrs. Chow (second row, left), Mrs. Wong (second row, center), Rev. Richard Tang Lee (third row, second from left), Lin G. Chow (third row, far right), and several unidentified persons are shown in this 1960 photograph of a church outing. (Courtesy of Elinor Lee Cheung.)

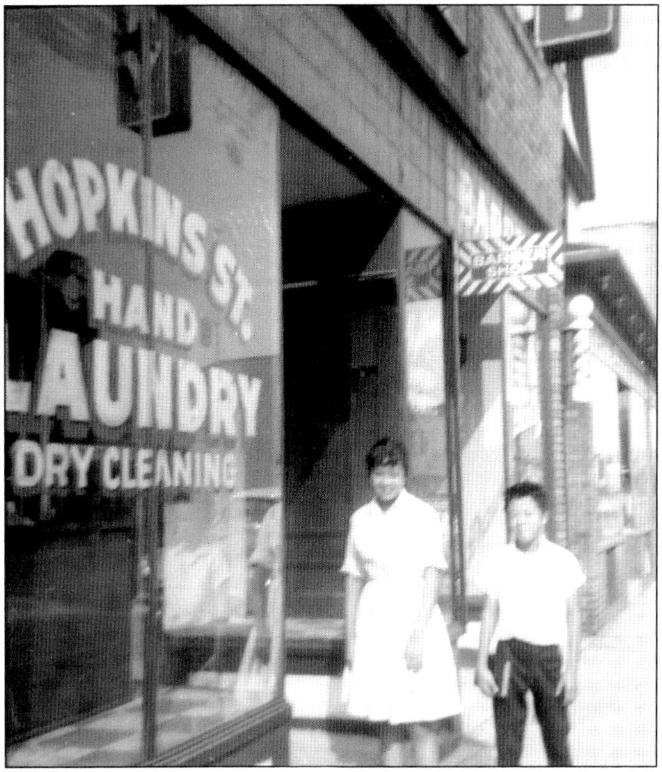

Lily Chow (age 14) and her brother Eddie Chow (age 13) are shown in front of the laundry operated by their father, Lin G. Chow, on North Hopkins Street in this photograph dated 1962 or 1963. (Courtesy of Elinor Lee Cheung.)

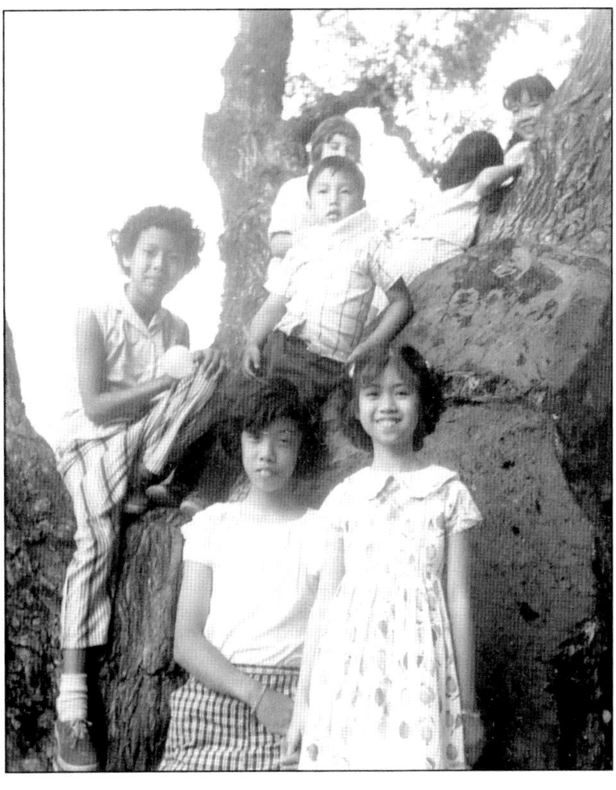

Elinor Lee Cheung (front left), Anna Moy (front right), Rose Fong (middle left), Tommy Moy (center), Pat Schweitzer (top center), Sally Moy (top right center), and Lily Chow (top right) are shown having fun climbing trees in this 1960 photograph taken during a group outing of several families to a Milwaukee park. (Courtesy of Elinor Lee Cheung.)

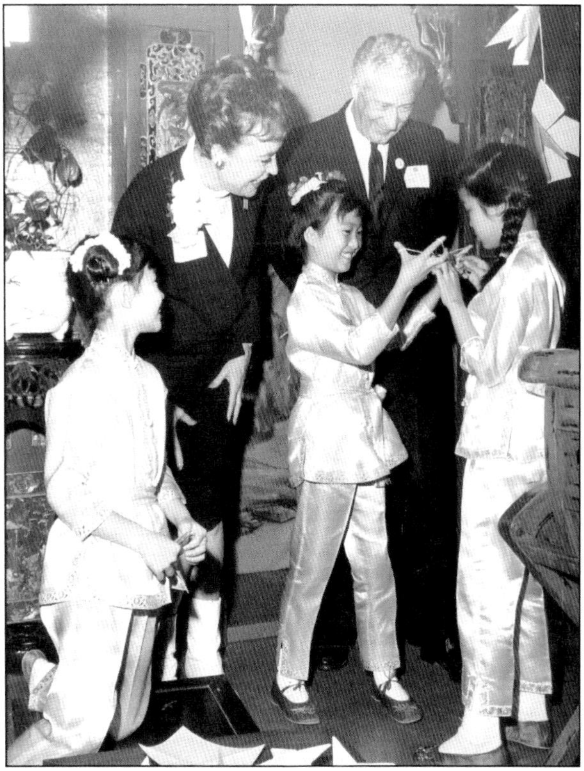

Three young performers at the Holiday Folk Fair are shown demonstrating a Chinese string game in this 1960s photograph. The performers were likely children of members of the Chinese American Civic Club. (Courtesy of the International Institute of Wisconsin.)

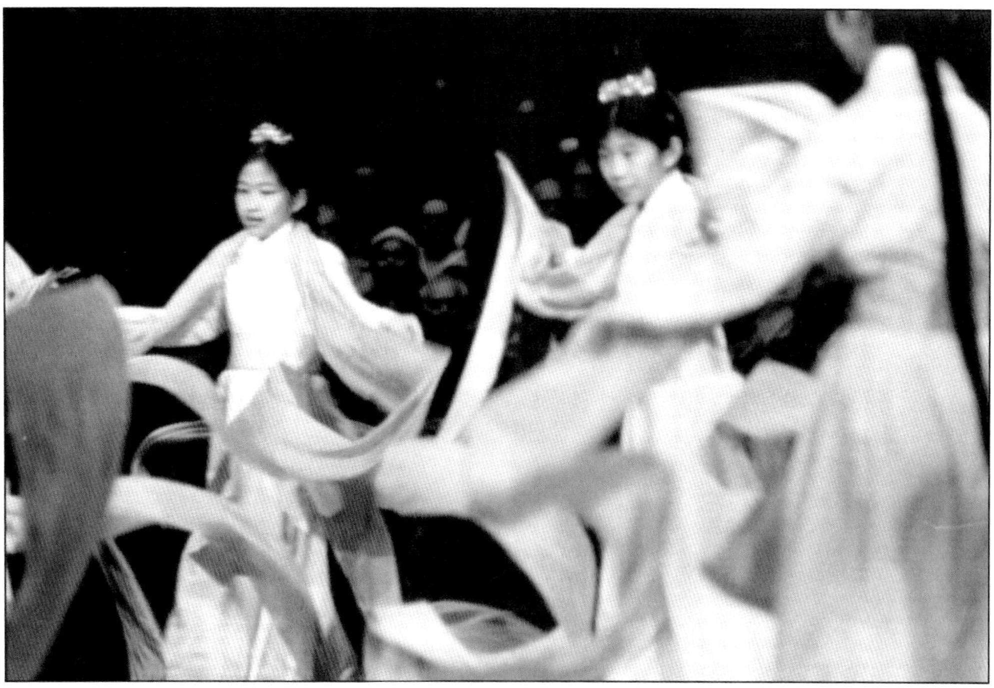

A Chinese children's group is shown in this 1960s photograph performing a ribbon dance at the Holiday Folk Fair at the Milwaukee Arena. The performers were likely children of members of the Chinese American Civic Club. (Courtesy of the International Institute of Wisconsin.)

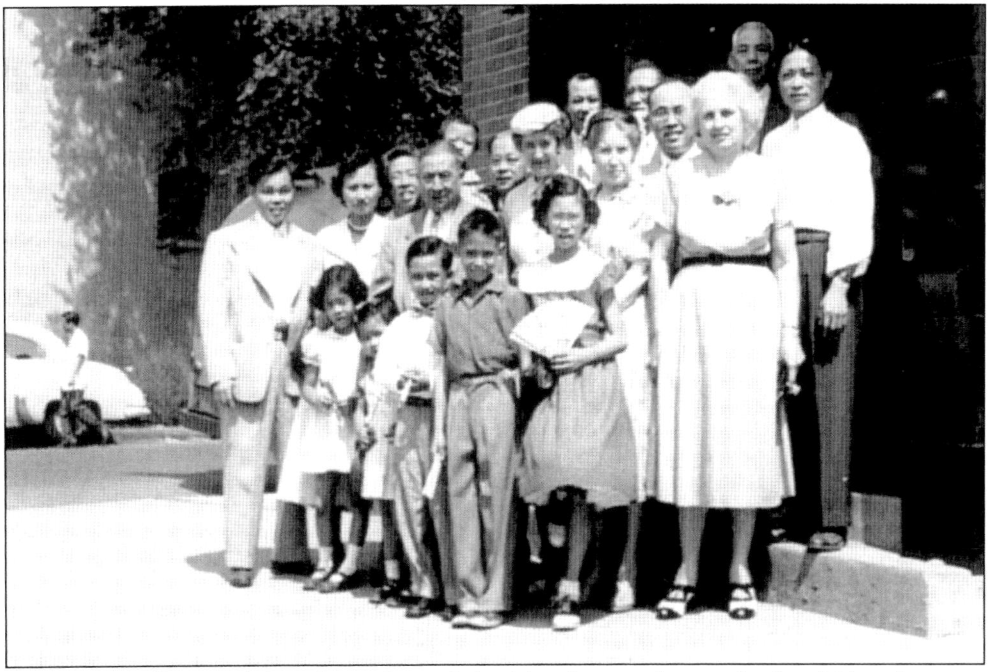

Eva Johnson (front right) and members of the Moy, Lee, and several other Milwaukee area Chinese families are shown in this late-1950s photograph during a visit to a church in Chicago's Chinatown. (Courtesy of Elinor Lee Cheung.)

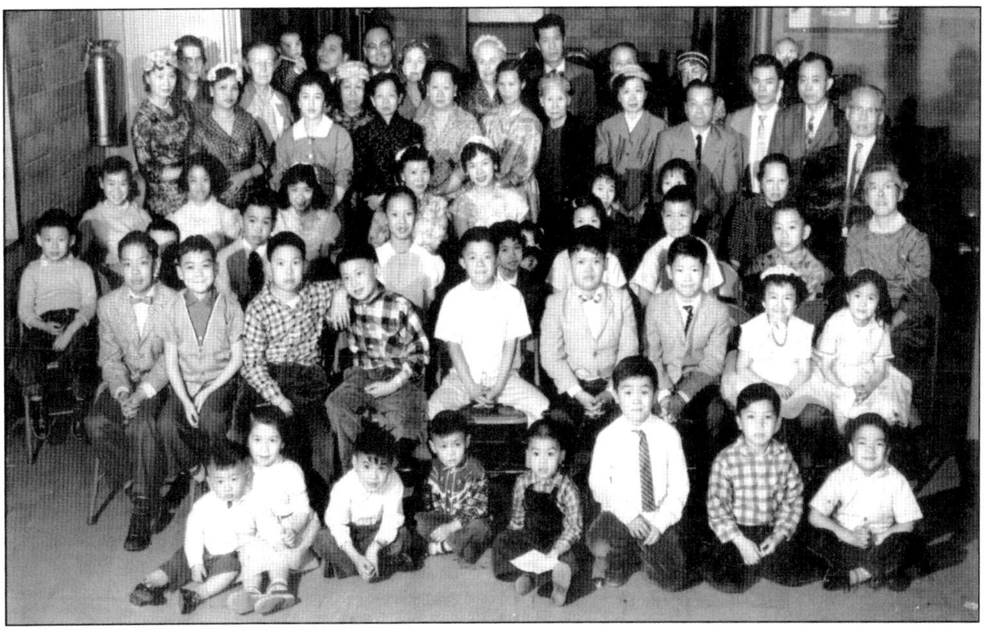

Many Chinese community members moved to the Garfield Avenue Baptist Church, 210 West Garfield Avenue in Milwaukee. This photograph was taken in 1961 at the first Easter program held for the Chinese at the Garfield Avenue Baptist Church. Individuals shown in the photograph are primarily members of the Toy, Moy, Chow, Lee, Wong, Fong, Leong, Huey, and Hong families. (Courtesy of Sally Moy Klatt.)

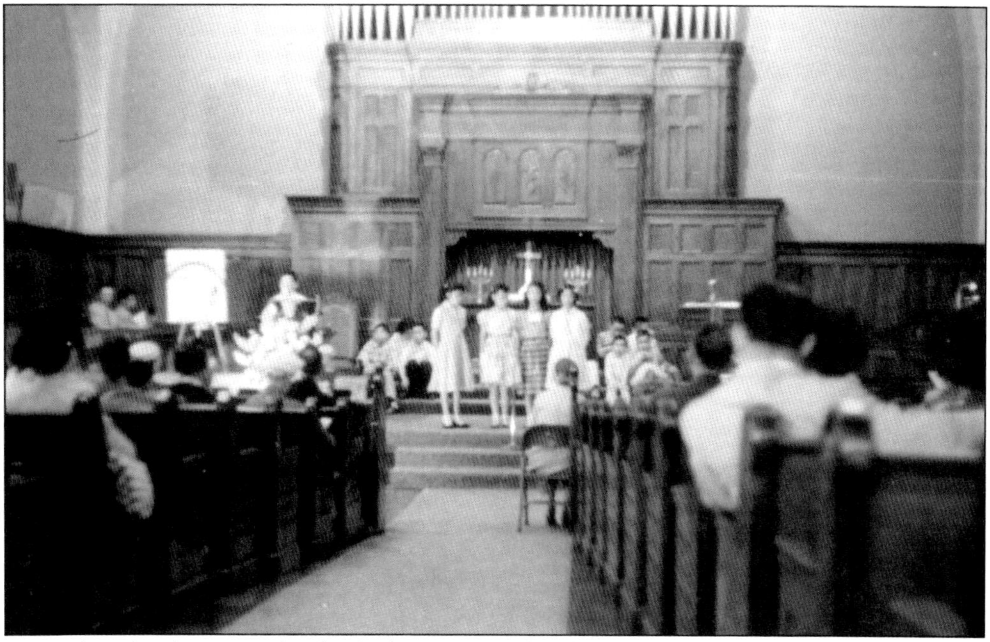

A Sunday school program for the Ogden Baptist Church, on East Ogden Avenue in Milwaukee, is shown in this early-1960s photograph. The girls standing on the steps include Lily Chow (left), Norma Lee (second from left), and Elinor Lee Cheung (right). (Courtesy of Sally Moy Klatt.)

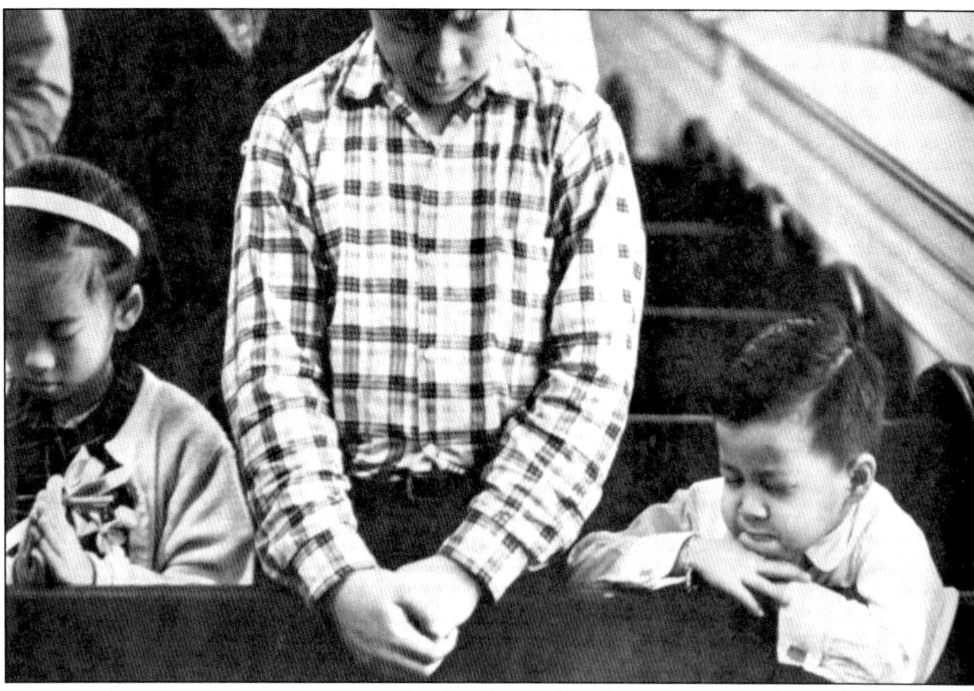

Dale Yee (age 5, with eyes closed) and his brother Bobby (age 12, standing) are shown praying during a communion service held at the Chinese Mission, 911 East Ogden Avenue, in downtown Milwaukee. This photograph first appeared in a photo essay on the Milwaukee Chinese community published in the *Milwaukee Journal* in 1961. (Courtesy of the Milwaukee Journal Sentinel.)

Lillian Wong (standing) is shown teaching Chinese characters to children at a Sunday school class held at the Garfield Avenue Baptist Church, 210 West Garfield Avenue in Milwaukee. This photograph first appeared in a photo essay on the Milwaukee Chinese community published in the *Milwaukee Journal* in 1961. (Courtesy of the Milwaukee Journal Sentinel.)

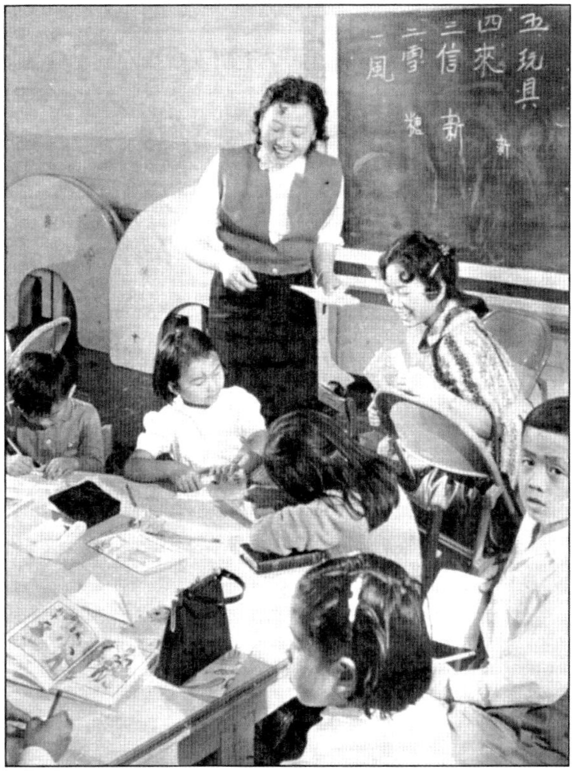

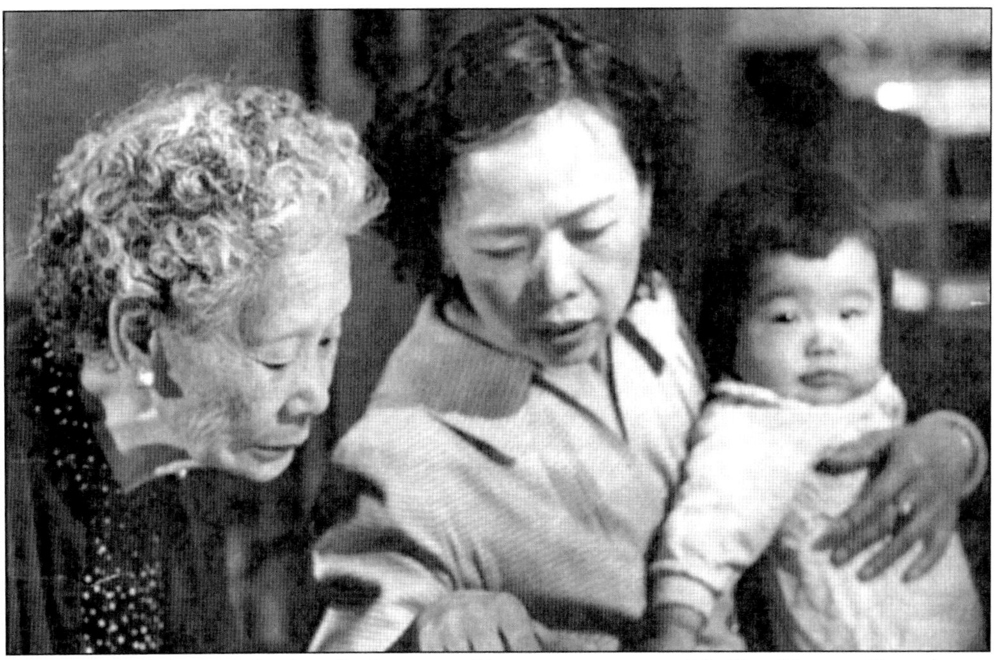

Learning English was a big hurdle for many Chinese newcomers. MayYun Ng, age 70, is shown studying English with Won Gim Toy, who is holding her daughter Anita Toy in this photograph, which first appeared in a photo essay on the Milwaukee Chinese community published in the *Milwaukee Journal* in 1961. (Courtesy of the Milwaukee Journal Sentinel.)

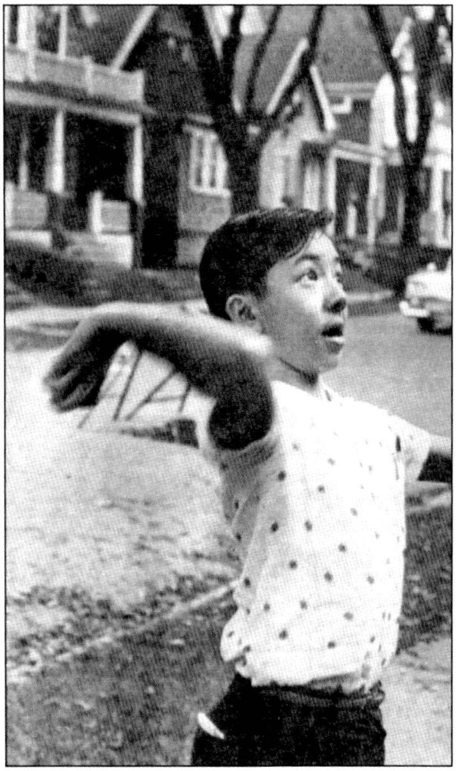

Mario Chou, a 12-year-old resident of Milwaukee whose parents were of Chinese descent and living in Cuba, is shown in this photograph, which first appeared in a photo essay on the Milwaukee Chinese community published in the *Milwaukee Journal* in 1961. Mario was sent to live with relatives in Milwaukee due to unrest in Cuba. Mario spoke Spanish but no Chinese, while the opposite was true for his guardians, Mr. and Mrs. Yat Ming Lowe. The photograph below shows Mrs. Yat Ming Lowe giving testimony before county judge Rudolph Mudroch to obtain legal guardianship for Mario Chou. (Courtesy of the Milwaukee Journal Sentinel.)

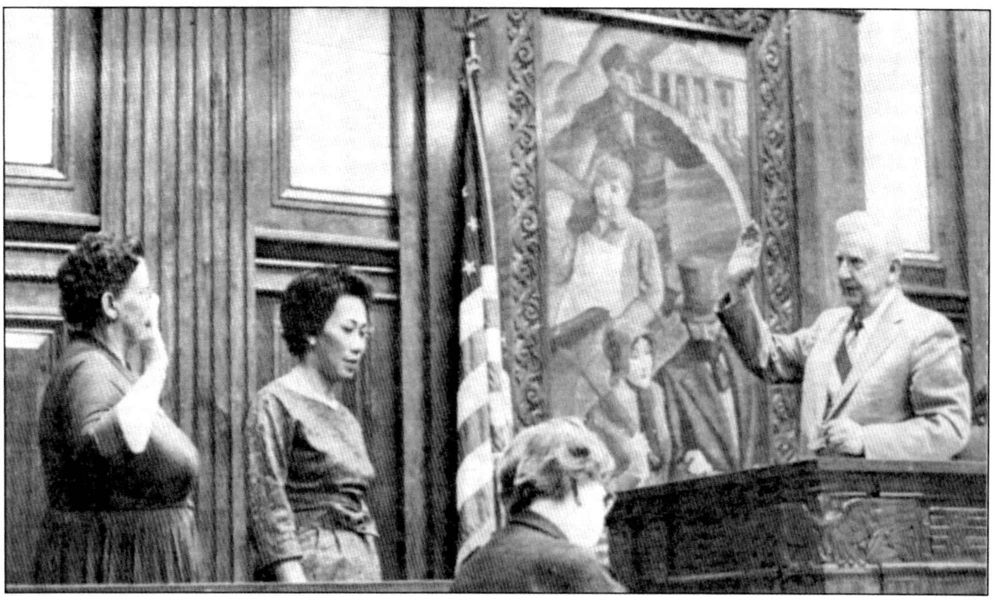

Philip Toy, a son of Dr. David Toy and Mary Jane Toy and a grandson of Moy B. Toy, is shown getting ready for school in this photograph, which first appeared in a photo essay on the Milwaukee Chinese community published in the *Milwaukee Journal* in 1961. (Courtesy of the Milwaukee Journal Sentinel.)

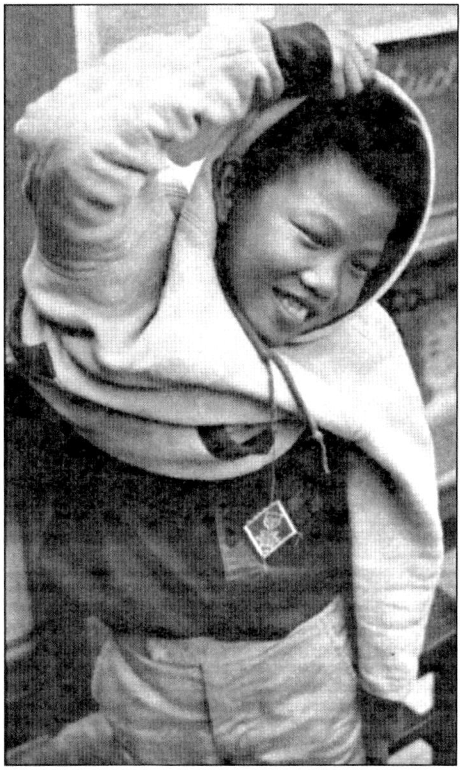

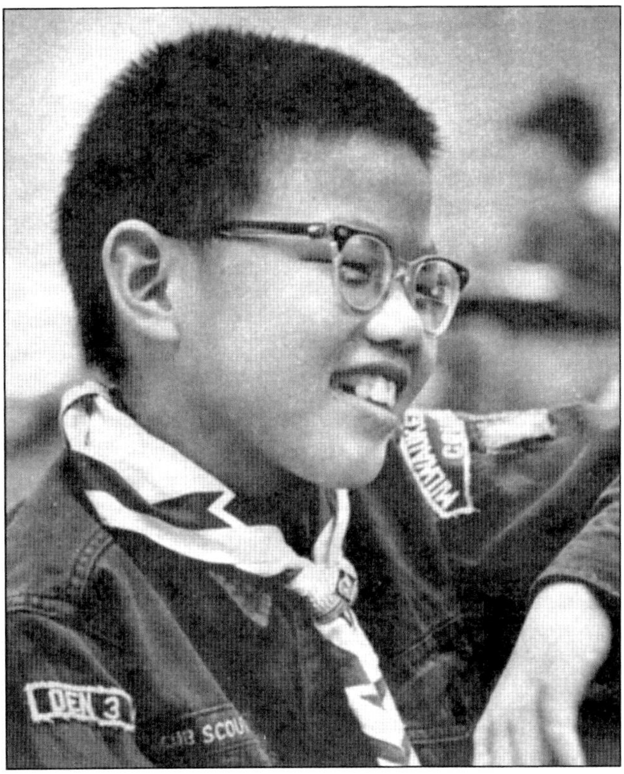

Leland Toy, a member of Cub Scout Pack 47 and a son of Dr. David Toy and Mary Jane Toy, grandson of Moy B. Toy, and great-grandson of Charlie Toy, is shown in this photograph, which first appeared in a photo essay on the Milwaukee Chinese community published in the *Milwaukee Journal* in 1961. Leland later became a master kite builder, known internationally for his innovative designs. (Courtesy of the Milwaukee Journal Sentinel.)

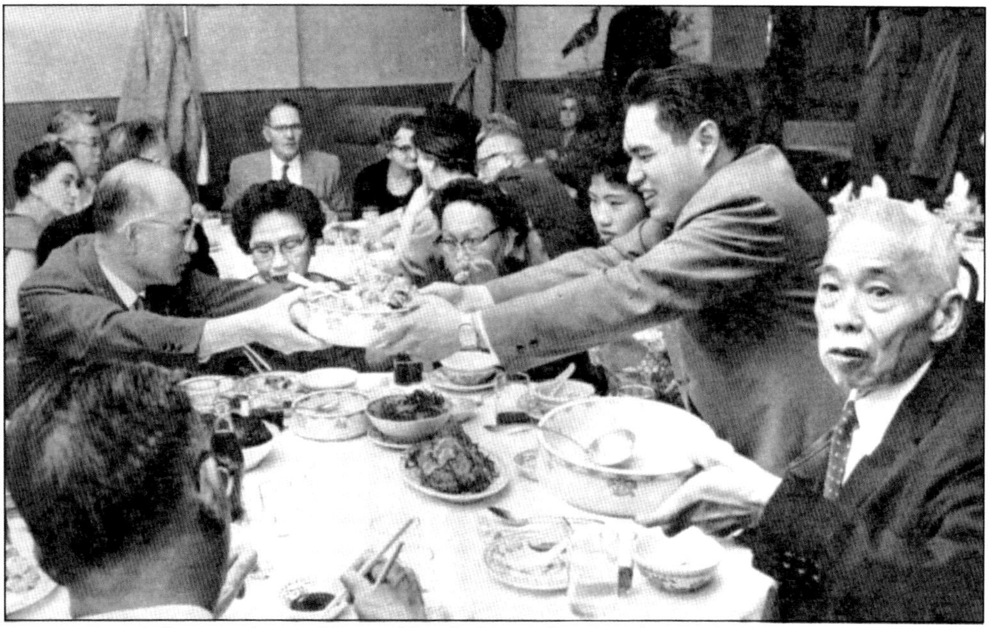

A reception following the wedding of Linda Moy of Milwaukee and Bow Huie of Chicago is shown in this photograph, which first appeared in a photo essay on the Milwaukee Chinese community published in the *Milwaukee Journal* in 1961. Also shown in the photograph are Anthony Woo (on left, receiving dish), Mr. Huie (on right, passing dish), and Charlie Hong (lower right). (Courtesy of the Milwaukee Journal Sentinel.)

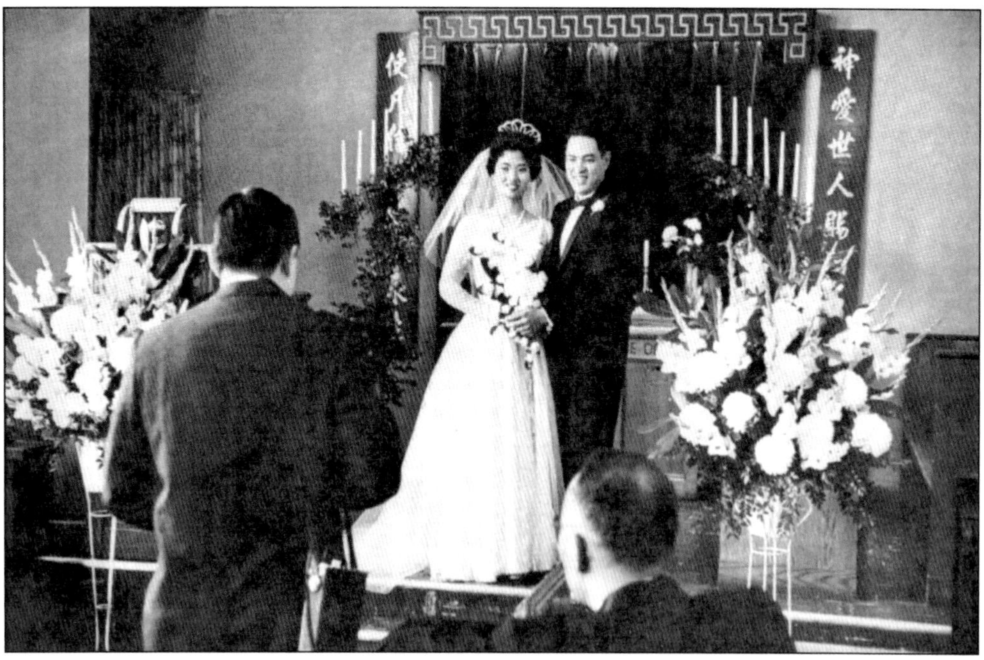

The wedding of Linda Moy of Milwaukee and Bow Huie of Chicago, which was held at the Chinese Union Church in Chicago and conducted in Chinese, is shown in this photograph, which first appeared in a photo essay on the Milwaukee Chinese community published in 1961 in the *Milwaukee Journal*. (Courtesy of the Milwaukee Journal Sentinel.)

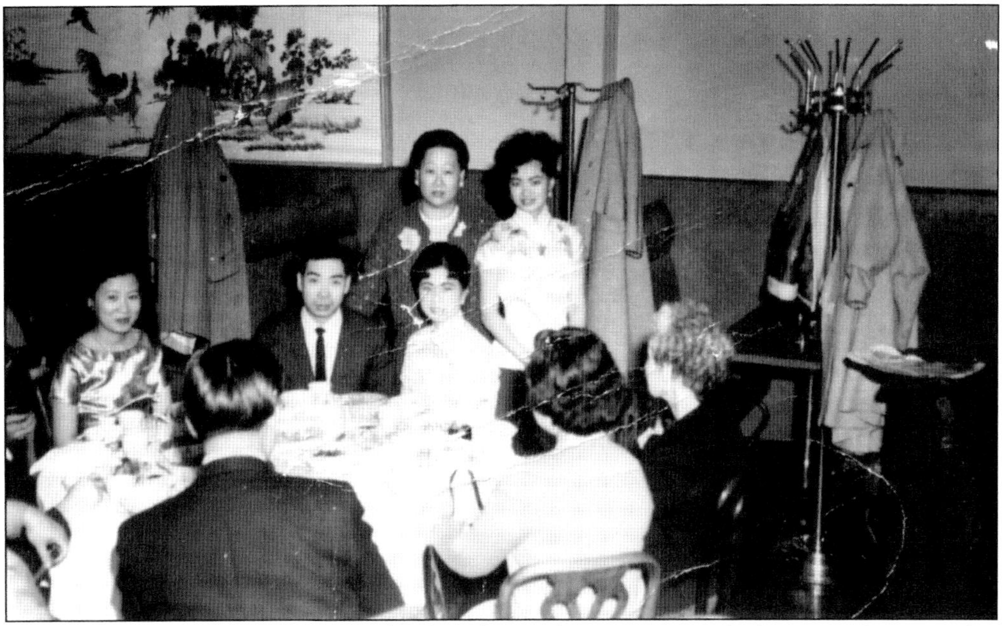

A wedding reception for Sue Moy of Milwaukee and George Tom of Chicago is shown in this photograph dated 1961. The reception was held at Lotus Restaurant on 733 North Third Street. Sue (right) is standing with Marianne Fong, who owned Moy Restaurant on West Wells Street in Milwaukee. Seated from left to right are Lillian Wong, Kenny Fong, and his wife Mae Fong. (Courtesy of Sally Moy Klatt.)

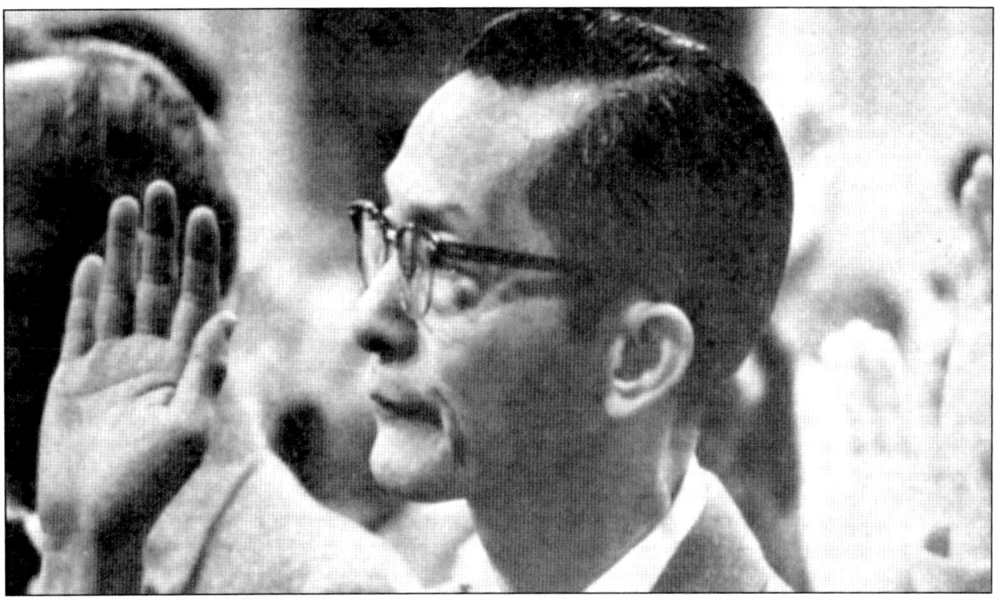

Howe Chan is shown taking the oath of citizenship in this photograph, which first appeared in a photo essay on the Milwaukee Chinese community in the *Milwaukee Journal* in 1961. Chan operated a grocery for seven years in Mississippi before coming to Milwaukee after his son entered the University of Wisconsin medical school. Chan was a waiter in a restaurant at the time of this photograph. Chan was married to Jennie Chan, who is shown on photographs on pages 69 and 122. (Courtesy of the Milwaukee Journal Sentinel.)

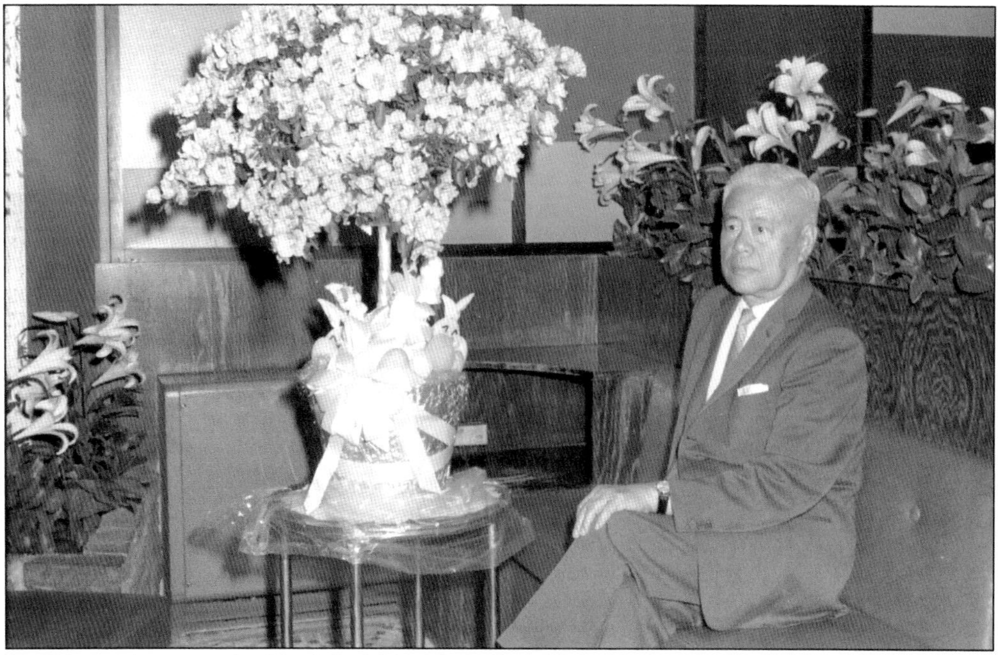

Joe Wong, a longtime leader of the Milwaukee Chinese community, is shown in this photograph dating from the early 1960s. The photograph was taken in La Joy Restaurant, at 4730 West Lisbon Avenue. The restaurant was opened at this location by Joe Wong in 1932 and remained open for over 65 years. (Courtesy of Paul Wong.)

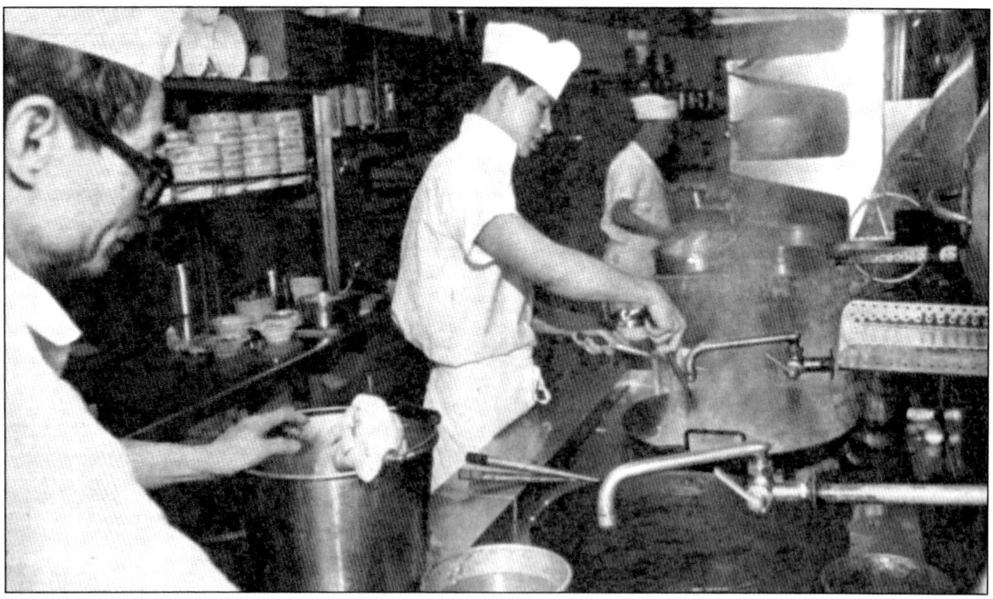

This photograph of the kitchen in La Joy Restaurant first appeared in a photo essay on the Milwaukee Chinese community published in the *Milwaukee Journal* in 1961. Chuck Moy, a kitchen supervisor for La Joy Restaurant, is shown in foreground. At the time of the photograph, there were reportedly 22 Chinese restaurants in the Milwaukee area that were estimated to directly or indirectly support approximately half the local Chinese population. (Courtesy of the Milwaukee Journal Sentinel.)

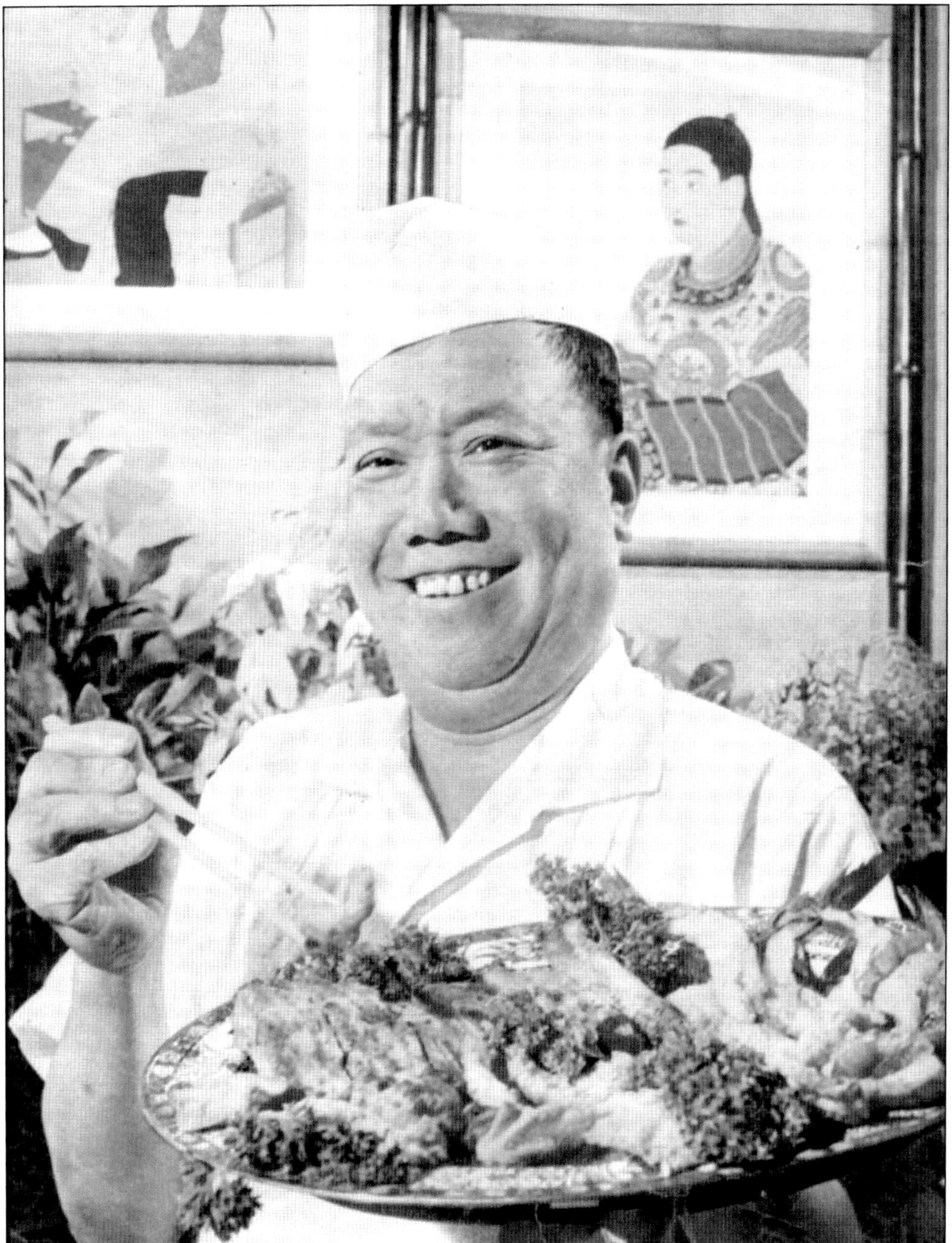

This photograph shows Arthur Lee, a cook specializing in Cantonese foods, with a plate of one of his specialties. This photograph first appeared in a photo essay on the Milwaukee Chinese community published in the *Milwaukee Journal* in 1961. (Courtesy of the Milwaukee Journal Sentinel.)

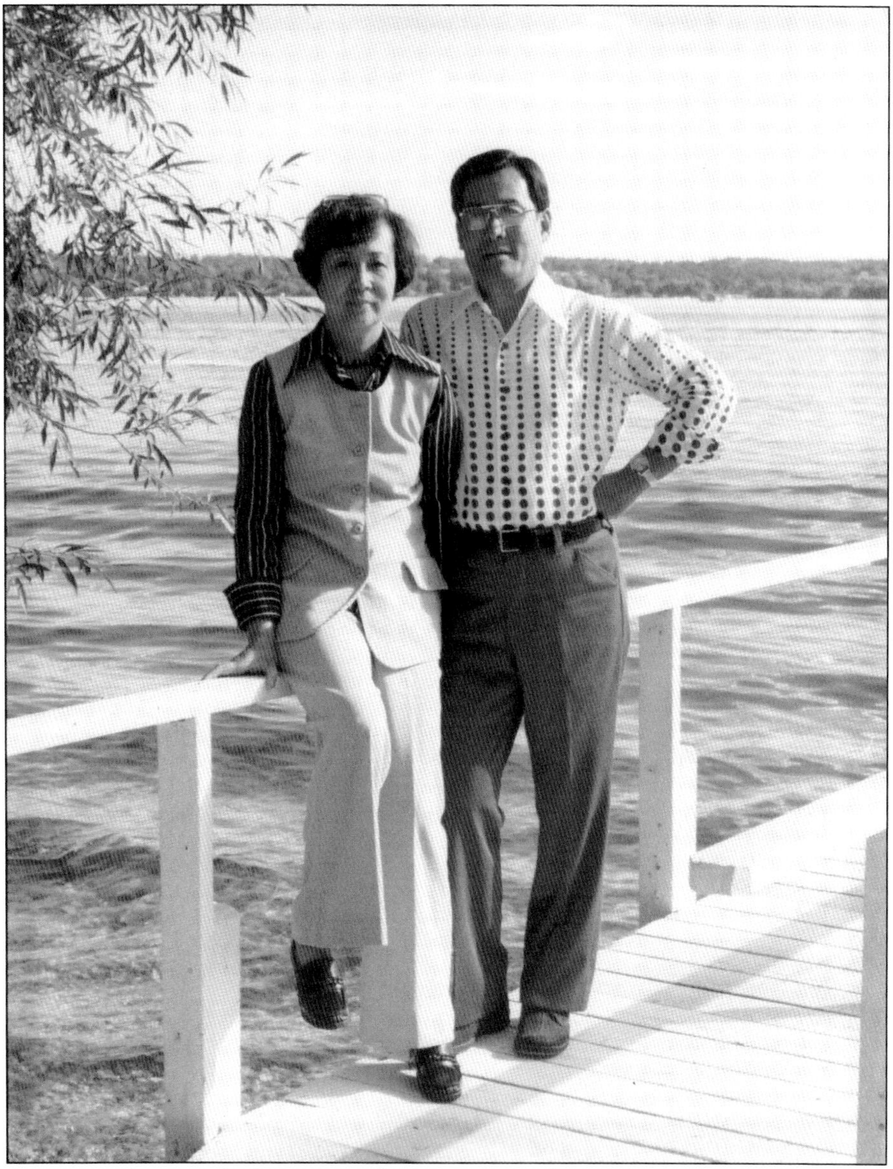

This late-1960s photograph shows Rev. Charles Y. Ho, and his wife, Susan, on a religious retreat at Green Lake, Wisconsin. Reverend Ho moved with his family to the Milwaukee area in 1966 to assume leadership of the Chinese Baptist Mission of Greater Milwaukee. In 1968, Reverend Ho helped found the Community Baptist Church at 120 North Seventy-third Street in Milwaukee. In 1983, Reverend Ho received a special award from the Metropolitan Milwaukee Civic Alliance for his distinguished service to refugees, which included helping more than 880 refugees from around the world to settle in Wisconsin. As a student leader in China in the 1930s, Reverend Ho helped tear down a sign prohibiting the entrance of dogs and Chinese into Huangpu Park in Shanghai. The tearing down of the sign (or a similar incident) was memorialized by Bruce Lee in a scene in the movie *Fists of Fury*. During World War II, while still in China, Reverend Ho worked as a surveyor for the United States 14th Air Force, a legendary air force unit more commonly known as the "Flying Tigers." Reverend Ho retired in 1986 but remains active in the Chinese community. (Courtesy of Rev. Charles Y. Ho.)

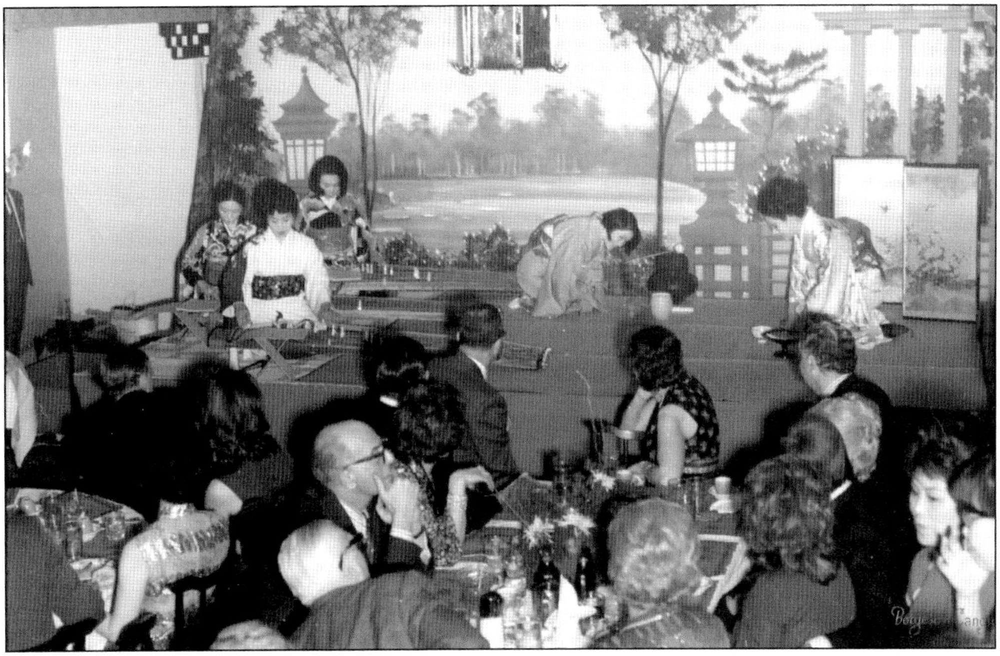

The grand opening of Toy's Chinatown Restaurant at 830 North Third Street in downtown Milwaukee is shown in this 1968 photograph. Guests at the event included many notable figures from Milwaukee, as well as at least 20 members of the local news media. (Courtesy of the Toy family.)

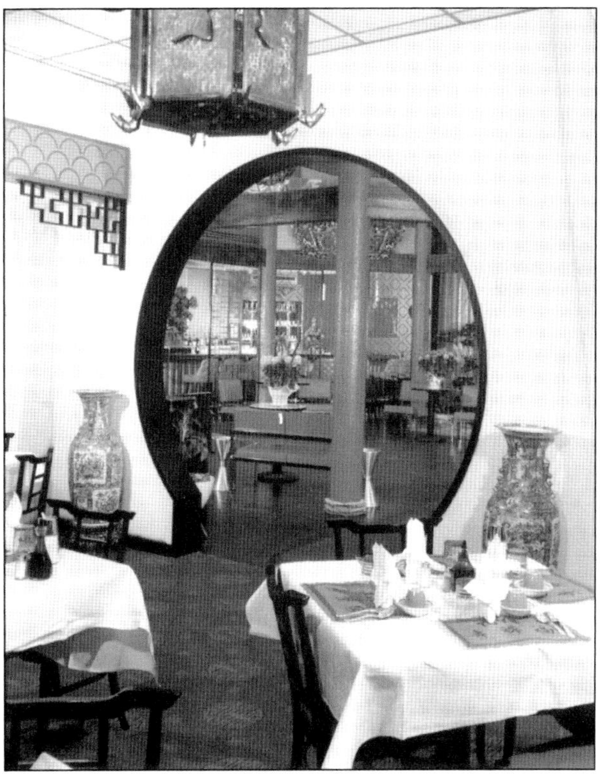

The interior of Toy's Chinatown Restaurant at 830 North Third Street in downtown Milwaukee is shown in this photograph dated 1968. The restaurant was opened by Moy B. Toy in 1968 and was operated by the Toy family until sold in 1988. The restaurant remained open for 14 additional years under the ownership of Paul Wong and Edward Chin. (Courtesy of the Toy family.)

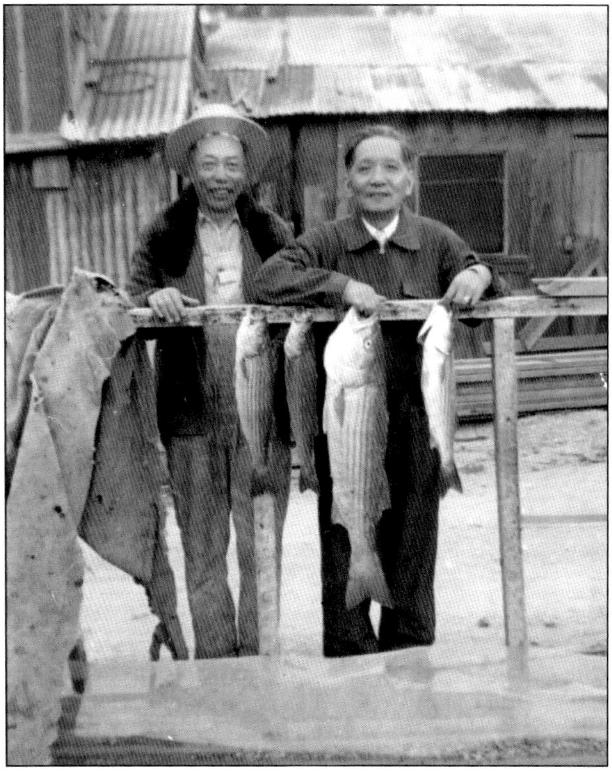

This photograph, dated approximately 1960, is of Moy B. Toy and an unidentified friend on a fishing outing in Wisconsin. Moy B. Toy was an avid fisherman and one of many Milwaukee Chinese who took advantage of Wisconsin's hunting and fishing recreational opportunities. (Courtesy of the Toy family.)

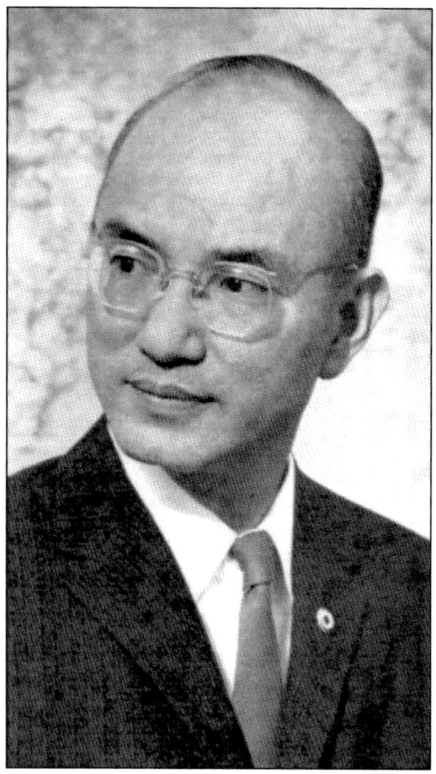

Anthony Woo, an engineer for Allis-Chalmers Manufacturing Company in West Allis, was a leader of the Milwaukee Chinese community in the 1950s and 1960s. He immigrated from Taishan in southern China to Milwaukee in 1931, where, in 1936, he graduated with honors from Marquette University. This photograph first appeared in a photo essay on the Milwaukee Chinese community published in the *Milwaukee Journal* in 1961. (Courtesy of the Milwaukee Journal Sentinel.)

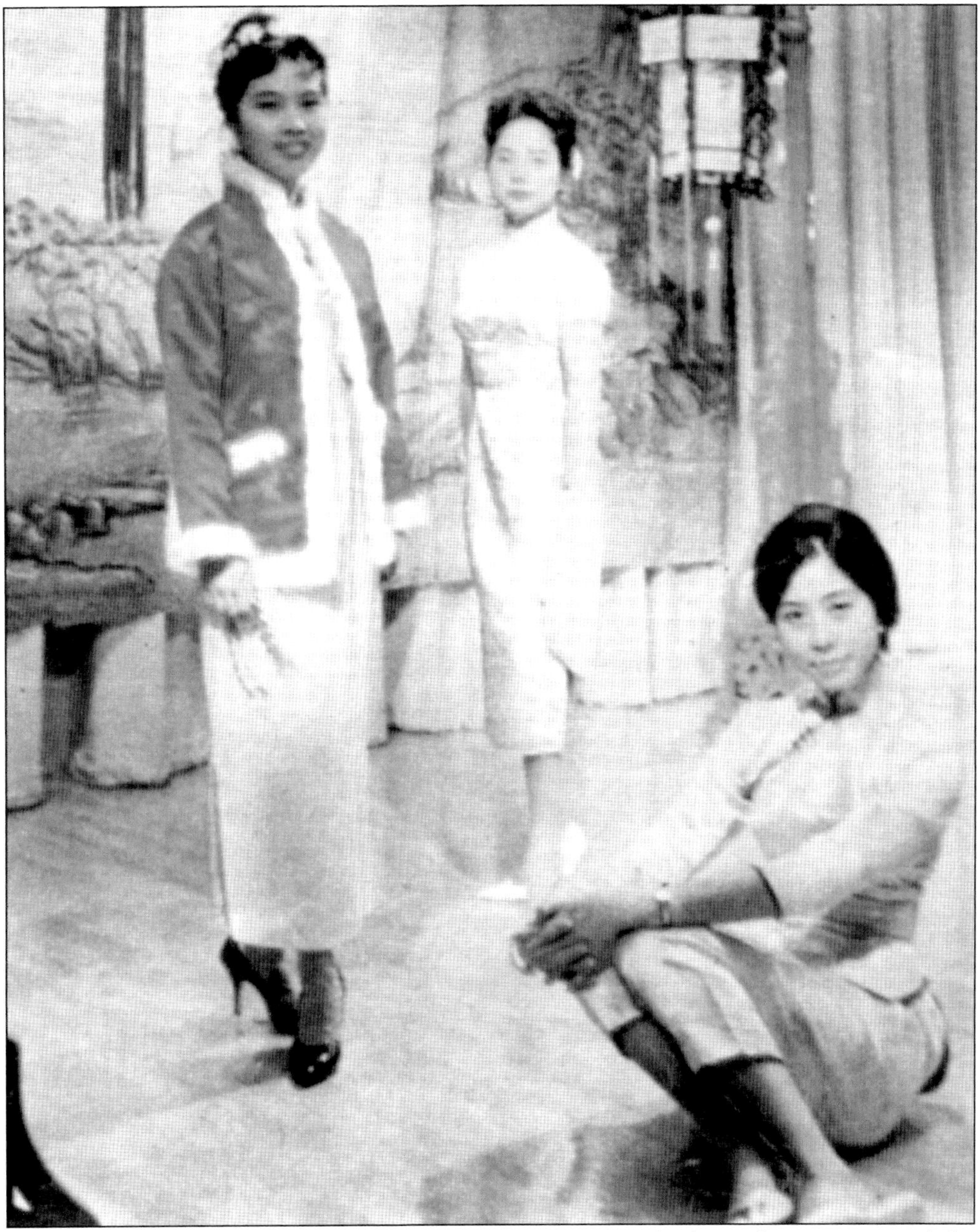

A public celebration was held in Shorewood in 1961 to mark the 50th anniversary of the founding of the Republic of China. Members of the Chinese community performed a program at the St. Robert School auditorium that included songs in Chinese, dances, and musical performances. A "China night" event was sponsored by the Chinese Student Club of Milwaukee, an organization that was devoted to fostering understanding between China and the United States. The women in the photograph include (from left to right) Mrs. Philip Chen, Grace Lum, and Esther Chan. Mrs. Chen, an immigrant from Taiwan, and Chan, an immigrant from Hong Kong, were both students at Alverno College at the time of this photograph, which first appeared in a photo essay on the Milwaukee Chinese community published in the *Milwaukee Journal* in 1961. (Courtesy of the Milwaukee Journal Sentinel.)

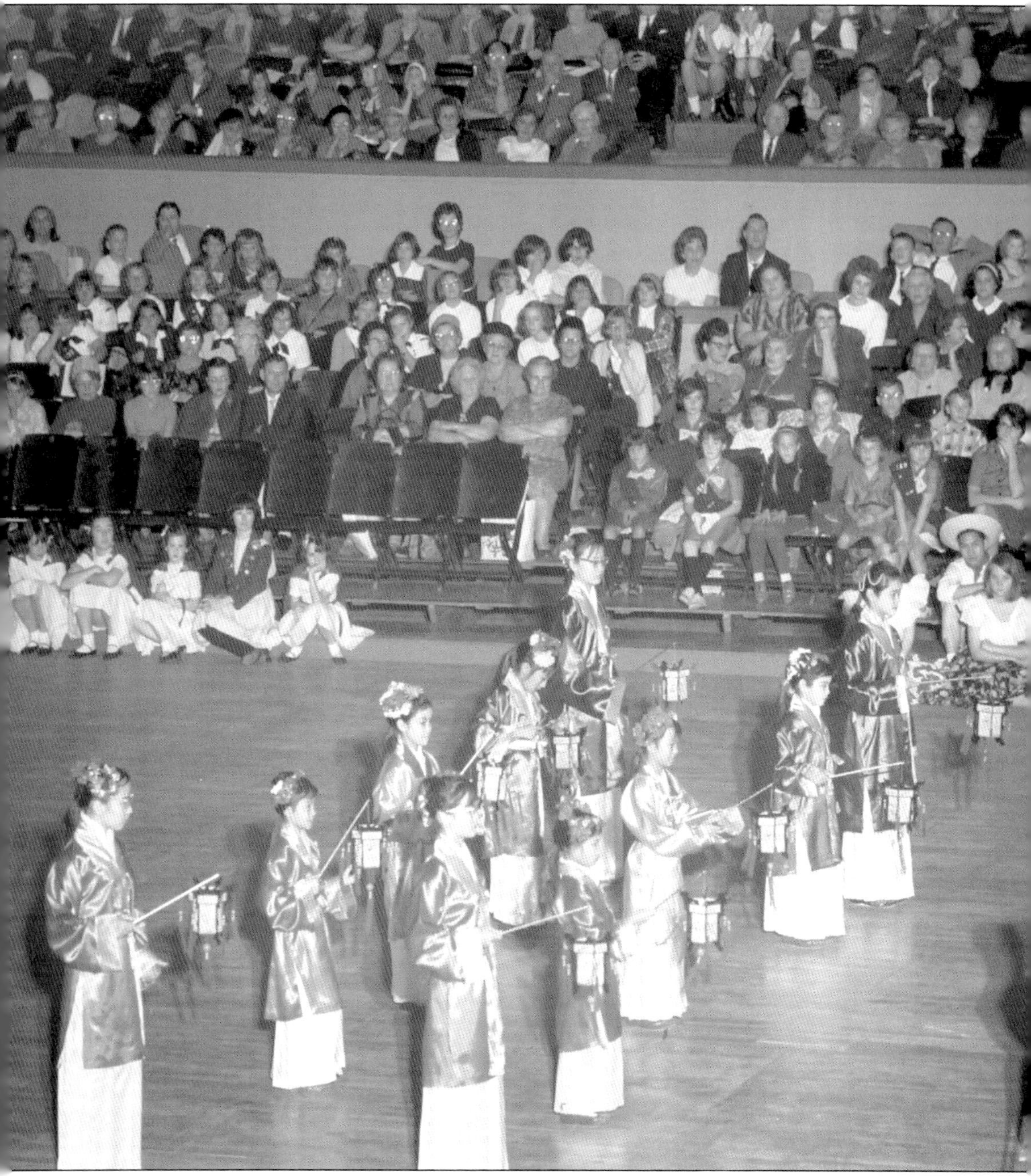

A Chinese children's group is shown performing the Lantern Dance in this photograph taken in 1965 at the Holiday Folk Fair at the Milwaukee Arena. The performers reportedly were all children of members of the Chinese American Civic Club. (Courtesy of the International Institute of Wisconsin.)

Seven

New Arrivals 1976–1989

During the 1970s and 1980s, the number of Chinese living in the greater Milwaukee area continued to increase. Economically, with more restaurant owners, medical professionals, engineers, and educators, they no longer relied predominantly on the laundry trade. The year 1976 was significant in marking the death of Mao Zedong, spurring dramatic changes to occur in China several years later. In 1979, diplomatic relations between the United States and China were reestablished, leading to the first officially sanctioned immigration from the Chinese mainland to the United States since the Communist government came to power in 1949.

China's Cultural Revolution (1966–1976) resulted in the near extinction of the university system in China. However, by 1976, universities started accepting students again. University students graduating from Chinese universities in the early 1980s came to the United States in large numbers to pursue advanced degrees in engineering, science, and other academic areas. Many chose to remain in the United States after obtaining their degrees, especially after the June 1989 incidents at Tiananmen Square.

Several Chinese who came as students to the Milwaukee area from Taiwan, Hong Kong, and other southeast Asian countries during this period subsequently started their own professional practices after working in area companies for several years. Examples include Philip Hung (American Institute of Architects), who started one of the first Chinese architectural and engineering firms in Milwaukee during the 1970s; Danny Ho (professional engineer) and Ming-Ta King (professional engineer), who started Horwood Engineering and Precast Engineering in the late 1970s; and Terry Ni (professional engineer) and Nick Ni (professional engineer), who started T N and Associates, Inc., in the 1980s.

After the early 1980s, an increasing number of Chinese immigrants arrived from mainland China from outside the traditional Taishan area that was the origin for many of the earlier Chinese immigrants to Milwaukee. Businesses pursued by Chinese in increasing numbers during this period included dental and acupuncture clinics and new variations of Chinese restaurants (including Chinese buffet system restaurants and sushi restaurants). Many of the restaurants were started by recent immigrants from Guangdong and Fujian provinces in southeast China. The years 1975 and 1976 also marked the beginning of the arrival of large numbers of Hmong refugees to Wisconsin and the Milwaukee area who had previously immigrated out of China in the 1800s from the south of China to Laos and other southeast Asian countries.

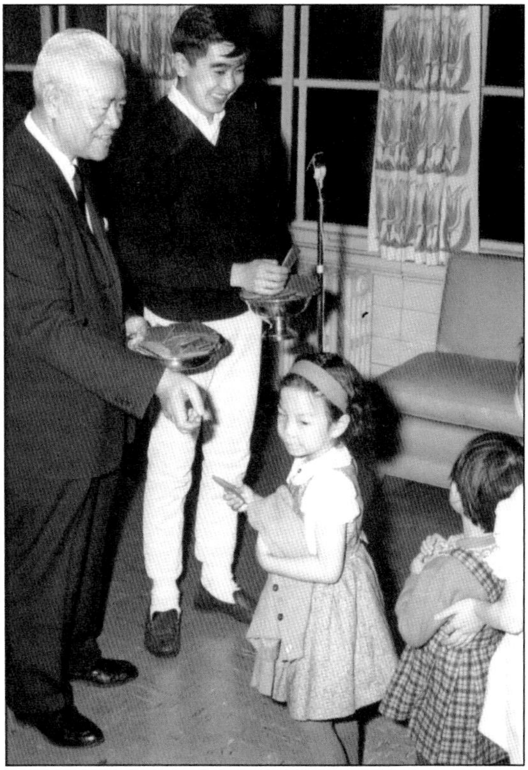

This photograph shows Joe Wong (left) and Harvey Wong (middle) practicing a traditional Chinese New Year custom of adults handing out small red envelopes containing money to visiting children or young relatives. The envelopes, named *hong bao*, were colored red to symbolize good luck, and the amount of money in the envelope typically coincided with a lucky number. (Courtesy of Paul Wong.)

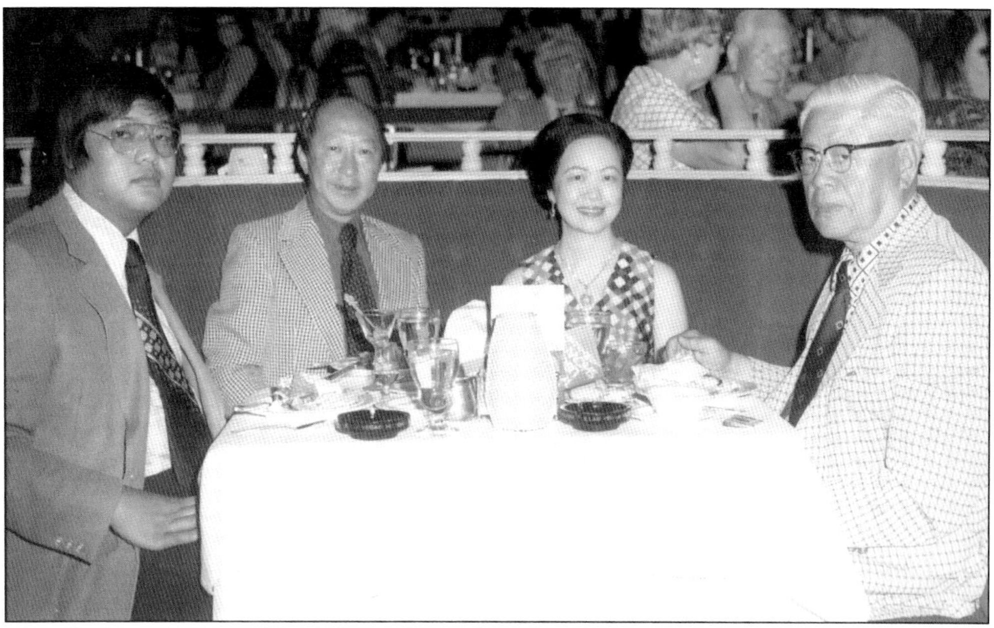

This photograph shows, from left to right, Richard Chin; Dr. William Wong and his wife, Julie Wong; and Joe Wong. Dr. William Wong was a prominent Milwaukee dentist whose clients included many of the Milwaukee Braves baseball team. Dr. Wong served as a dentist with the United States Army in China during World War II where his patients included Chiang Kai-Shek, and where he met his wife, Julie. (Courtesy of Paul Wong.)

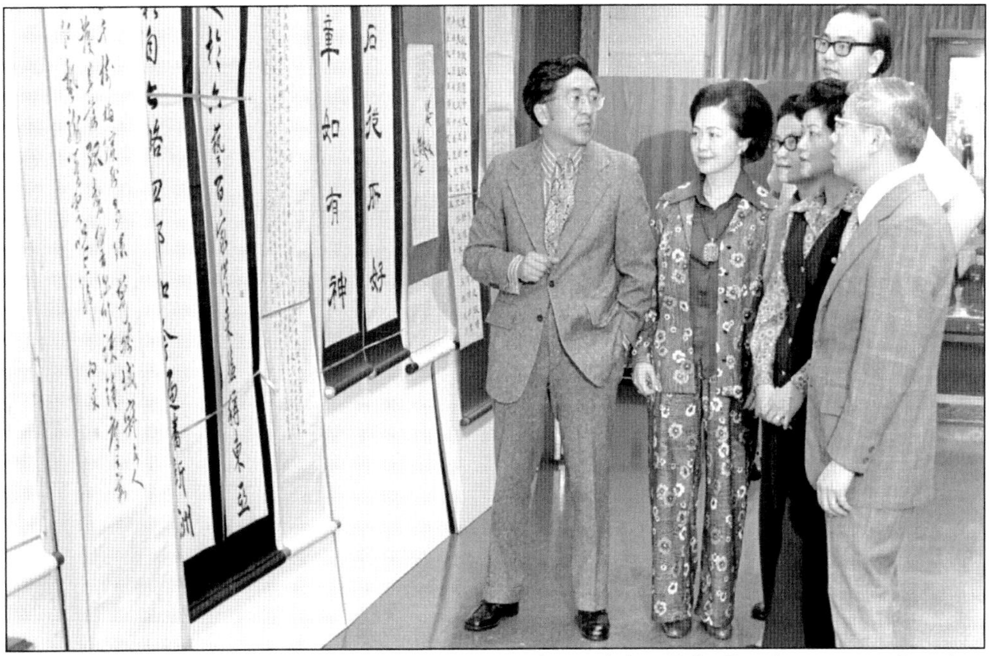

This 1970s photograph shows several visitors to the Holiday Folk Fair being introduced to Chinese calligraphy. For nearly 2,000 years, calligraphy was considered the highest art form in China. However, this art form is dying out in modern China, as well as in the second (and later) generation Chinese Americans. (Courtesy of the International Institute of Wisconsin.)

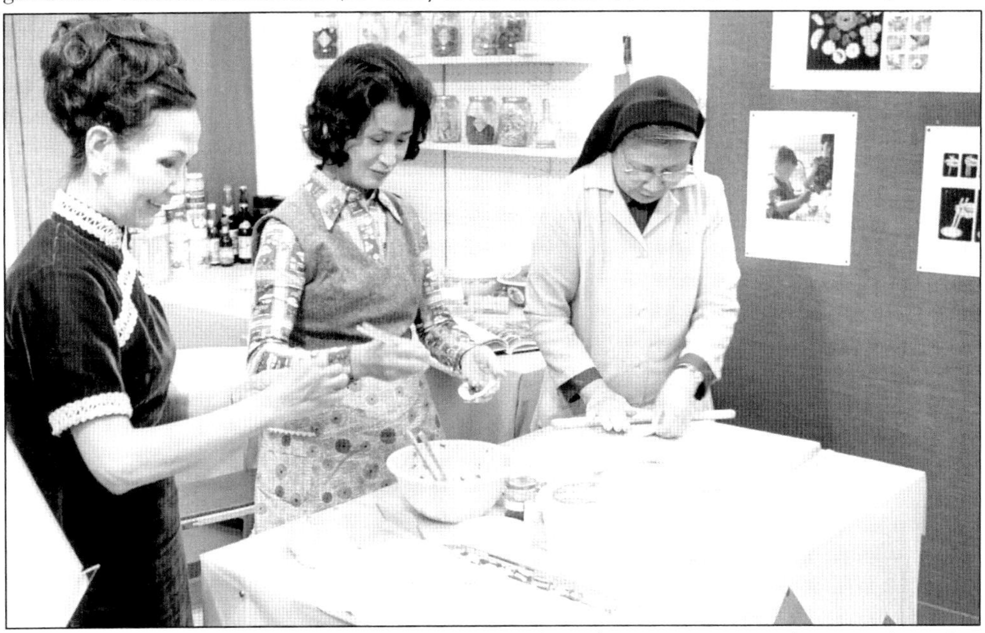

A local Chinese nun and fashionably dressed Milwaukee Chinese women are shown in this 1970s photograph preparing a favorite Chinese dish: dumplings (or *jiaozi*), as part of a demonstration at the Holiday Folk Fair. Dumplings were considered to be one of the most delicious northern Chinese foods (as well as one of the most time-consuming dishes to prepare). (Courtesy of the International Institute of Wisconsin.)

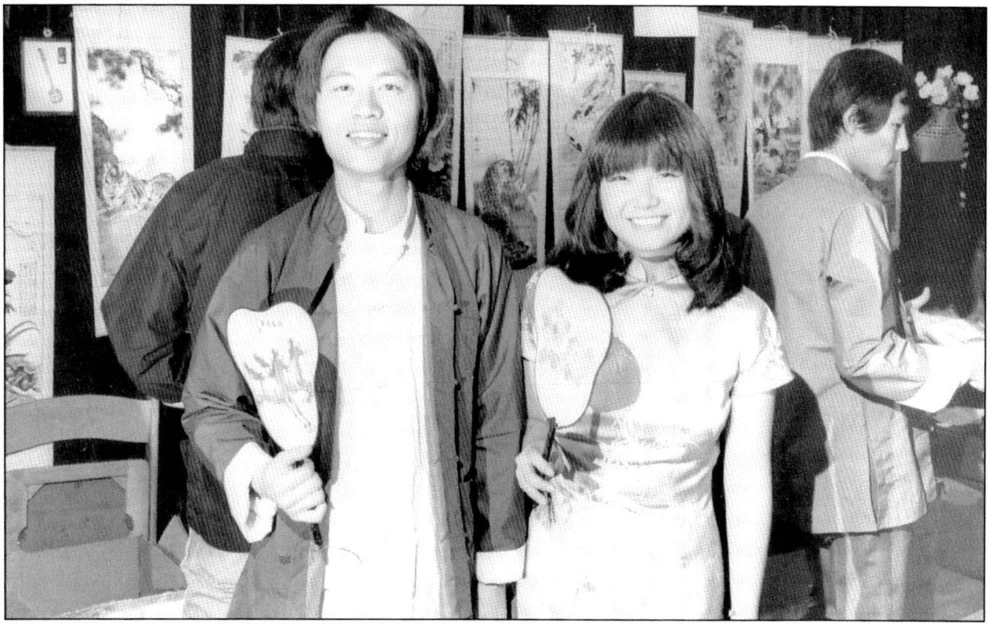

This 1986 photograph shows a presentation of Chinese traditional clothing by local Chinese residents at the Holiday Folk Fair. The man's costume is called *magua* and was popular from 1900 through 1949 in Shanghai and large urban areas of China. The woman's dress is called *qipao* and was popular among affluent members of Chinese society. (Courtesy of the International Institute of Wisconsin.)

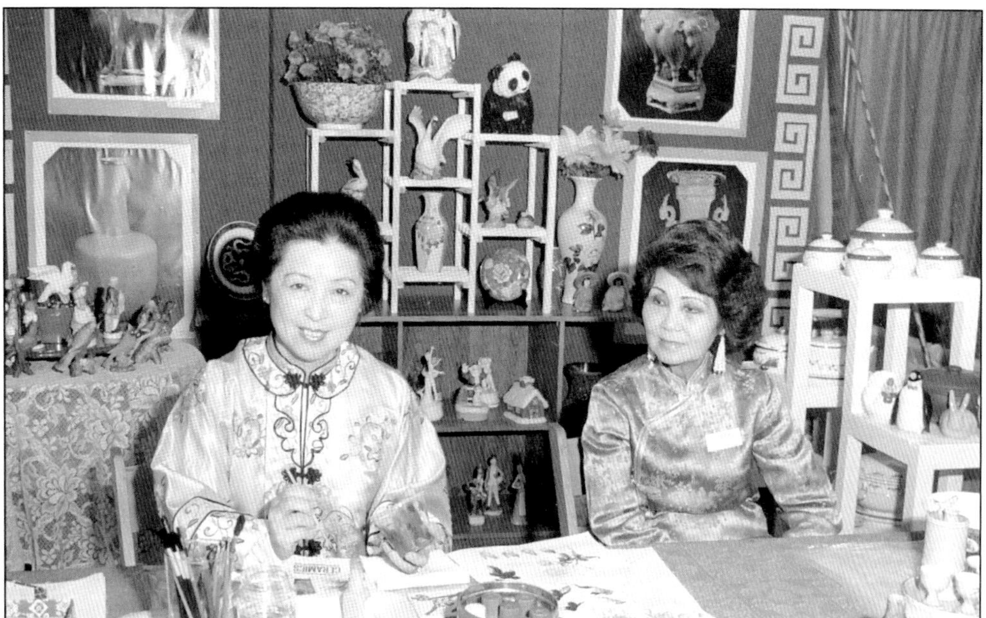

Two local Chinese residents (Sengchi Chen, left, and Lulin Chang Walter, right) are shown in this late-1970s or early-1980s photograph at the Holiday Folk Fair. The women are demonstrating traditional Chinese pottery and other crafts. (Courtesy of the International Institute of Wisconsin.)

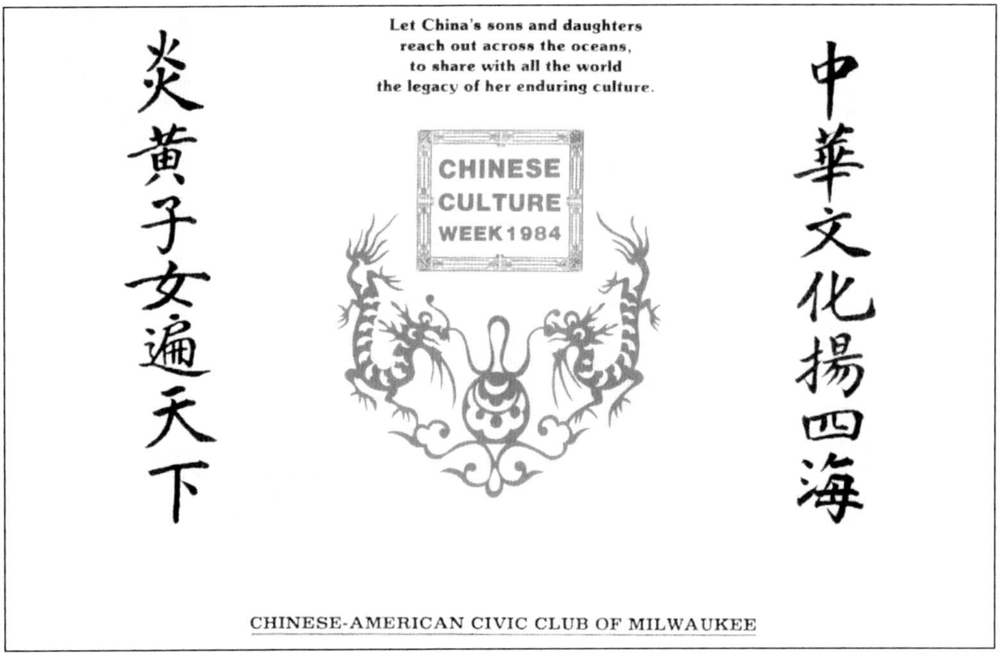

In 1984, the Chinese American Civic Club presented Chinese Cultural Week at the Milwaukee Public Museum. Chinese Cultural Week was hosted by the Milwaukee Public Museum from January 28 to February 4, 1984, and included cultural performances, games, special displays and exhibits, and a Lunar New Year's party. (Courtesy of Lulin Chang Walter.)

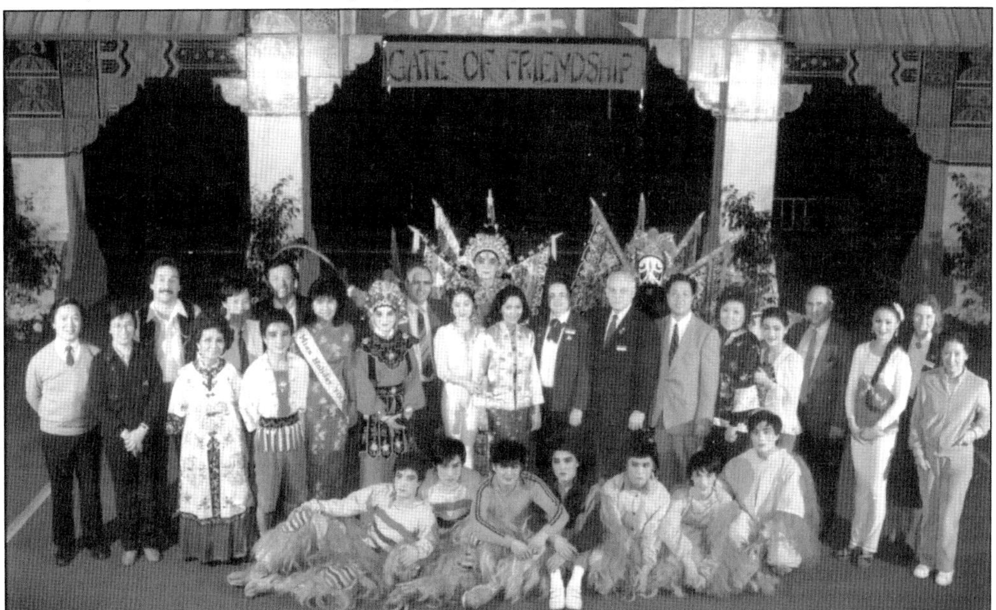

Organizers of Chinese exhibits pose at the Holiday Folk Fair in 1986, when Chinese were selected as the honor group and featured at the fair. Chinese participation in the Holiday Folk Fair dates back to at least the 1940s, when Chinese booths were operated at the fair by members of the Chinese American Civic Club, as a means to present Chinese arts, crafts, food, and culture. (Courtesy of Lulin Chang Walter.)

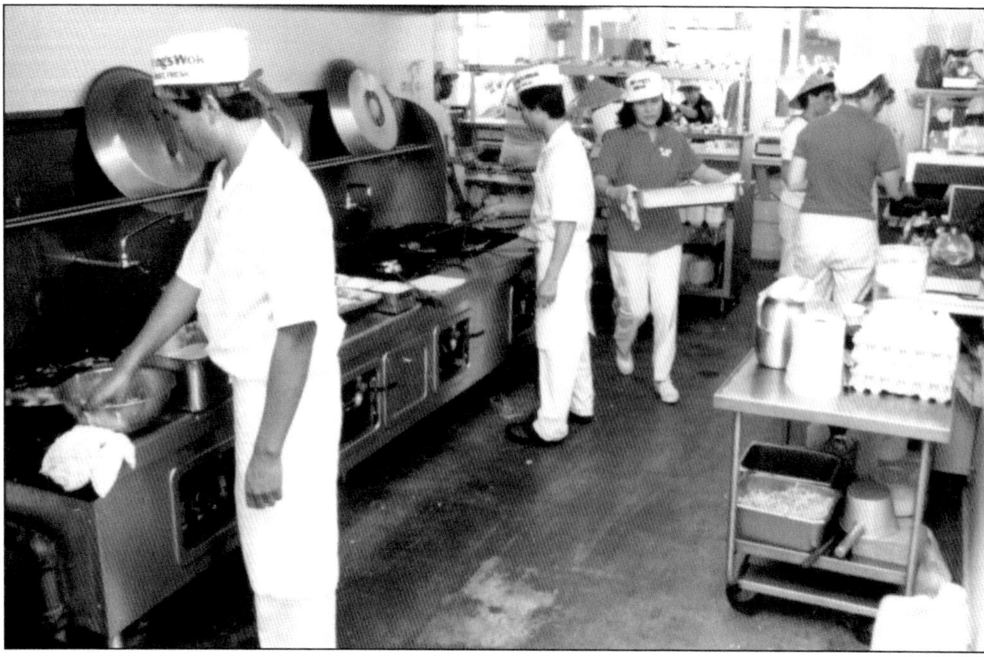

This is a photograph of the kitchen for a Wong's Wok at the Milwaukee Summerfest grounds. Wong's Wok was a Milwaukee Chinese fast-food chain started by cousins Edward Chin and Paul Wong of Milwaukee that grew to 11 outlets. The chain was started in the late 1970s to provide an alternative to the slower-paced traditional Chinese restaurants. (Courtesy of Paul Wong.)

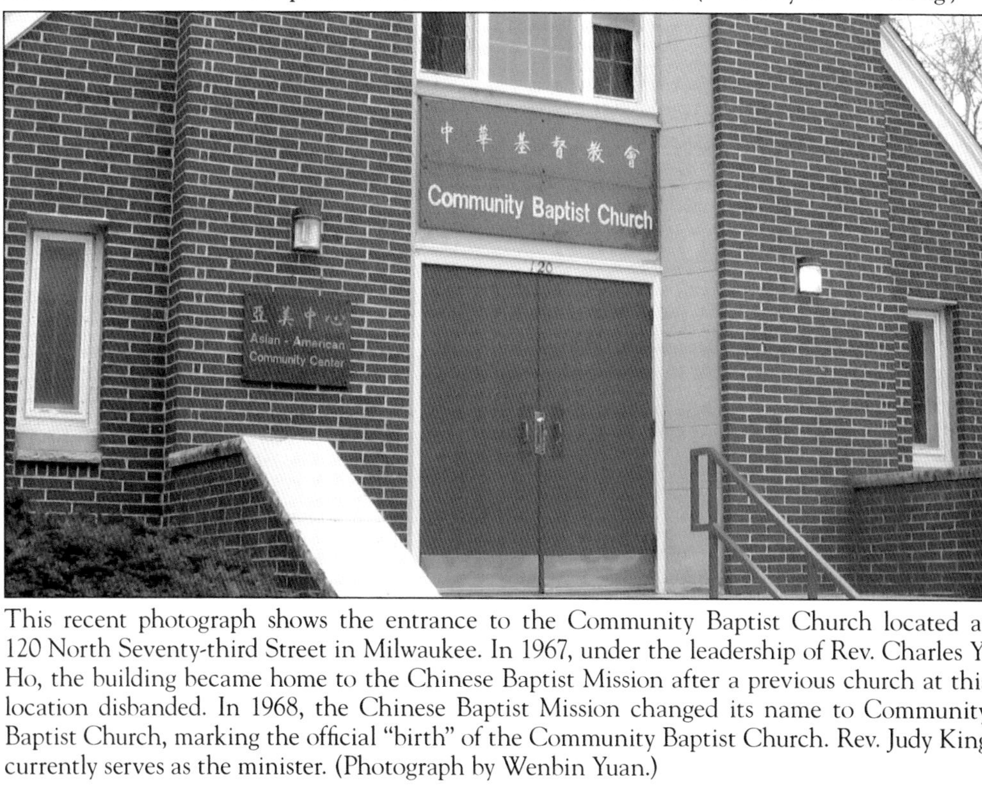

This recent photograph shows the entrance to the Community Baptist Church located at 120 North Seventy-third Street in Milwaukee. In 1967, under the leadership of Rev. Charles Y. Ho, the building became home to the Chinese Baptist Mission after a previous church at this location disbanded. In 1968, the Chinese Baptist Mission changed its name to Community Baptist Church, marking the official "birth" of the Community Baptist Church. Rev. Judy King currently serves as the minister. (Photograph by Wenbin Yuan.)

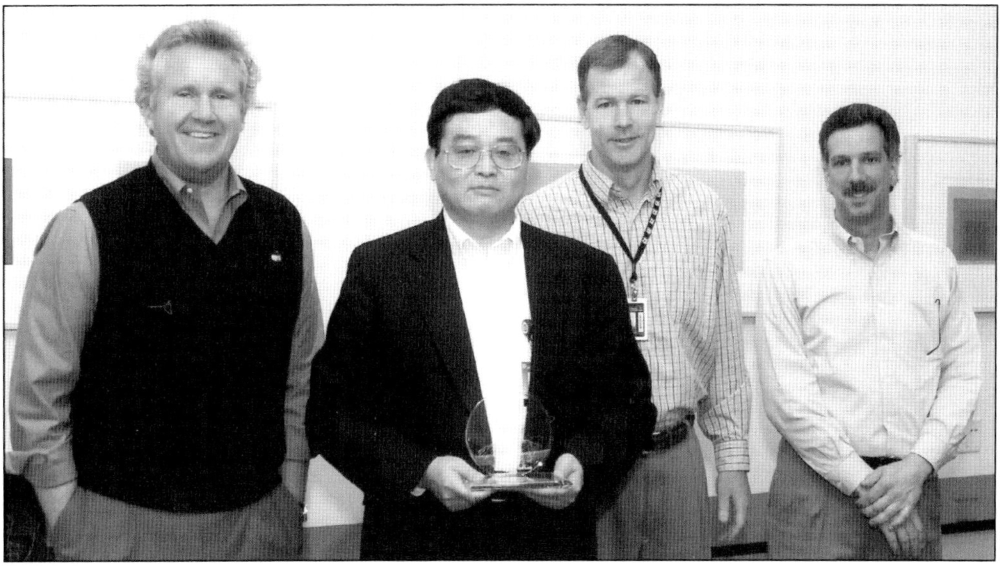

In the 1980s, an increasing number of Chinese immigrants arrived from mainland China from outside the traditional Taishan area that was the origin for so many earlier Chinese immigrants to Milwaukee. Dr. Jiang Hsieh, who holds over 100 patents, arrived in 1980 and eventually became a chief scientist in the Applied Science Laboratory of GE Healthcare Technologies. In this photograph, Dr. Hsieh (second from left) is shown receiving the GE Edison Award for his contributions to advanced computed tomography (CT) technology. Others shown include Jeffrey Immelt (left), Scott Donnelly (third from left), and Gene Saragnese (right). (Courtesy of Jiang Hsieh.)

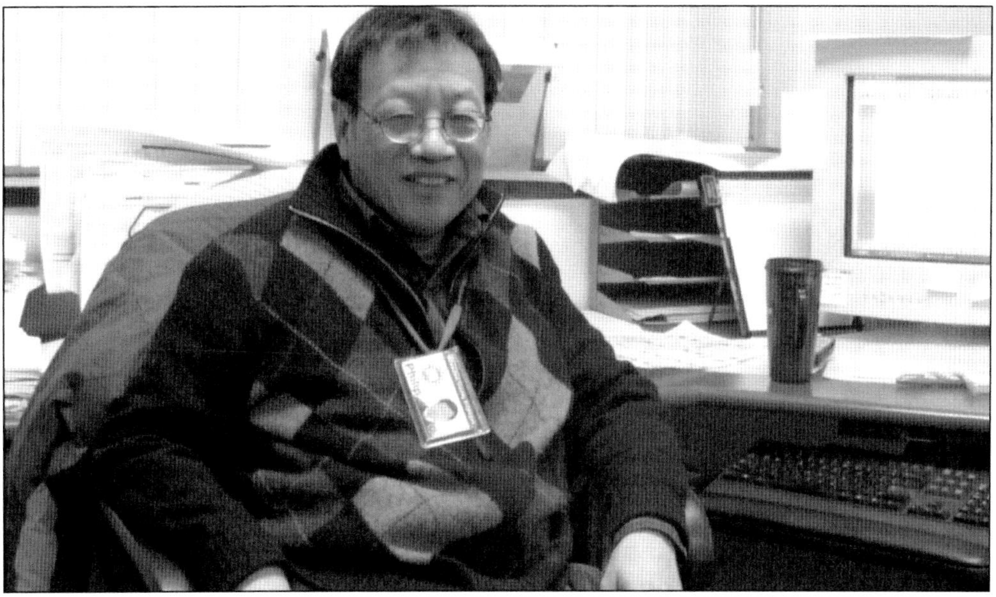

Philip Hung (American Institute of Architects), an architect for Milwaukee County, is shown in his office in this recent photograph. Hung may be the first Chinese architect certified by the State of Wisconsin and worked for his own firm for several years before joining Milwaukee County. Hung is a member of the "brain drain," a term used for professionals with advanced degrees who immigrated in large numbers to the United States from Taiwan and Hong Kong in the 1960s and 1970s. (Photograph by Wenbin Yuan.)

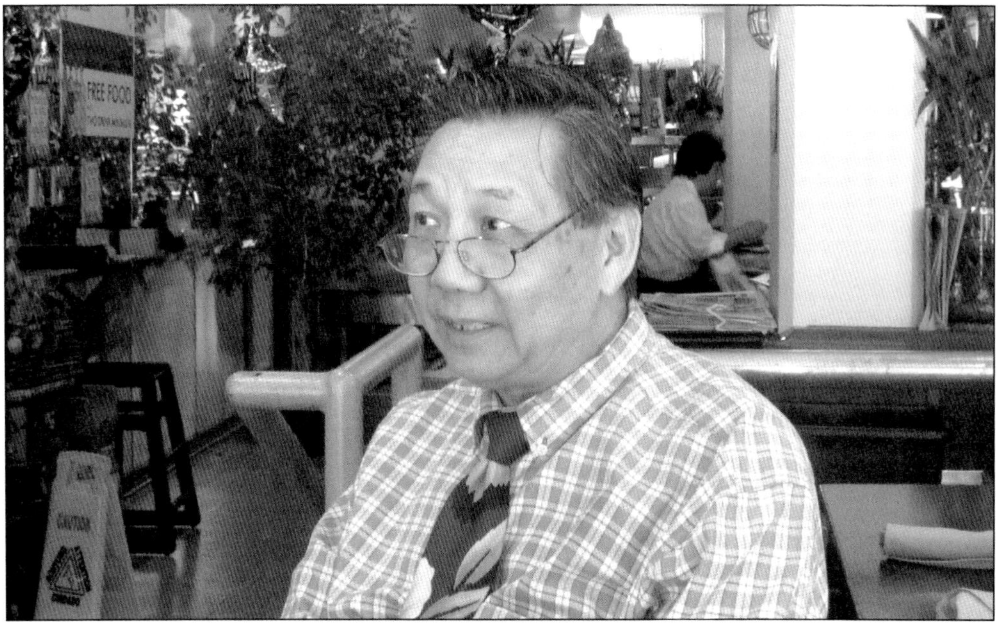

Robert Cao owns the China Gourmet Restaurant located at the intersection of North Water Street and West Wells Avenue. Cao is a member of a newer generation of Chinese restaurant owners who immigrated to the United States from Taiwan in the 1960s. The newer generation of restaurant owners has changed the appearance of Chinese restaurants, from the traditional dim lighting and dark colors to a more modern, brighter look, offering a variety of Asian foods. (Photograph by Wenbin Yuan.)

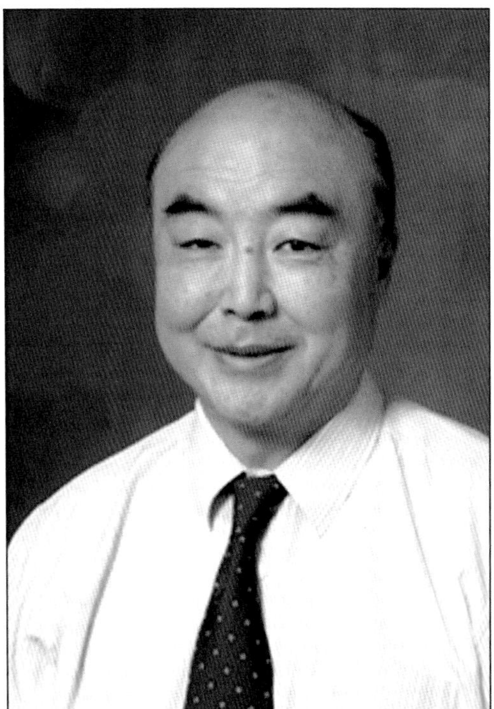

Dr. Xin Feng, shown in this recent photograph, is an associate professor of electrical and computer engineering at Marquette University who came to the United States from mainland China in the early 1980s and joined the faculty in Marquette University in 1988. Dr. Xin Feng is also an active leader of the Milwaukee Chinese Christian Church. It should be noted that Marquette University has been a frequent choice of Milwaukee area Chinese seeking university degrees since at least the 1930s. (Photograph by Wenbin Yuan.)

Eight

The Rise of China 1990–2007

The Tiananmen Square protest of 1989 had a significant influence on Milwaukee's Chinese community. The Chinese Student Protection Act of 1992 and other legislation resulted in more than 53,000 mainland Chinese students becoming permanent residents of the United States during the 1990s, most of whom were professionals studying for advanced degrees in science, engineering, medicine, and other desirable fields.

The population of the Chinese community in the Greater Milwaukee area grew rapidly after 1990. Although the 2000 census reported only 1,232 Chinese living in the city of Milwaukee, this number is misleading. As of 2007, it was estimated that there may be as many as 25,000 persons of Chinese heritage living in the five-county Greater Milwaukee area, including over 20,000 Chinese, Taiwanese, and Hmong recorded directly by the census data, and an estimated 5,000 students, temporary workers, and persons of mixed Chinese ancestry.

Milwaukee Chinese continued to play a significant role in events such as the International Folk Fair, as well as the Asian Moon Festival, which was held at Maier Festival Park from 1994 to 2005. Chinese, Taiwanese, and Hmong were identified as 3 of the 14 ethnic groups represented at the festival.

Another recent influx of Chinese immigrants to the Milwaukee area are an estimated 500 Chinese children adopted by primarily non-Chinese Milwaukee area families since mainland China opened its doors to international adoptions in 1992. A Chinese school named the Cricket Academy was organized by a group of the parents, to provide an opportunity for the children to learn Chinese language and culture, and currently has over 300 students. Other Chinese schools, such as the Mercan Chinese Language Institute, which opened in the South Tower at Mayfair Mall in 2007, were established to teach Mandarin Chinese to non-Chinese Americans.

The span of 1990 to 2008 was marked by the start-up of several new Chinese organizations to serve the changing needs of the community. These included the Milwaukee Modern Chinese School organized in 1994, the Milwaukee Chinese Community Center established in 2005, the Association of Chinese Scientists and Engineers (ACSE), the Society of Chinese American Professors and Professionals, and several social clubs, in particular Yi Fans Club, which was organized in 2007 after Chinese basketball star Yi Jianlian was drafted by the Milwaukee Bucks.

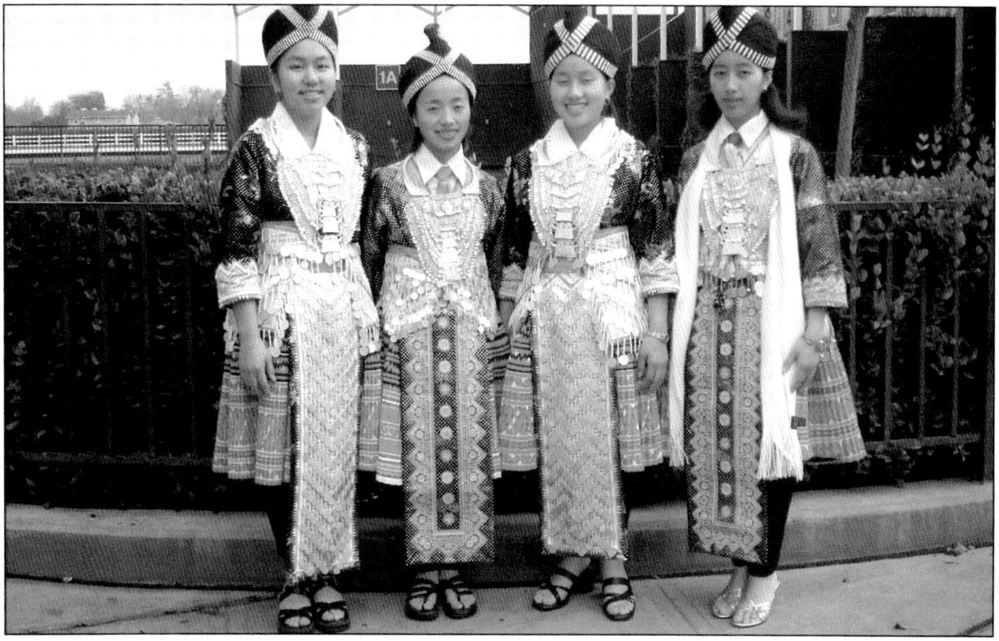

Yang Cheng (second from the left) and several of her friends are shown wearing traditional Hmong clothing in this photograph taken at the Asian Moon Festival, which was held from 1994 through 2005 at the Summerfest Grounds on Milwaukee's lakefront. Yang Cheng is a marketing professional at the Falk Corporation. The population of Hmong in the Milwaukee area and in Wisconsin as a whole in 2007 was estimated to be approximately 14,000 and 50,000, respectively. Currently the Hmong community in the Milwaukee area has its own newspaper, chamber of commerce, radio station, and cultural center. (Courtesy of Yang Cheng.)

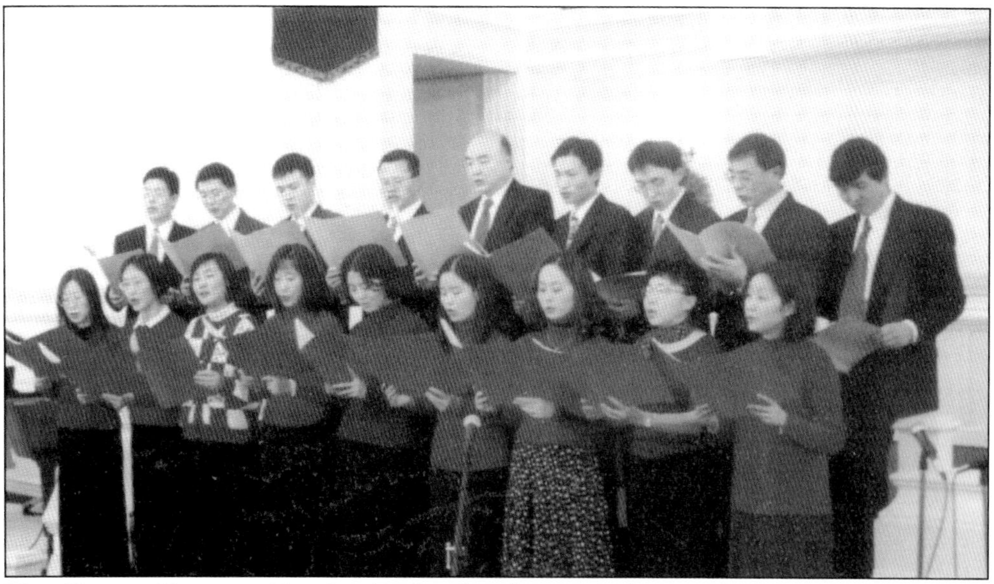

The Chinese Christian Church of Milwaukee (CCCM) choir is shown in this photograph dated 2003. Most church members are immigrants from mainland China or Taiwan. CCCM reportedly is the largest Chinese Christian church in Milwaukee, with an active congregation of approximately 400 members. (Courtesy of CCCM.)

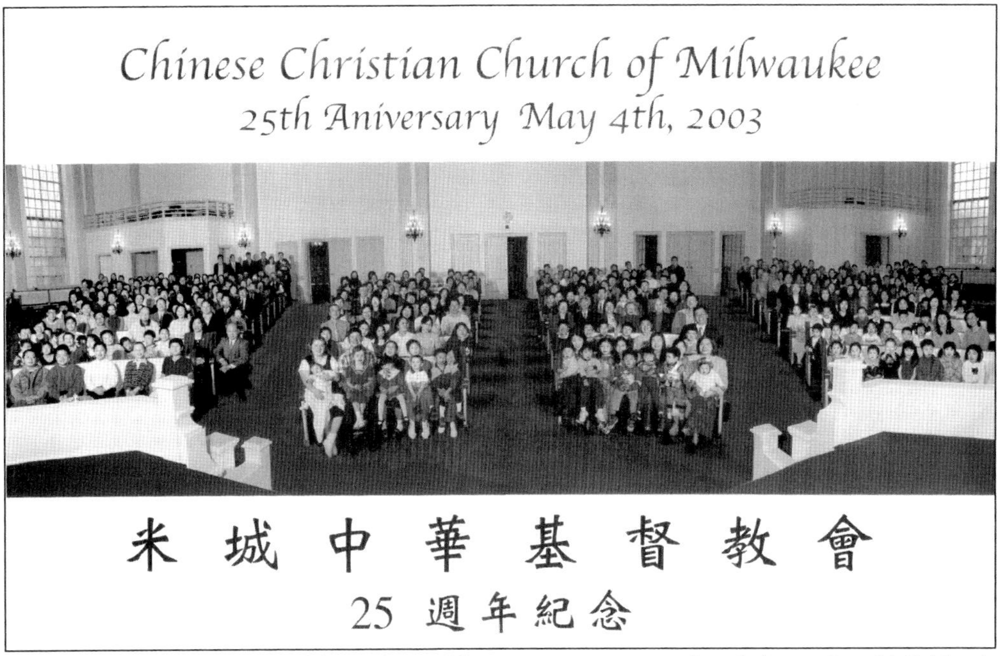

On May 4, 2003, CCCM celebrated its 25th anniversary in its church located at 3069 North Downer Avenue in Milwaukee. The church was purchased using over $1 million in donations from members of the congregation. (Courtesy of CCCM.)

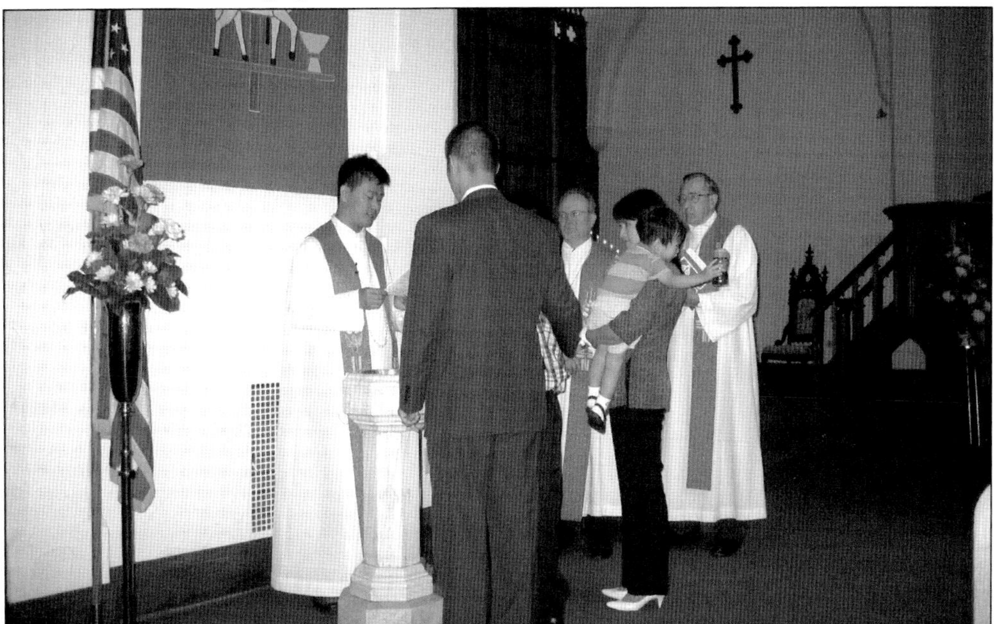

Rev. Joshua Yu is shown, in this photograph dated 2007, giving a blessing to members of the congregation of the St. John's Lutheran Church as it celebrated its 125th anniversary. The church has a service in Mandarin to serve the local Chinese community. Reverend Yu is one of several recent Chinese immigrants who have become local church leaders. (Courtesy of Rev. Joshua Yu.)

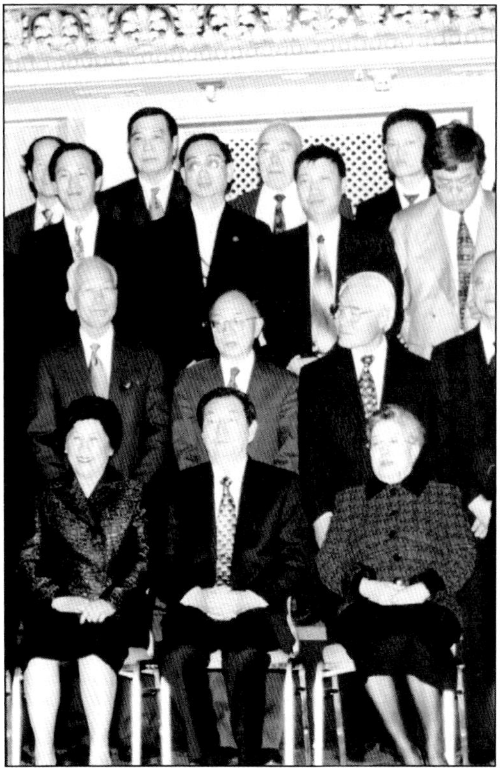

Dr. Guanyuan Jin, M.D., of Milwaukee is shown (third row, second from the right) in this photograph meeting with Chinese premier Zhu Rongji (first row, center) and cabinet members in Beijing as part of a cultural exchange with China. He represented the Association of Chinese Scientists and Engineers (ACSE). Dr. Jin is a practitioner of Chinese traditional medicine and owner of Ace Acupuncture Clinic. (Courtesy of Guanyuan Jin.)

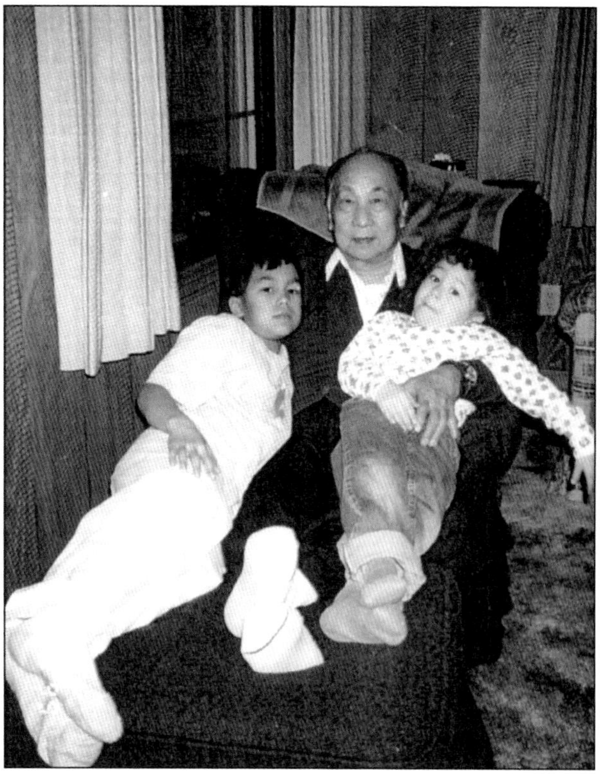

Dr. Thomas T. Tang relaxes with his grandchildren at his Brookfield home. Dr. Tang came to the United States in 1944 as a major in the Chinese army, assigned to help train several thousand Chinese pilots to be used in the air war against Japan. He stayed in the United States, earning both a doctor of philosophy and doctor of medicine degree before moving to the Milwaukee area and working as a professor of medicine at the Medical College of Wisconsin until his retirement in 1986. (Courtesy of Dr. Thomas Tang.)

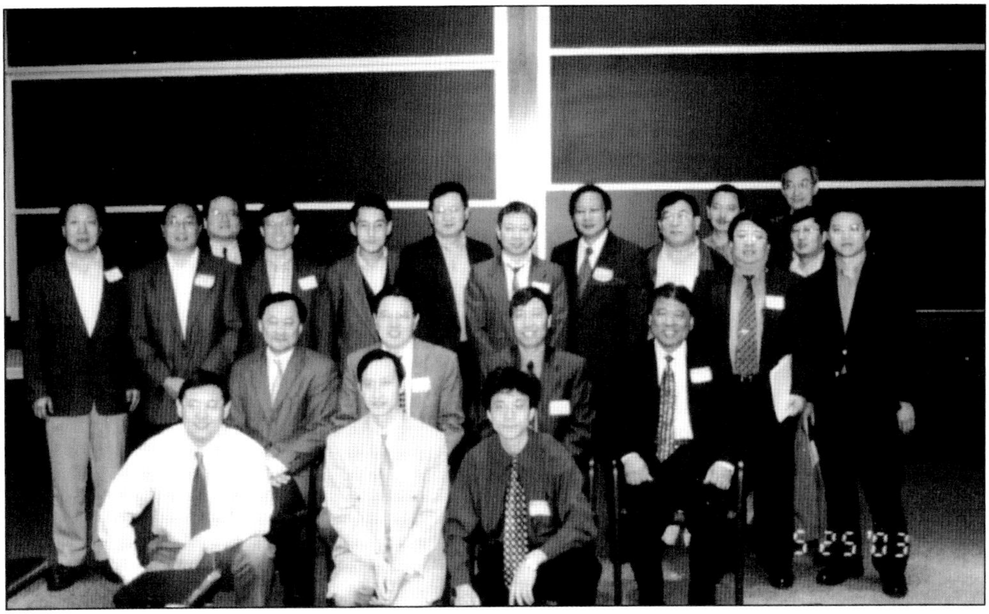

This 2004 photograph shows the founding members of Society of Chinese American Professors and Professionals (SoCAPs). Among those shown are Dr. Guanyuan Jin, Dr. Shijiang Li, Dr. Ai-Ping Zou, Dr. Zhong-Ren Peng, and Dr. Guokui Liu. The idea for forming SoCAPs was initiated by Dr. Guanyuan Jin and Dr. Shijiang Li. Dr. Jin., who came to Milwaukee in 1989, is one of the first State of Wisconsin–certified acupuncture doctors. (Courtesy of Guanyuan Jin.)

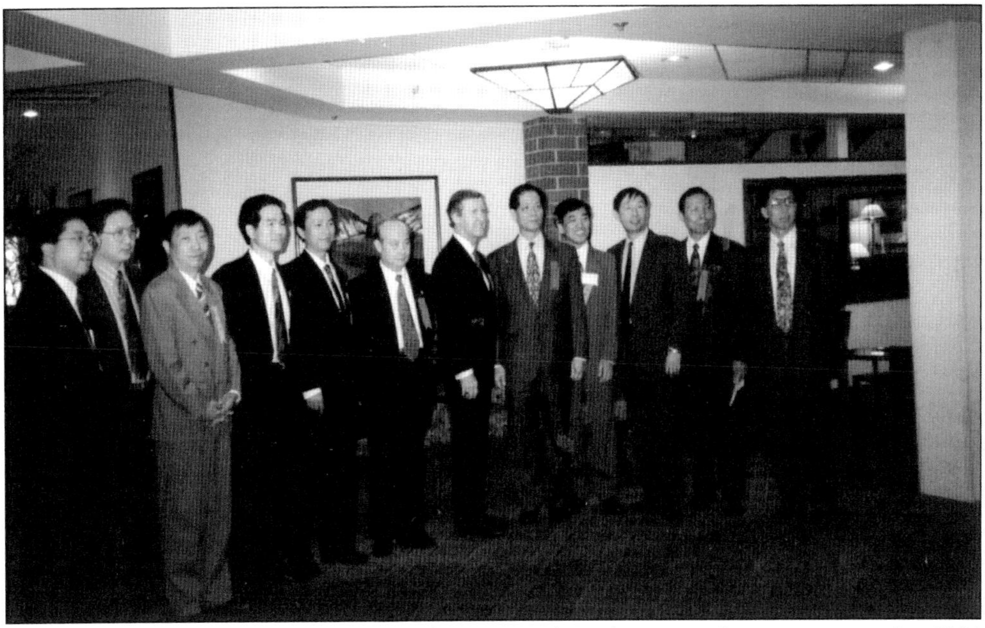

Delegates of the ACSE organization are shown attending the national convention in this 1996 photograph, which included keynote speaker Secretary of Defense William Cohen (sixth from right) and the general counsel of China (seventh from right). ACSE was started in 1994 by two Milwaukee area Chinese doctors, Dr. Shijiang Li and Dr. Guanyuan Jin. (Courtesy of Guanyuan Jin.)

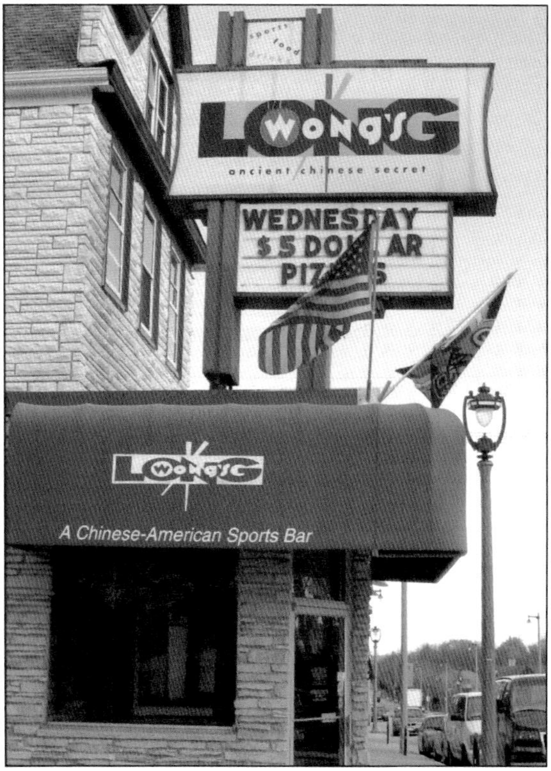

This photograph shows the exterior of Long Wongs, a Chinese American sports bar opened by Paul Wong in 2004 at the corner of North Fifty-second Street and West Bluemound Road in Milwaukee. Paul Wong, whose family has operated Chinese restaurants in Milwaukee since 1904, was the cofounder of the Wong's Wok Chinese fast-food restaurant chain. (Photograph by Wenbin Yuan.)

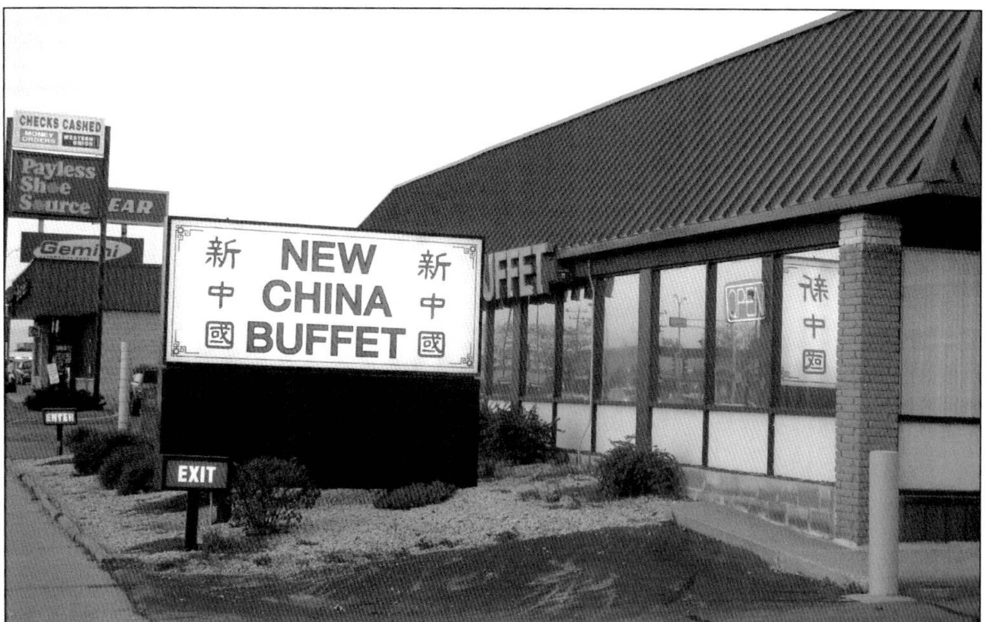

The New China Buffet is shown in this recent photograph and is part of a chain of similar restaurants opened in Milwaukee and other cities in the United States during the 1990s. Many of the restaurants have been owned and operated by immigrants during the last 20 years from Fujian Province in mainland China. (Photograph by Wenbin Yuan.)

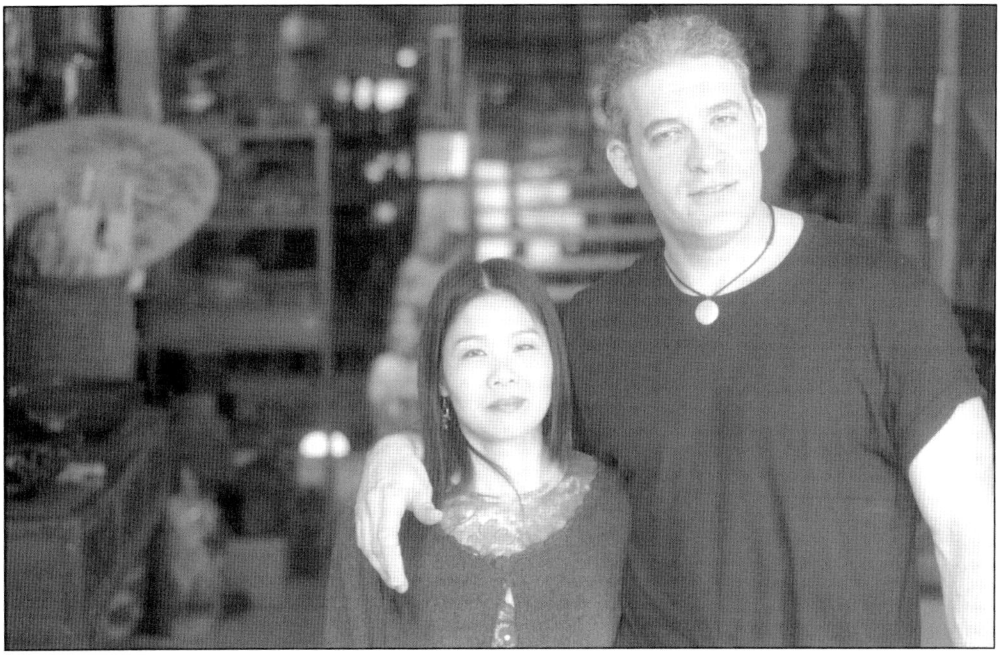

Pauline and Eli Rosenblatt own Artasia, which is located at 181 North Broadway in the Milwaukee Historic Third Ward. Pauline is a native of Taiwan, and Eli is a Milwaukee native. Both worked in Taiwan and China before deciding to open an Asian artifacts and art gallery in Milwaukee in 1992. (Photograph by Wenbin Yuan.)

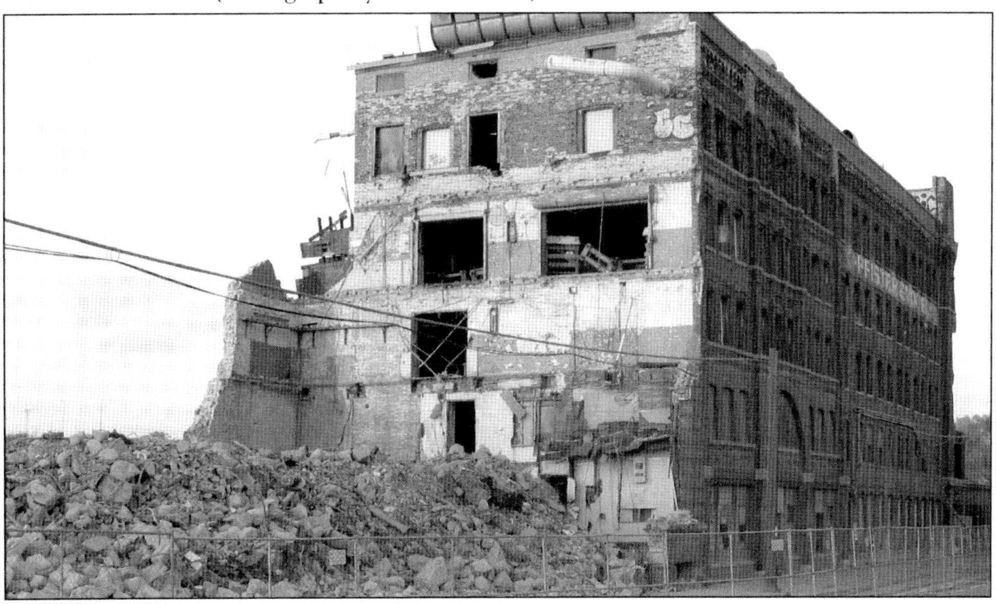

A. F. Gallun and Sons Tannery is located adjacent to the Milwaukee River in downtown Milwaukee. At one time, the tannery was one of the four largest in the United States, and Milwaukee was the largest tanning center in the world. Although the tanning industry in the United States had been in decline for many years, the rise of China as a low-cost manufacturing center during the 1990s was the final factor to almost completely ending the tanning industry in Milwaukee. (Photograph by Wenbin Yuan.)

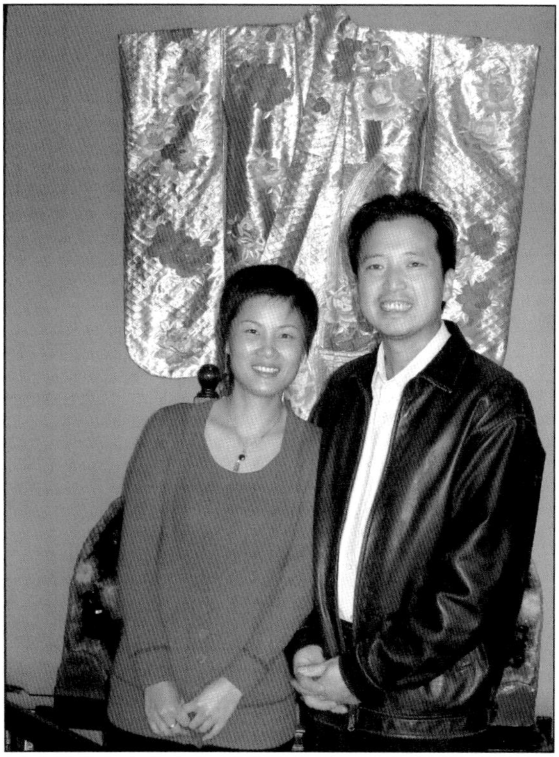

Fujiyama Restaurant is located at 2916 South 108th Street in West Allis. It features an upscale Japanese menu and was started in 2004 by Vicky and Billy Ni, who are both immigrants from Fujian, China. The Nis are representative of a new generation of Chinese immigrants who are working in what would generally be considered one of the traditional businesses for Chinese Americans, but with a nontraditional approach—a primarily Japanese menu selection. (Photograph by Wenbin Yuan.)

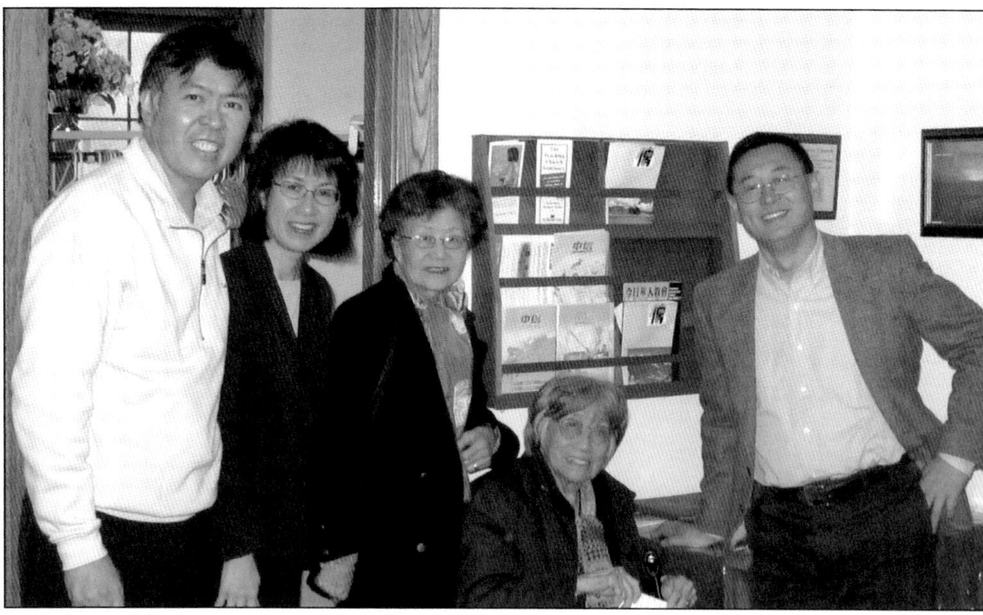

This 2007 photograph was taken at the Community Baptist Church and shows, from left to right, Dr. Walter Wong (a neurologist and former president of the Milwaukee Chapter of the Organization of Chinese Americans), Rev. Judy King (pastor at the church), Betty Eng and Jennie Chan (longtime church members), and Wenbin Yuan (the author and president of Dakota Intertek Corporation, a Milwaukee area engineering and contracting firm). (Photograph by Wenbin Yuan.)

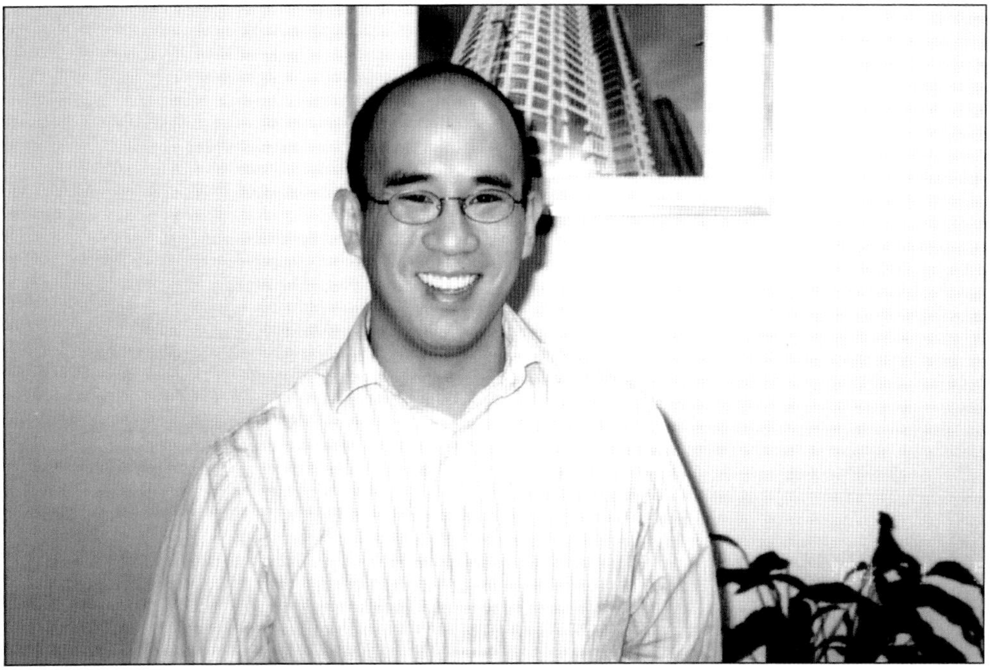

This photograph dated 2008 shows Jerry King (professional engineer), a structural engineer who is also the chief executive officer of Precast Engineering, a company founded by his father, Ming-Ta King, in 1978. The company currently has nearly 50 employees. (Photograph by Wenbin Yuan.)

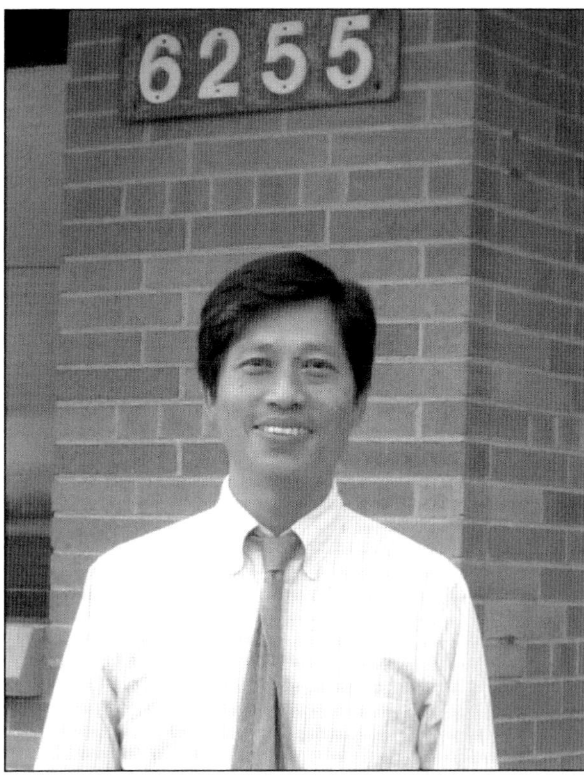

This recent photograph shows Dr. John Lin, who in 1993 founded AD Electronics and Lin-Engineering, Inc., in the Milwaukee suburb of Greendale. The two manufacturing firms have a total of approximately 100 employees. (Photograph by Wenbin Yuan.)

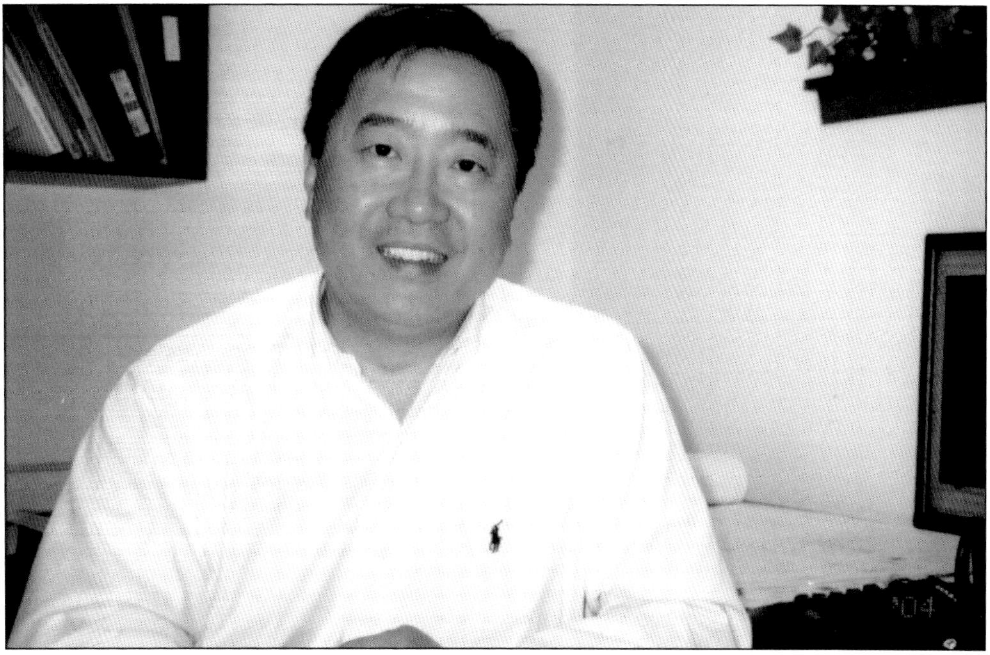

This recent photograph shows Dr. Junyi (John) Wang in front of the Midwest Structure Engineering offices, a company that he founded in 1999. Dr. Wang is a structural engineer and an active church elder at the CCCM. Dr. Wang immigrated to the Milwaukee area from Taiwan in the 1980s. (Photograph by Wenbin Yuan.)

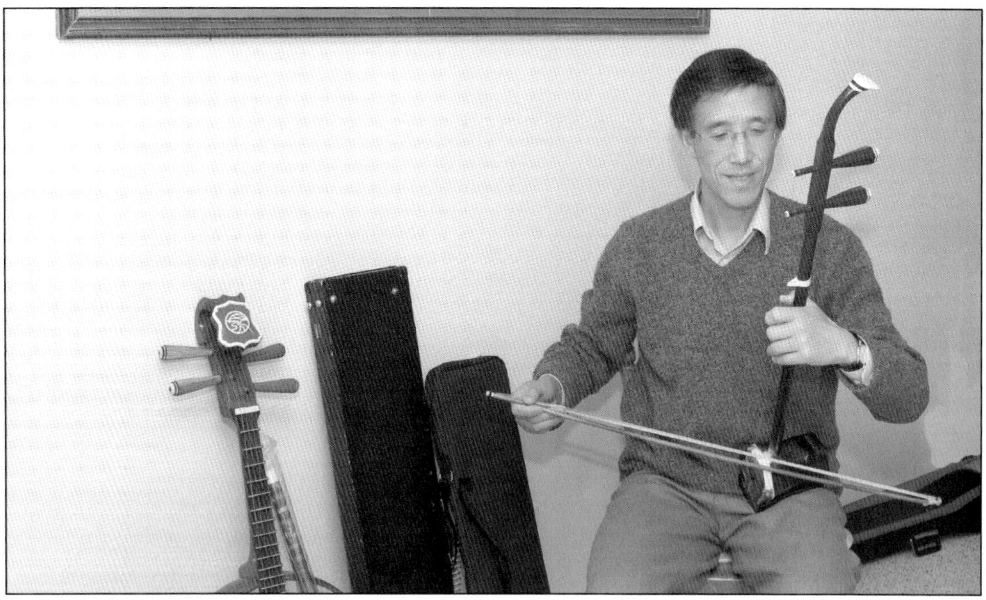

Dr. Qiuzhen Xue is a principal engineer at GE Healthcare who came to the United States in the mid-1980s to obtain his doctorate from the University of Wisconsin–Madison and moved to Milwaukee following his graduation. Dr. Xue is a painter and musician who performed in a Chinese music ensemble and who remains active in teaching traditional Chinese instruments to students in the Milwaukee area (such as the erhu being played by Dr. Xue in this recent photograph). (Courtesy of Dr. Qiuzhen Xue.)

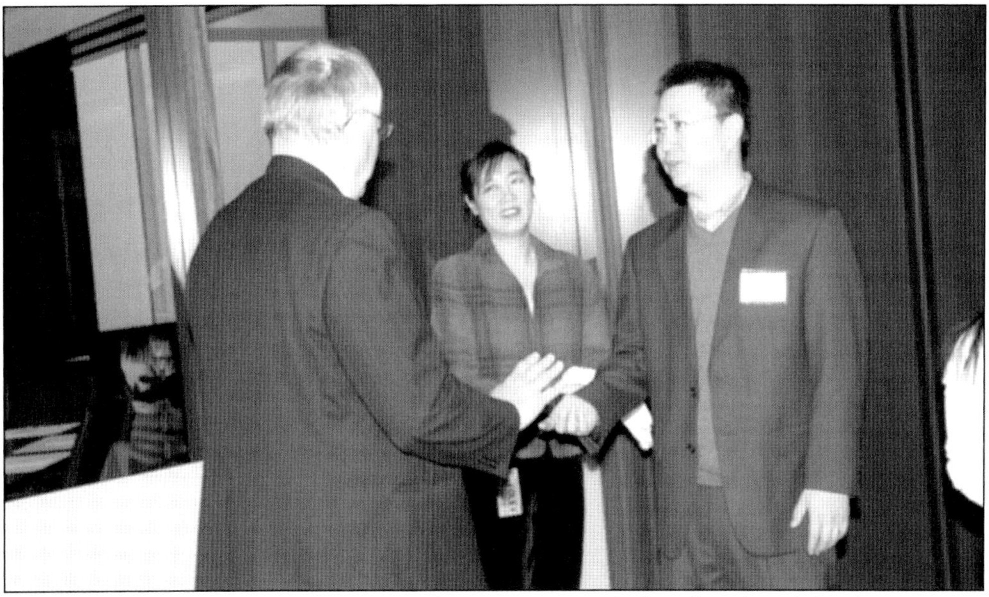

This photograph, dated February 2, 2008, shows Dun Wang shaking hands with local community leaders at an inaugural ceremony and reception held to celebrate the launch of the *Milwaukee Chinese Times* newspaper, believed to be the first Chinese-language newspaper published in Milwaukee. The reception coincided with another notable event, which was a basketball game between the Houston Rockets and the Milwaukee Bucks, featuring the only two Chinese players in the National Basketball Association. (Photograph by Wenbin Yuan.)

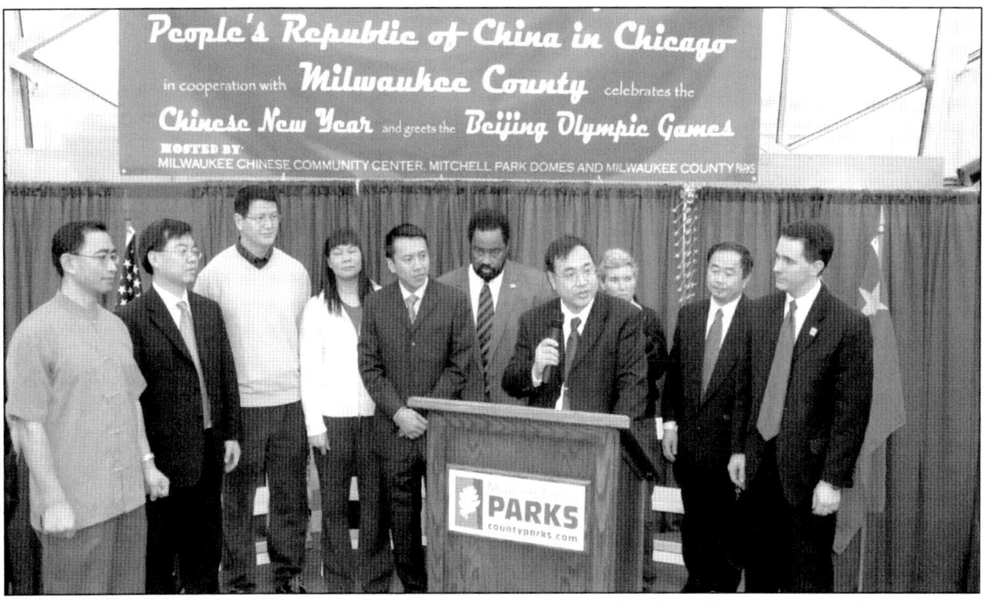

This photograph was taken at a Chinese New Year's event held on February 2, 2008, that was jointly sponsored by Milwaukee County and Milwaukee Chinese Community Center (MCCC). Shown in the photograph from left to right are Dr. Peng Gao; general counsel Ping Huang from the Chinese Consulate in Chicago; Jingliu Yi and Meiling Mai (parents of Milwaukee Bucks basketball player Yi Jianlian); Qun Li; ? Miller; Dr. Liang Tang; Dr. Liangheng Qiu; and Milwaukee County executive Scott Walker. (Courtesy of Yi Hong.)

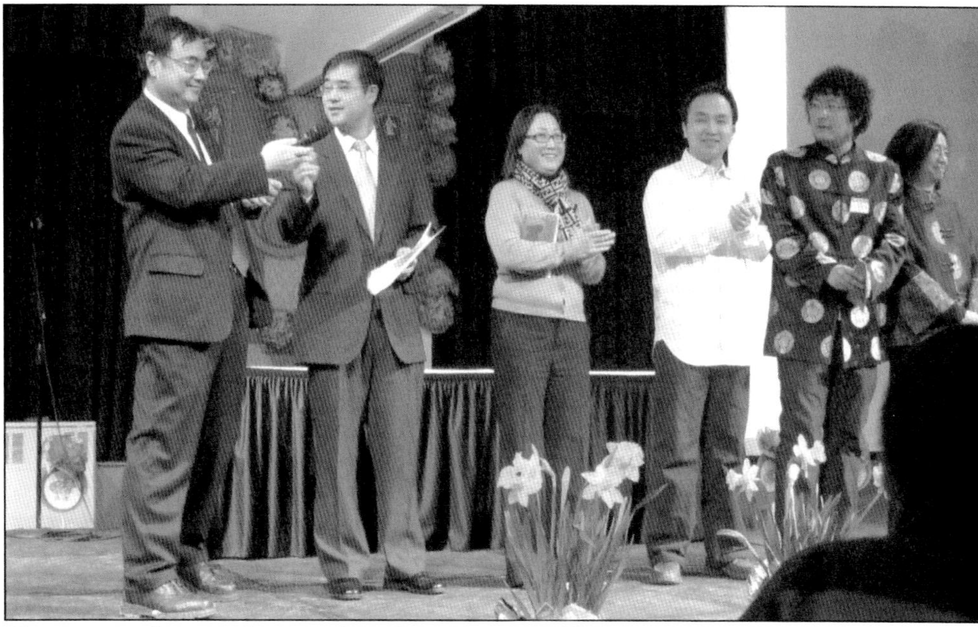

This recent photograph was taken during a joint Chinese New Year's party organized for the past seven years by representatives of six Milwaukee area Chinese organizations. These organizations include Milwaukee Modern Chinese School (MMCS), ACSE, the Organization of Chinese Americans (OCA), and Chinese student associations at the Medical College of Wisconsin, Marquette University, and the University of Wisconsin–Milwaukee. (Photograph by Wenbin Yuan.)

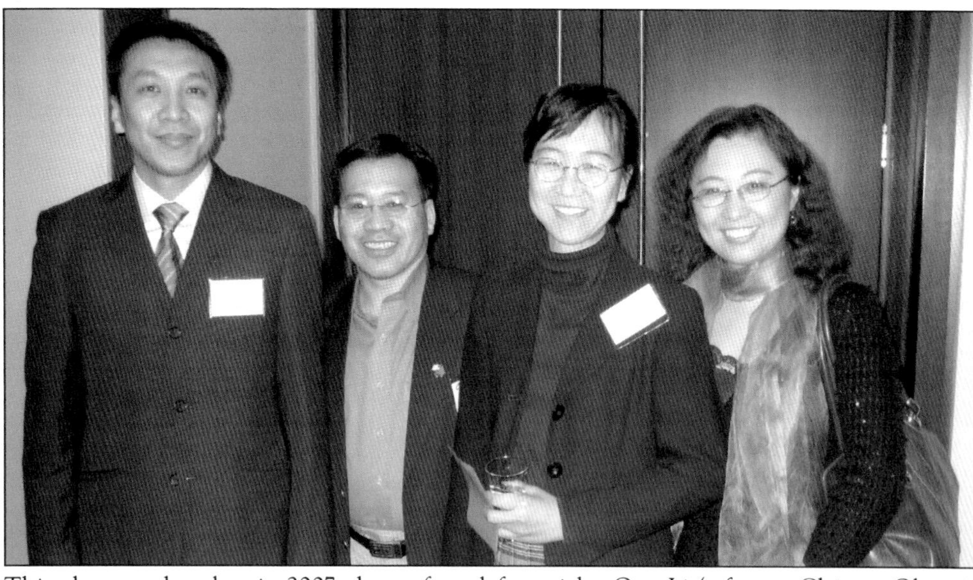

This photograph, taken in 2007, shows, from left to right, Qun Li (a former Chinese Olympic basketball team captain and a personal coach for Milwaukee Bucks player Yi Jianlian), Charles Vang (president of Hmong Chamber of Commerce in Milwaukee), Beng Yeap (a Chinese immigrant from Malaysia who is a government official working for the Department of Commerce), and Dr. Connie Li (chief executive officer of TranSmart and TrafficCast International, who was recently recognized as a Woman of International Influence). (Photograph by Wenbin Yuan.)

This 2007 photograph shows Yi Jianlian, a professional basketball player who was drafted by the Milwaukee Bucks in the first round of the 2007 NBA draft. The two games against the Houston Rockets during Yi's rookie season were each estimated to have been watched by more than 200 million Chinese citizens. (Courtesy of Zhengjiang Sun.)

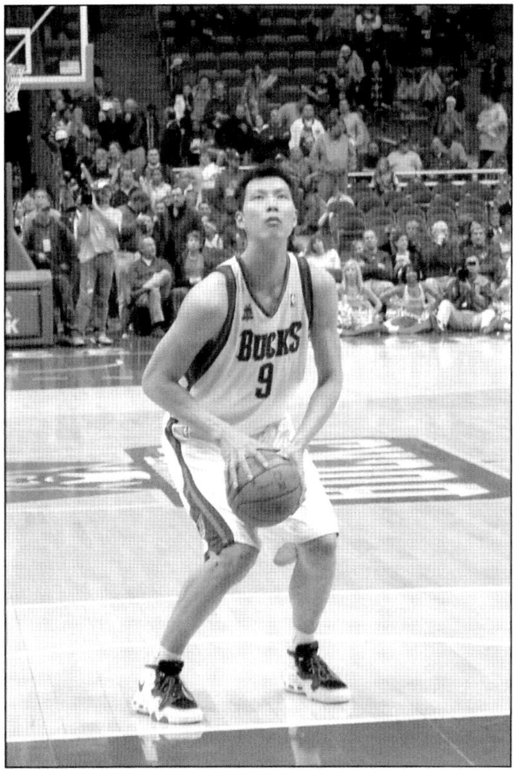

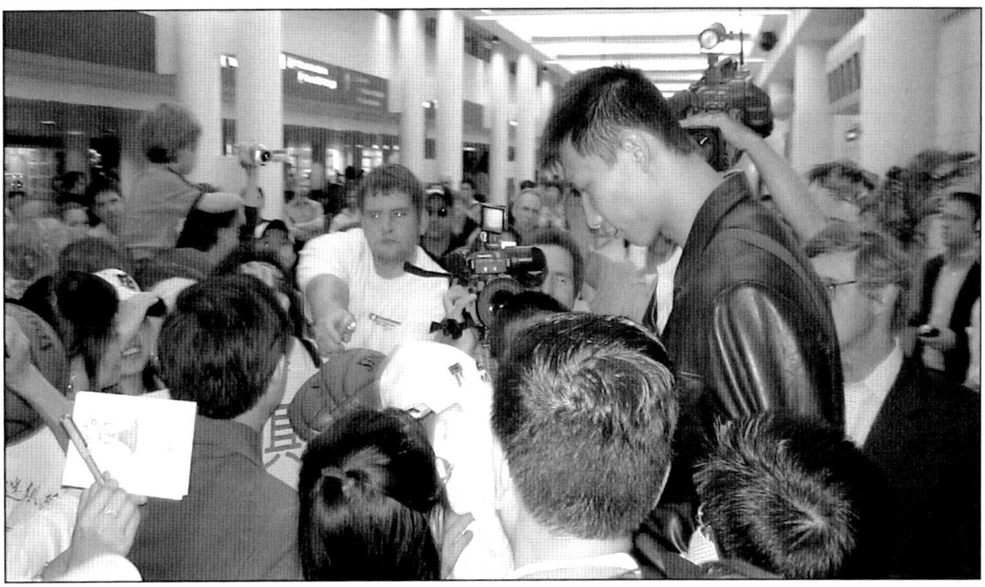

This photograph was taken in October 2007 at the arrival of Milwaukee Bucks basketball player Yi Jianlian at O'Hare International Airport in Chicago. Yi was an instant celebrity upon his arrival at the airport and was greeted by members of a fan club (Yi Fans Club) organized in Milwaukee. The fan club currently has more than 1,000 registered members and is led by Dr. Dian Wang, M.D., of the Medical College of Wisconsin. The presence of Yi has made Milwaukee one of the United States cities most widely recognized in China. (Courtesy of Dr. Mingtao Jiang.)